Global History

Bruce Mazlish, Carol Gluck, and Raymond Grew,
Series Editors

Conceptualizing Global History,
edited by Bruce Mazlish and Ralph Buultjens

FORTHCOMING

Global Civilization and Local Cultures,
edited by Wolf Schäfer

Global History and Migrations,
edited by Wang Gungwu

Conceptualizing Global History

Conceptualizing
Global History

EDITED BY
Bruce Mazlish
and Ralph Buultjens

Westview Press
BOULDER • SAN FRANCISCO • OXFORD

 # 28214094

Global History

Copyright © 1993 by Westview Press, Inc.

Published in 1993 in the United States of America by Westview Press, Inc., 5500 Central Avenue, Boulder, Colorado 80301-2877, and in the United Kingdom by Westview Press, 36 Lonsdale Road, Summertown, Oxford OX2 7EW

Library of Congress Cataloging-in-Publication Data
Conceptualizing global history / edited by Bruce Mazlish and Ralph
 Buultjens.
   p.   cm. — (Global history)
 Includes bibliographical references.
 ISBN 0-8133-1683-9 (cloth). — ISBN 0-8133-1684-7 (pbk.)
   1. History—Philosophy.   2. History—Methodology.   I. Mazlish,
Bruce, 1923–   .   II. Buultjens, Ralph.   III. Series.
 D16.9.C633   1993
 901—dc20   93-25123
                                                                              CIP

Printed and bound in the United States of America

      The paper used in this publication meets the requirements
 (∞) of the American National Standard for Permanence of Paper
      for Printed Library Materials Z39.48-1984.

10   9   8   7   6   5   4   3   2   1

Contents

PART THREE
An Overview

An Introduction
to Global History

Bruce Mazlish

More than a century and a half ago in his essay "Signs of the Times" (1829), Thomas Carlyle sought to discern the shape of his own time, the early nineteenth century. He wrote: "Were we required to characterize this age of ours by any single epithet, we should be tempted to call it, not an Heroical, Devotional, Philosophical, or Moral Age, but, above all others, the Mechanical Age."

Today, we find the signs of the times pointing to a new destination. Ours, to put it categorically, is an Age of Globalization. In the Carlylean spirit, we can say that the most significant fact of our time and one that gives meaning to many other important trends and events is that we are entering a global epoch. Marshall McLuhan intuited some of what was happening when he wrote about the "global village"; but the term *village* is singularly superficial and misleading, as a look at what follows will show.

Historians and social scientists know that nothing is completely new. For example, some scholars have claimed to discern a major industrial movement in the fifteenth century, anticipating Carlyle's "industrial revolution" (he helped coin the phrase and give it currency) by four centuries. Similarly, we can recognize that there was a kind of globalization around the fifteenth century when the earth was first circumnavigated, making us see it as spatially "whole." A comparable step was taken in the nineteenth century when time zones were standardized, thus bringing the world's populations closer on the temporal plane. One task of global history, then, will be to look back selectively and detect earlier signs of the global epoch now upon us. Yet the conceptualization and practice of global history must start from our present position, where new factors building on the old have given a different intensity and synchronicity to the process of globalization.

What are some of these new factors? The starting point for global history lies in the following basic facts of our time (although others could be added): our thrust into space, imposing upon us an increasing sense of being in one world—"Spaceship Earth"—as seen from outside the earth's atmosphere; satellites in outer space that link the peoples of the earth in an unprecedented fashion; nuclear threats in the form of either weapons or utility plants, showing how the territorial state can no longer adequately protect its citizens from either military or ecologically related "invasions"; environmental problems that refuse to conform to lines drawn on a map; and multinational corporations that increasingly dominate our economic lives.

These and other "signs" require us to design a new perspective to guide our understanding of what is happening around us. A new consciousness is needed to help us view these developments along with other more traditional ones and to give meaning to them. A new subfield of history—clearly defined in terms of its differences and similarities with, for example, world history—must be created. Global history as a new perspective, consciousness, and discipline must be conceptualized and then exemplified. This book is an attempt to start on these tasks.[1]

I

In this introduction, I shall try to sketch some of the key problems and possibilities that lie ahead, a number of which are further developed in the chapters that follow. Among the topics to be treated are: the historiographic problem; the nature of previous attempts at some form of global vision; the existence of an antecedent Darwinian vision of the "economy of nature"; the challenge of creating institutions other than the nation-state as the subject matter of history; the possibility of global public opinion as an ethical force; the issue of identity; the nature of global communications; the context of global time/space; and, lastly, the policy implications of global history. It must be emphasized that all these topics are interacting and overlapping.

II

There are particular historiographic problems in trying to come to terms with the new historical reality, and it is wise to start with these. Global history, to state the first postulate, is contemporary history. In the eyes of some historians, contemporary history is not history at all; they feel that the lack of a long-term, traditional perspective precludes the possibility. Yet Herodotus started with a contemporary event, the Persian-Athenian War, and wrote a "history," i.e., an "inquiry" into the events surrounding him, that is generally recognized as the beginning of the discipline. His record and analysis then became the basis of "Greek history," as studied by subsequent scholars.

One might also argue that, whether acknowledged or not, all history is contemporary history in the sense that the perspective brought to bear on past events is necessarily rooted in the present. In this light, global history may simply be more conscious of its perspective and interested in focusing it more directly on contemporary happenings, as well as on the past. Serious problems of selectivity or documentation then remain, as they do with any history.

Almost at the other end of the spectrum from contemporary history, but differing from global history, is the effort to encompass all of history, not just the recent past, in one sweeping account. The product of such an effort has often been called "universal history." This genre, too, emerged around the fifth century B.C., at the beginning of Greek historiography, in the effort to encompass the notable happenings of all the poleis and their neighbors.[2] At the time, these happenings seemed to be universal to the Greeks; from our perspective, they are parochial, centered as they are on only a small part of the globe. (For example, Chinese and Indian histories are nonexistent in these accounts.)

Another contender for an ecumenical perspective is "world history." Unlike universal history (though the terms *universal, world,* and *global* are vague and their usage is varied), world history is very much alive today. It spearheads the effort to transcend Eurocentrism (with only partial success, in my opinion) and to give equal voice to the past of all peoples. It includes distinguished practitioners in its ranks, such as William McNeill, Philip Curtin, and others, who have written exemplary scholarly works in a broad vein. It is making its way into high-school, college, and university curriculums, though in varying degrees. There are world history journals and a professional association.

World history also has, not unexpectedly, major problems. Does it transcend the nation-state or too often simply place one national history next to another? Does it lose sight of the crucial factors shaping events, in the otherwise laudable efforts to foster multiculturalism and to avoid one point of view? Does it apply more to the distant past than to the modern period? Does it have no real principle of selectivity, thus leaving nothing out?

One variant of world history is the Braudelian. The great *Annales* historian, Fernand Braudel, claimed that he was practicing "global" or "total" history. His usage of the terms global and total, however, was limited and erratic. "What the *Annales* proclaimed," he told us, "was a history whose scope would extend to embrace all the sciences of man—to the 'globality' of all the human sciences."[3] Here, the emphasis was on interdisciplinarity. He next wrote, "To have seized upon the entire past of a province, observing it both in its historical reality and its geographical aspects, is that not, to use a recent expression, to achieve 'global thought,' the only form of history capable of satisfying us now." Here, he had in mind an all-encompassing treatment, whatever the subject.

Fundamentally, Braudel used the term *global history* in the sense of there being no boundaries to his understanding of a subject.[4] Such global history, however, is very different from what is being discussed in this book. First, like most efforts at world history, Braudel's focused on the premodern periods; his works stopped at 1800. Second, unlike many other world historians, Braudel stressed material factors far more than mental factors and shortchanged the way consciousness could affect material forces. Similar limitations apply to the work of his disciple Immanuel Wallerstein and his study of "world systems" (though lately he has extended his time frame).

Many of these efforts at world history—Braudelian and non-Braudelian—and, indeed, some efforts at universal history are extremely valuable and sometimes overlap with what I am calling global history. They need far more investigation (see the chapters by Manfred Kossok and Wolf Schäfer). I have noted them, superficially, for comparative purposes. What needs to be said forcefully, however, is that they are generally not global history as conceptualized here. Although the lines are not rigid, and a terminological quarrel is unhelpful, one must nevertheless seek as much clarification and useful distinction in this matter as possible. The conscious decision of global historians to start from the globalization proceeding apace today is one essential difference. (How far this perspective can be extended into the past is a major subject for further reflection and work.)

Yet another postulate of global history is that it seeks to transcend the nation-state as the focus of history, while recognizing that the nation will persist as a powerful form of social action and that national histories will still be written. The hope is that the latter, too, can be newly viewed through the global history perspective.

A further critical characteristic is that no *single* global history is anticipated. In spite of the fact that there are definite factors of globalization of the kind enumerated earlier, we must shun a new version of Whiggish history where all lines lead to a preordained destiny. Instead, we can conjecture that there are and will be many global experiences, i.e., encounters between local situations and global pressures or between particular peoples and the forces of globalization. Each of these experiences will require its own history, as part of our increased awareness of global history.

At this point, the question of method arises. Will global history be primarily a matter of *narrative* or *analysis*? (See the chapters by Raymond Grew and Neva Goodwin.) The answer must be in the doing, but my suspicion is that, like most history, it will be some combination of the two.

I suspect that the experience of globalization will best be dealt with by narrative and that the structures and processes involved in globalization will be handled by analysis. Time, however, will tell.

If the major actor or subject in historical study is no longer to be the nation-state (though it will certainly remain important) or empire, one question arises naturally: Who or what *is* the prime actor or subject of global history? Again, time will tell us. Some provisional candidates, however, are movements, such as the women's and environmental causes; nongovernmental organizations (NGOs), such as Amnesty International or Human Watch (whose strictures may rapidly be replacing those of religion in the setting up of an international conscience); and multinational corporations.

Some of the consequences following from the actions of these new actors may be intentional and others unintentional. Such consequences, newly conceptualized, may include the study in historical terms of such topics as investment (especially related today to multinationals; for the latter, see the chapter by Richard Barnet and John Cavanagh), ecological effects, the spread of human rights, and so forth. Along with factors of globalization, these actors and consequences may take center stage in global history.

Large questions, of course, persist: What documentation allows us to write history centered on the actors suggested here? How do we select the important material from the overwhelming amount of data available? What happens to traditional subjects, such as social stratification, when there is no bounded society? Global history clearly cannot be achieved in a day.

It follows from what has been said that global history must be interdisciplinary and more given to team research than the usual history. It must also be more willing to risk pursuing leads that may prove false and be more experimental and inventive than traditional history. As I have argued, humanity is now entering upon a new epoch—a global epoch—and it is only natural that this will call forth novel and sometimes erratic ways of comprehension.

Yet in spite of global history's provisional nature, we are not totally without initial guidance. Global history can be thought of as a diagram, in which a process called globalization gives rise to global consciousness or perspective, which, in turn, gives rise to global history; this then informs the globalization process itself, further heightening global consciousness, ad infinitum (the idea for this diagram comes from Margaret Herzig). However, written global history must be specific, based on empirical data, and carried out in historiographic terms that are traditional, if sophisticated.

With this accepted, a preliminary definition of global history encompasses several factors. Put negatively, it is neither Eurocentric, nor focused on the nation-state, nor a single, Whiggish entity. More positively, it starts from the existing factors of globalization—seen as novel at least in degree—and in their interactions; it focuses on new actors of various kinds; it is dramatically concerned with the dialectic of the global and the local (recognizing, for example, that the global helps create increased localism as a response); it embraces the methods of both narrative and analysis as befitting the specific phenomena under investigation; and it necessarily relies a good deal on interdisciplinary and team research.

Perhaps the single most distinguishing feature is that of perspective, awareness, or consciousness (to use a number of overlapping terms), as combined with the lived reality of globalization.[5] A global perspective, based on the features enumerated earlier, is then used to guide research interests and to offer a definite principle of selectivity.

III

Until recently, Marxism and capitalism contended for global hegemony. And throughout history, certain religions have made global claims. For example, Catholicism embodies universal and ecumenical aspirations, as its name implies. So does Islam. Judaism makes no such claims, but in a perverse fashion, it has sometimes been labeled an "international" conspiracy.

Marxism, a secular claimant, appears now to be a failed globalism. In its heyday, however, "the International" expected to shape the entire world in its image, and it went a fair way toward doing so. Even in non-Communist countries, fellow travelers thought of themselves as part of an "imagined" international community, to use Benedict Anderson's phrase; they owed it their prime loyalty and were accused of disloyalty by their nation-states. (Catholics have often been seen in a similar situation.)

Though Karl Marx himself was scornful of competing nationalisms (while nevertheless being a German chauvinist) and dismissed them as competitors for the workers' allegiance, Marxism fell far short of its global rhetoric in practice and lapsed into "national" Marxisms. Josef Stalin's "socialism in one country" was the first example, subordinating other nationalisms to its supposed internationalism. Mao Tse-tung's "socialism with Chinese characters" was and still is the second most prominent example. We hear the worldwide claim in his "100 Flowers" speech, when he declared, "The Chinese entered an entirely new era, both in thought and in life. They found Marxism-Leninism, a *universal* truth which is applicable anywhere" (italics added).[6] The more limited version emerged in his *On Practice*, where he concluded, "There is no abstract Marxism, only specific Marxism. So-called specific Marxism is Marxism given *na-tional* form" (italics added).

Marxism's failure at global hegemony has, however, helped prepare the way for other forms of globalization, as I will show. Indeed, Mikhail Gorbachev's historic efforts at reforming the Soviet Union, which unintendedly led to its downfall and transformation, can be viewed as one of the factors favoring global history. *Perestroika* and *glasnost* helped supply the political context in which global history could flourish, for they ended the superpower contest—the Cold War—that beclouded our perception of common global problems and challenges. (Although Russia did not experience the Western Renaissance or Reformation, it has been going through the throes of "modernization," thus participating in the experience—and problems—increasingly common to all parts of the globe.)

Capitalism, too, has had global pretensions. These have taken the form of wishing to convert the whole world to its doctrines, generally disguising national economic ambitions in the rhetoric of free trade and frequently realizing these ambitions through imperialism. Decolonization has ended the latter aspect of capitalism, and, like the decline or fall of Marxism (with its own form of imperialism), it has become a precondition for what I am calling global history.

Capitalism's aspirations, however, survive in a form different from that of mere colonization. In its more self-interested shape, though couched in universalistic rhetoric, it can be found in Lord Cromer's statement on Egypt: "The future of Egypt [read any other colony] lies not in the direction of a narrow nationalism, which will only embrace Egyptians . . . but rather in that of an enlarged cosmopolitanism."[7] Of course, Lord Cromer had in mind Westernization or "modernization" on the model of Great Britain (and in its interest). A more benign and important expression of this idea can be found in the introduction to *The Protestant Ethic and the Spirit of Capitalism*, where Max Weber declared that "in Western civilization only, cultural phenomena have appeared which (as we like to think) lie in a line of development having *universal* significance and value."[8]

Weber's analysis, with its emphasis on Western science's incessant probing and on capitalism's inexorable expansionism (thereby echoing Marx), caught at the truth at the time he was writing. Not unexpectedly, his view was Eurocentric for it envisioned the spread of the Western model to the rest of the world, without much modification or feedback.

One very important result of the exit of both Marxist and capitalist forms of imperialism and their attendant ideologies (though capitalism is currently experiencing a kind of resurgence) is that the division into first, second, and third worlds is now ended. The notions of a first (capitalist) and a second (Communist) world are losing their meanings completely. That of a third (developing) world still retains some significance (see the chapter by Ralph Buultjens), but it is fading and, in turn, being replaced by a North/South dichotomy.

The concept of global history seeks to transcend the first/second/third world dichotomy and to envision future change—development?—as being open-ended and shaped by all populations of the world, even if differentially. (This can also be cast in terms of the global/local issue or, in world-systems phraseology, the core/periphery division.) Moreover, there is an emerging awareness that unbridled economic development is bringing unacceptable costs to the environment and other sectors (see the chapter by Neva Goodwin) and that the so-called Western model can no longer be pursued even if it were thought desirable. It is this perspective that helps guide the writing of global history.

IV

The Darwinian model differs from the capitalist and Marxist models. Its essence is a "global" theory of the "economy of nature." The latter phrase was the one Charles Darwin used; we would say the "ecological whole." It embodies the notion that all parts cohere in one system and are interdependent and that what affects one part will affect the rest. To take an example Darwin used, the number of cats affects the number of rats, which affects the number of bumblebees, which affects the amount of clover, and so on.

Darwin drew much of his inspiration from geology. It was from this emerging discipline of the nineteenth century that an awareness of global physical nature first emanated (from the inside of the globe; in our time, we see it coming from outside—from space). As William Buckland remarked, "The field of the Geologist's inquiry is the Globe itself."[9] This sense of worldwide upheaval and change was expressed most powerfully by Charles Lyell, and it was from him that Darwin took inspiration and extended the notion to biological nature.

Darwin's other inspiration was Adam Smith (whom he read along with Thomas Malthus). Smith wrote of "the wealth of nations," envisioning countries in an open international system. As Arnold Toynbee observed in 1884 in his pioneering treatment of the industrial revolution Smith believed "that all the nations in the world should be considered as one great community. We see how widely he had departed from the old national system of economics, by contrasting the mere title of his book, *The Wealth of Nations*, with that of Mun's treatise, *England's Treasure in Foreign Trade*. This cosmopolitanism necessitated a detailed refutation of the mercantile system."[10]

In these examples, we see a convergence of global visions working itself out on the theoretical plane. These and other global conceptualizations help prepare the way, intellectually, for our understanding of the globalization now taking place. Thus, global history, though new both in the factors that it deals with—for they are emergent—and in the way it conceptualizes them, draws upon antecedent theories.

V

From the seventeenth century more or less to the present, the dominant focus of most historical writing (which means Western writing) has been the nation-state. As manifested in the 1648 Peace of Westphalia, religious affiliation was uncoupled from nation-state loyalty. Similarly, state sovereignty effectively displaced feudal attachments. Needless to say, this was not an all-at-once event but a gradual process.

At the same time, nationalism emerged as the glue holding together the nation-state. Occurring first in seventeenth-century England, it spread to France and America and then, in more conservative form, to Germany and Russia.[11] It is imperative to realize that this nationalism was "constructed," or "imagined."[12] In any case, the nation-state claimed legitimacy as the representative of all its members, either as citizens or as part of a mystic entity, and it claimed their loyalty on this same basis.

Today, however artificially and even fragilely constructed, there are about 190 nation-states. Each is legally sovereign over its own territory. Each, in theory, is an autonomous economic unit, whose well-being is measured in terms of gross *national* product. If we move from these legal and theoretical definitions, however, we find that each, to a greater or lesser degree, has lost effective control over its separate destiny as a result of the global factors enunciated earlier.

Will the nation-state, therefore, vanish from the stage of history? Eric Hobsbawm has proclaimed that nationalism in the late twentieth century is "no longer a major vector of historical development."[13] A recent issue of *The Economist*, on the other hand, declared that "nationalism, perhaps called tribalism, is an enduring phenomenon."[14] A judicious view, I believe, would see the nation-state persisting as a widespread form of organization, with nationalism as an underpinning, but changing with varying degrees of rapidity as it confronts the challenges of globalization. Thus, one task of the global historian is to continue to study the nation-state in its local experiences and manifestations, under the impact of the global factors.

Perhaps the more interesting question for global history, already touched upon in terms of actors, is: What institutions will replace or supplement some of the functions of the nation-state? The answer emerging at the present time seems to be twofold: on one side, for example, multinational corporations, NGOs, or regional trade and/or political groupings, such as the European Community (EC); on the other side, national splinter groups (potentially breaking up existing nation-states), such as Catalans seeking greater autonomy and looking to the EC instead of to Madrid or Croats escaping from a dissolving Yugoslavia.

Beyond these developments is the expanded activity of the United Nations. Only the future historian will know what institutional changes in the UN are in the offing. But one thing can be said with certainty: While the UN's functions and its capacity to execute them will expand, we are not about to move to a world government or a world state in the near future.

The other likely and portentous development is the emergence of an "imagined" global community. It is much too early to descry its dimensions or to describe its features, although the global historian doing empirical work will be on its track. We can say that if the nation-state was largely defined by its enemies and mainly in military terms, the new global community is also initially taking its definition from its enemies. In this case, however, the enemies are transnational threats of an environmental, economic, and nuclear nature, to name a few, and the entity being threatened is not only the nation-state but also a global community—humanity. (Incidentally, this sort of shift in the enemy will probably entail a new definition of treason and treasonable actions.) In sum, a number of the new institutions studied by global historians still largely exist in the "imagination."

VI

Increasingly present—and not just in the imagination—is the force of global public opinion. One of the most exciting developments in this regard is the emergence of international human rights as a measure of states (for an extended development of this idea, see the chapter by Louis Menand). It builds on the age-old fear of appearing "barbarian" but in greatly strengthened form. It is connected, of course, to increasing communications, made possible by global satellites. Now, seeing one's own actions, past and present, through other eyes ("would someone give us the giftee," as Robert Burns said) is facilitated and made necessary by the omnipresent TV and radio.

The ethical force of human rights is superseding both religion and science in this regard. The various religions, though they have often claimed to be universal, are not, in fact, accepted globally as moral legislators. Indeed, many of the world religions are rivals.

From the seventeenth century until recently, science was thought of as a universal good. Through empirical science, it was hoped, men and women of diverse views could overcome ideological differences by means of established "fact." Joseph Glanvill expressed a common belief in the 1600s when he prophesied: "[Science] will in its progress dispose mens Spirits to more calmness and modesty, charity and prudence in the Differences of Religion and even silence dispute there. For the free sensible knowledge tends to the altering the Crasis of mens minds and so cures the Desease at the root; and true philosophy is a Specifick against Disputes and Divisions."[15]

This view of science is now contested. At the most basic level, it is recognized that "fact" does not dictate "value." Further, the impartiality and objectivity of science itself is under attack from social constructionists and others. The charges need not be rehearsed here. While some, such as Bernard Williams, hold to the view that science, unlike ethics, will ultimately converge to a unified understanding embodied in a universal discourse, many others see mere paradigms—often Western, masculine, and so forth—in the guise of "universal" truths.

Into the void left by religion and science (whatever the ultimate judgment as to the latter's validity may be) has stepped a global concept: human rights. The nineteenth-century conservative Joseph De Maistre argued that he saw Frenchmen and Germans but never Man; today, in contrast, many take up the Enlightenment's dedication to humans, although in new form.

This is not to say that the issue is uncontentious. For example, in many parts of the world, there is little recognition or desire for "human" rights (which are often seen as merely "Western"). Thus, Amartya Sen observed as a matter of fact (though he himself wished to change the situation) that "rural Indian women typically do not suffer from envy of the position of men, do not see their situation as one of painful inequality, and do not pine for reform."[16] A little over a century earlier, T. H. Huxley had asked, "Was our own Government wrong in suppressing Thuggee in India?"[17] The Thuggee question has merely taken on new form, with neither Great Britain nor any other single power now in a position to seek to impose its will on other countries. Instead, we have the force of global public opinion, however shaped.

The modern argument takes the following form. On one side, the localists argue for particularism, pluralism, relativism, national autonomy, and so forth. On the other, many globalists argue that if nations have the right to tell their regions how to behave, why does humanity not have the right to tell all nations how to behave toward their own populations? Human rights proponents argue that there is a radical condescension involved when foreign scholars and local nativists can say, "Let them treat their women [or whatever] as they want; it's their custom."

There is, clearly, a legitimate conflict over the extent of external inter-
ference and local indifference. Human rights, not located in any one
country but taking global form, may be able to transcend some of the
battles. A few examples of voices raised in this regard will suffice. Eduard
Shevardnadze, the former Soviet foreign minister, declared, "To think of
democracy and freedom as Western values is complete arrogance, a Western delusion of grandeur. Universal human values cannot be reduced to
just Western ones." And Lin Binyan, the Chinese dissident, insisted,
"Humanism isn't the privilege of the West. It's a kind of insult to think
human rights don't matter as much in China."[18]

Whatever the rightness or wrongness of the arguments, the human
rights movement must be recorded as a matter of historical fact (see the
chapter by Louis Menand). The Helsinki Final Act of 1975 has had widespread repercussions. The Charter 77 movement, for instance, founded by
Vaclav Havel and others in response to Helsinki, became a powerful force
in Czechoslovakia. There, it was declared an "open community of people
of different convictions . . . to strive individually and collectively for the
respect of civil and human rights in our own country and throughout the
world."[19] And even further from the West, in Mongolia, the Mongolian
Democratic Association—a small group of students and intellectuals—
celebrated International Human Rights Day, December 10, 1991, in Ulaan-
baatar.[20]

Clearly, human rights are one facet of the policy implications of global
history. They are tied to the notion of a global village, linked by satellite
communication. In turn, the awareness of human rights links diverse
peoples in the new global community—a spiritual community gradually
becoming a defined subject of study for global history.

VII

Some of the challenges posed by global history to traditional notions of
national loyalty and localized notions of rights can be stated in terms of
identity. The concept of identity has come into widespread usage, in
regard to both the individual and the group. It should be noted that it is,
in fact, a Western-derived notion.

My intention is not to engage in an extended discussion of the origins
or nature of the term *identity*, or to make normative claims here; I merely
want to offer a few observations suggesting its possible role in global
history.[21]

First of all, it should be obvious that humans have multiple identities.
One may be a member of a family, a tribe, a nation, and humanity at one
and the same time, not to mention an ethnic group, a religious body, and
so forth. The next observation is that these multiple identities are hierar-

chical, in that some will take precedence over others (although possibly at varying times). One litmus test is to ask for which group a person is willing to die.

In our context, the important identities are those that are religious, ethnic, and/or national. Should identities be considered real or imagined? The debate over this question has primarily focused on primordial ties—ties that are presumed to be more basic, more unthinking, more "given" than others. In late nineteenth-century sociology, for example, they were conceptualized by the German sociologist Ferdinand Tönnies in terms of *Gemeinschaft*, in opposition to *Gesellschaft*. Thus, he spoke of a "community" as bound by ties of blood, land, and kinship—"organic" ties—in contrast to the mechanical and artificial bonds of "society."[22]

In more recent times, the issue of primordial ties has been taken up by anthropologists, spectacularly so by Clifford Geertz, as well as by sociologists. As with communities, much of the debate has raged over the issue of whether the ties are "real" or constructed. The very word *primordial* carries with it the connotation of unconstructed, that is, previous to conscious thought (though an argument can be made that, even if unconscious, ties can be "constructed").

Geertz's emphasis, for example, has been on describing such ties as symbolic processes, which clothe persistent patterns of social interaction with meaning. Nevertheless, as Allan Hoben and Robert Hefner pointed out, the clear implication of Geertz's work is that primordial ties are "in some sense the unreflexive product of a given social world, something that emerges quite spontaneously and thus without encouragement from higher-level political organizations. An individual is born and bred into them, so to speak, rather than being self-consciously instructed in their meaning or self-interestedly motivated in their pursuit."[23]

Clearly, the issue is a vexed one, and it vexes much work on questions of national or ethnic identity, among others. And it will vex any effort to think about a global identity. But having indicated the troubling nature of the subject—and stating my own view that primordial ties are, in fact, constructed—I now want to explore a different question about identity.

Can we identify the processes, political and psychological, involved in making a group identity? If so, can we then see how these or similar processes might serve in the construction of a global identity (not doing away with but adding to the others)?

This topic, again, is a huge and complicated one, whose fringes I merely touch upon. Certainly, land is frequently a factor in a person's sense of identity: "I come from X land." Of course, X has not always existed in a given form—in that sense, it is constructed—but *some* territorial base seems favorable for group identity. Will the "globe" (Spaceship Earth) supply that base in the future?

What of ethnicity, the extended form of kinship? Again, ethnicity is not an eternal affinity but the result of migrations, breeding patterns, and so forth. Nevertheless, existing ethnic feeling is a powerful bond. Like other badges of difference, it serves to mark an in and an out group, a demarcation seemingly essential to the group's definition. What counterpart can there be on the global level?

Further, over the last few centuries, a new form of identity—nationalism—has come into being. As modern democracy and industrialism, along with other novel forces, disrupted older social ties and called into question the legitimacy of hereditary monarchies and empires, the "nation," seen as something above personal, class, or any other interest, came to claim one's being. Can global history transcend these national ties and lay claims of its own on humans everywhere?

Of the numerous other factors in identity, I will look at only one more here, a psychological one (reserving language for separate treatment later in this introduction). Case study after case study suggests that a key factor in the rise of ethnic or national identity is a sense of humiliation. If members of a group feel insulted and humiliated, their self-worth is eroded. In reaction, they become assertive and claim to be special, indeed, superior, and they clothe themselves in a unique identity. In almost all cases, that unique identity, by definition, is closed to others.

On the face of it, it would seem impossible to build a global identity from a sense of humiliation (or from many of the other psychological building blocks of ethnic or national identity). Nor can it be exclusive. What psychological factors, then, can be identified as constituting a global identity?

In this regard, several further questions are pertinent. Are some identities pathological and others healthy? That is, do some ethnic and national identities entail projections of such an evil nature that extermination of the "other" becomes requisite? Would global identity be free from such pathological elements? Can a global identity be forged without some variant of them? To raise such questions is to indicate the nature of the inquiry that must be pursued.

It should be made clear, however, that whatever the nature of global identity, it will be different from earlier claims to some version of universality. It will recognize other, multiple forms of identity, and it will honor and prize these local forms along with its new global affirmation. Earlier cosmopolites sought to detach themselves from their local ties. Thus, as Moses Finley told us, the philosophical schools after Aristotle— the Cynics, Stoics, and Epicureans—"dismissed the Greek *polis* as meaningful; they depoliticalized ethics and sought virtue within the individual independent of the social relationship in which he lived. 'I am a *cosmop-*

olites', Diogenes the Cynic is supposed to have said, a citizen of the cosmos, the universe."[24]

François-Marie Voltaire could proudly declare, "I am a citizen of the world." But this was mere rhetoric. His world was that of Europe, which meant mainly Western Europe, and Voltaire was the quintessential Frenchman. Any global identity will have to be based on the reality of globalization—an actual, lived experience. It will exist because all members of the globe are subject to the same powerful factors of globalization described earlier. As a result, they may begin to have a shared identity, standing above all others, as the national stands above the regional and the regional above the more local. In short, global identity, if it is to emerge, will have to be constructed out of common global experiences, whose dimensions and ways of forging identity are not yet clear.

VIII

Language, along with territory, ethnicity, common history, and so forth, seems to play a major role in the formation of communities and identities. What will be the language component of global community and identity? Again, I will only touch on a matter requiring extensive research and development.

Claims to a universal language have been made in the past. The Christian West has asked, "What language would the first man have spoken?" and devised experiments to find out (such as isolating newborn children, which would not be permissible today). Latin was long vaunted as a universal language, and in Islam, the claims for Arabic have been set forth.

Let us look further at Latin for a moment. In fact, it was a parochial Western language, whose claims rose and fell with the reach of the Roman Empire and then of the Christian church. What is of interest for our purposes is that it served to link a large part of the known world (leaving aside major areas such as China and India, no small omission) in the time of Roman and Christian domination. This linguistic domain was largely shattered, however, with the rise of the vernaculars during the Renaissance. That rise, in turn, was correlated with the subsequent coming of nationalism.

A fascinating account can be secured from Lucien Febvre and Henri Martin's *The Coming of the Book*, much of which was then summarized and linked directly to nationalism by Benedict Anderson.[25] Their thesis was that the invention of the printing press around 1459 (based on inspiration from China) took on capitalist trappings in the form of the book trade.

That trade was international or at least inter-European. Readers of the books formed the embryo of an imagined community.

That community was the Republic of Letters, in which Voltaire claimed membership. The paradox is that, although most books were printed in Latin, the new press also fostered the emergence of vernacular literature—a much wider market, bringing in non-Latin readers—by reducing dialects to a uniform language. These languages could then become the basis of national communities and ultimately of nationalism.

Still, the quest for universality persisted, even if expressed in many tongues. Thus, Johann Wolfgang von Goethe came to speak of a "world literature." Although he bridged the classical and the romantic movements, it was the romantics in nineteenth-century Europe who truly opened the way to a transnational literature, at least in principal. They did this by extolling the exoticism of non-Western art and literature, based on different canons but nonetheless on equal terms with the works of classical antiquity and the Renaissance.

George Eliot expressed a European version of this attraction to the different when she praised William Wordsworth and Wilhelm von Riehl (a German writer) for their interests in the local and in the "real language of men." The link of this interest and the construction of a transnational community was made clear in a passage from her *Mill on the Floss.* "'Nay, Miss, I'n no opinion o' Dutchmen. There ben't much good i 'know-in' about *them*,'" said Luke, the head miller. To which the heroine, Maggie, answered, "'But they're our fellow-creatures, Luke—we ought to know about our fellow-creatures.'"[26]

Knowing about our fellow-creatures is an intention of romantic and world literature. But in fact, it does not get us very far. Large numbers of people in the world are illiterate. Only an elite, though a substantial one, can be said to read in any language. And much of so-called world literature is written in the European languages, especially English, of course.

Can English claim to be on its way to becoming a global language? There is no question that it is becoming a sort of lingua franca (to the dismay of the French, as well as many others). Yet there are obvious limitations to the use of English as the daily language of a global culture.

A different sort of contender for universal discourse is mathematics. Yet though mathematics does transcend all vernaculars, it, too, is inherently limited in reaching a wide populace, partly because of its abstract nature.

Are there any other candidates for a global language? A closer glance at one of the factors that make global history—satellite communications—may point to other possibilities. I will touch on the role of satellite communications via its expression in three modes. The first is computer language. Indeed, it is computer technology—in itself a powerful force bringing about global history—that makes possible satellite communi-cation, and computer language is rapidly becoming a form of global connection.

So, too, is global TV, with its use of visual images accessible to all humanity. They form part of the new, shared global language. This is a topic on which much expansion is possible (radio, for example, certainly warrants discussion).

Lastly, music speaks in a more or less universal tongue (see the chapter by John Joyce). Whether in the form of rock and roll or even classical music, this wordless tongue speaks to all of us. As Seiji Ozawa, discussing classical music in Japan, said, "The impact of classical music . . . is without boundaries. It is classless, stateless and essential!"[27] Rock stars have be-come the new global heroes, and classical performers (conductors like Ozawa, as well as soloists of all kinds) have clearly also emerged as new "global actors."

Global history will have to study the spread of new forms of universal languages, as well as the more traditional ones of the written word. This empirical study must then be related to theories about an emerging global community and identity.

IX

What is our conception of the globe, on which we and our communities deport ourselves? How does it differ from previous conceptions? To suggest the importance of this subject for global history, I will make a few remarks about space and time, about cartography and calenders.

With maps, it is obvious that perspective is all. From what point is one conceiving the world? For modern Westerners, that point was deter-mined, until recently, by the period of the great discoveries, when the Atlantic nations began their seabound sweep across the world. David Harvey identified this moment with the introduction of the Ptolemaic map in Florence in 1400, based, as he put it, on mathematical principles and money, i.e., trade needs. "Thereafter," he declared, "it became pos-sible in principle to comprehend the world as a global unity."[28]

Such "global" comprehension, however, was still radically Eurocentric. Marshall G.S. Hodgson gave us some idea of the problem when he compared the Muslim and West European images of the world. The Muslims' images, he argued, were "noticeably more balanced." Where the Muslims divided the world into seven parts, the Europeans divided it into "only three, centered on the Mediterranean Sea (the lands north of it were Europe; those south of it, Africa; those east of it, Asia)." As Hodgson added, "Such a distribution was naturally totally inappropriate to the hemisphere as a whole."

The absurdity of the Eurocentric view (which was also ethnocentric, with its concept of "Orient" and "Orientalism") was disguised by the use of "a drastically visually distorted world map, the Mercator projection, which by exaggerating northward manages to make an artificially bounded 'Europe' look larger than all 'Africa', and quite dwarf that other Eurasian peninsula, India. In this way all the 'well-known' cities of Europe can be included, while the unfamiliar cities of India can be omitted."[29]

Paradoxically, it was the cities of India that first lured the New World discoverers onward. Having served this purpose, India then was pushed to the margin of the Mercator maps. The further paradox is that Western imperialism then put India back on the map; James Rennell, surveyor general of Bengal in 1777, "literally put India on the map with his comprehensive *Map of Hindoostan*."[30] Though the physical entity—India, as a whole—could not itself actually be seen, the mapping nevertheless created an "imagined" country and eventually a nationalism to go with it.

In discussing the history of cartography, with an eye toward global history, I must note that while spaces might be indicated, peoples might not. Thus, European maps and accompanying travelogues often depicted "empty" lands, as if the indigenous populations had disappeared into thin air.

In fact, there was a grain of truth to this representation. Much of the earth *was* empty in the sense of being sparsely populated. European populations could pour into them—North and South America, Australia, New Zealand—in seemingly unimpeded migrations. Even by the mid-eighteenth century, the time of Carolus Linnaeus, only about one-fifth of the earth's surface had been explored and something like one-tenth of its plants and animals discovered. Today, as Neva Goodwin points out in her chapter, the earth is known and "full"—at least of humans. And as Wang Gungwu demonstrates in his chapter, migrations now must be viewed in a different way for a global historical perspective.

Globalization, while changing our mapping of the world, is also changing the nature of that world and our existence in it. Most notably in the form of expansionist capitalism, it is annihilating space, both physically and socially, as events everywhere implode upon us simultaneously. As David Harvey noted, too, while reducing spatial barriers, multinational capital also favors small-scale, finely graded differences of place, with their particular labor supplies, infrastructures, resource mixes, and so on.[31] Or, to repeat, the more global, also the more local.

In the mid-nineteenth century, Thomas Macauley compared the globe, as something embracing the whole, and the Atlas, as something with a different country on each leaf or page.[32] It is clear that we need both. Further, we need new maps. Most maps today are still based on political divisions, that is, the nation-state. Some, of course, transcend national boundaries by focusing on geological features or rainfall or other natural phenomena. We might go further and regularly draw maps based on linguistic or ethnic or religious ordering, which would give a rather different view of the state of humanity. For example, a map showing twenty million Kurds, spread over a specific geographical terrain, might be as important as one showing eighteen million Iraqis. In short, global history might foster all kinds of new maps, especially those stemming from the new communications and cultural ties of our satellite age.

Above all, the emerging cartography will be developed from the perspective of outer space, seeing the globe as a whole. Weather coverage on TV already locates us above the earth, within the drifting clouds. Thus, not only nation-states but also Eurocentrism is being transcended in the course of "local" weather reports. Where New World voyages were primarily open to people in the Atlantic coast nations, space voyages are open, in principle, to almost anyone on the globe. The earth itself becomes the launching pad, and once in space, we see that the earth is, indeed, a globe. This is the new map on which all of us now increasingly chart our sense of ourselves as global beings.

The new spatial conception is matched by a new time sense. Time and space, in fact, have been compressed. The two concepts go together, and a few words will indicate the importance of time for global history. Our guide again can be David Harvey. As he pointed out, with the conquest of space through the railroad, telegraph, telephone, and radio, the way was prepared for international agreement on the meridian and time zones, as well as the beginning of the global day. The result, unfolding gradually even before 1884 and before any formal agreement, was a new sense of "simultaneity over space and total uniformity in coordinated and universally uniform time."[33] With global communications, the pace has accelerated even further.

The advent of the global day has been preceded and accompanied by that of the global year. The whole world is now more or less on the same calender.[34] This fundamental shift dates approximately from the late nineteenth century, when the Christian era system (beginning with the incarnation of Christ) by and large replaced the East Asian chronological systems. Based in China, for example, on sexagesimal cycles and dynasty names, these had existed for over 2,000 years. So, too, had the Islamic calender separated itself from the Christian, from the time of the hegira when Muhammad moved from Mecca to Medina (ca. 622-623 in the Christian calender).

In the late twentieth century, almost the whole world is on one calender. (Some cultures also retain the "old" calender; thus, the era names system is still in use in Japan, along with the Western calender.) Yearly time, as well as the dating of the day, has become global. In terms of global history, a single, accelerating time-space perspective is shaping human existence. Exactly how this is occurring and what its impact is on different people and localities will be a major research project for coming global historians. What I have offered here are only a few hints.

X

Up to this point, I have been sketching the definition, nature, and meaning of global history. I can now ask, in the most tentative manner: Does global history have policy implications? The answer is yes, as does all history. But it must immediately be added that such policy implications need to be predicated on actual, empirical work in global history. With this fully understood, a few suggestions may be in order.

Environmental impact statements are now common: Why not require global impact statements? These would be yearly or biennially prepared reports, describing and analyzing both the way globalization factors are affecting humanity and the way local and national decisions are affecting the globe. In fact, the reports could be part of the effort to understand the role of the state (i.e., the nation-state) and to write its history from a new perspective. For example, a military or economic decision on the part of a given state should be evaluated not solely in terms of its service to a presumed national interest but also in terms of a perceived global interest.

The Nuremberg trials tried to establish accountability under international law. Should we have nongovernmental "trials" of national leaders in the light of a global history perspective? Obviously, these would have no force other than that of opinion. They would have to be carefully prepared, as if they were legal trials, but recognizing that the criteria employed would not be juridical codes but historical standards. The dangers of tendentious trials and sensationalist publicity would have to be carefully guarded against. In short, such trials would have to be undertaken on the basis of serious historical scholarship—global in perspective and consciousness—and conducted in a sober and somber vein.

XI

As research or as policy, global history poses a host of problems (see the chapter by Raymond Grew). Some of them have already been touched upon. There is, for example, the question noted earlier: How does one do global history? What is the most useful methodology? The answer will probably be many voiced and dependent on the particular topic being studied. In any case, theory and empirical research must go hand in hand, as they should in all historical work.

Another problem concerns what topics should be investigated and how far back we should reach into the past. This book suggests a number of topics, and others will come readily to mind. Again, the answer on the time period to be covered will depend on the particular subject.

Then there is the question of institutionalizing the subject. If global history is a valid enterprise and if it is to flourish, concrete steps must be taken to ensure that it does thrive. For example, should there be a journal of global history?[35] Should sessions or panels be held at professional meetings? Should an association be formed? Should other new, more electronic connections be made? Even more delicate, can global history enter the curriculum of history departments as a regular subject, and can people in this new subfield be hired and tenured? It is in the context of such questions that the present series has been conceived as a way of fostering and disseminating the work of scholars who will be grappling with the challenge of conceiving and bringing global history into being.

XII

The chapters that follow offer further reflections on the nature of global history and some initial applications of the approach. These theoretical and applied efforts, like the present introduction, are primarily meant to be illustrative—to start a dialogue, to initiate efforts at a new way of conceptualizing parts of history.

I hope that each of the chapters, in turn, will serve as the spark for an entire volume in this series: e.g., on the comparison of universal, world, and global history; on migrations; on human rights; on the arts and literature; on multinationals and the economy; and on the environment. Other topics come readily to mind, such as the city in a globalizing society, science as a universalizing force, religion in the same mode, gender and global history, communications and media, and globalism and localism (indeed, a volume on this subject is already scheduled to appear next, edited by Wolf Schäfer).

The overall aim of the series and of this volume is to foster a new scholarly perspective, a new historical consciousness, and a new subfield of history—global history—that will have a major impact on the way we conceptualize our epoch and how we go about writing history and making policy in a world experiencing globalization. The ambitions of this enterprise are justified, we hope, by the vastness of the challenge posed for us by a universe that is enlarging and a globe that is shrinking.

Notes

1. I might note how this project originally came into being. In 1988, I participated in a seminar on "Global Issues," run by Neva Goodwin, a development economist. I was the only historian in a group consisting of economists, anthropologists, sociologists, and policymakers, and my mind became filled with the buzzword *globalization* and its attendant manifestations. The question, What is global history? (in obvious memory of E. H. Carr's book) immediately arose in this context. With the help of friends and other scholars, we organized a small planning meeting, and the resulting enthusiasm prompted us to go on to a larger, international conference at Bellagio, Italy, in the summer of 1991. Support for these meetings was given mainly by the Culpeper Fund, with further assistance from the Toynbee Foundation, the Rockefeller Brothers Fund (RBF), and the Rockefeller Foundation. For their generous support, I wish, on behalf of all of us involved in this enterprise, to express appreciation. A special debt of gratitude is owed to Colin Campbell, president of the RBF, for his continuing faith and excitement about the initiative.

2. See Charles W. Fornara, *The Nature of History in Ancient Greece and Rome* (Berkeley: University of California Press, 1983). Though their histories were wide-ranging, neither Herodotus nor Thucydides wrote universal history as such.

3. Fernand Braudel, "Personal Testimony," *Journal of Modern History* 44, no. 4 (December 1972), 457. The next quote is from p. 466.

4. Cf. Peter Burke, *The French Historical Revolution: The Annales School 1928-89* (Cambridge: Polity Press, 1990), 41, 46, and 113.

5. Roland Robertson, *Globalization: Social Theory and Global Culture* (London: Sage Publications, 1992), has done much to foster such a perspective using a sociological approach. His concern with globalization stems from his interests in the sociology of religion, international relations, and modernization theory. Other works to be consulted in this vein are Mike Featherstone, ed., *Global Culture. Nationalism, Globalization and Modernity* (London: Sage Publications, 1990) and, using an anthropological approach, Eric R. Wolf, *Europe and the People Without History* (Berkeley: University of California Press, 1982).

6. Mao was quoted in Dona Torr, *Marx on China, 1853-1860* (London: Lawrence & Wishart, 1951), xviii. The next quote is from Roderick McFarquhar, ed., *The Secret Speech of Chairman Mao* (Cambridge, Mass.: Harvard University Press, 1989), 114.

7. Quoted in Edward W. Said, *Orientalism* (New York: Pantheon Books, 1978), 37.

8. Max Weber, *The Protestant Ethic and the Spirit of Capitalism*, trans. Talcott Parsons (New York: Charles Scribner's Sons, 1958), 13.

9. Quoted in Charles Coulston Gillespie, *Genesis and Geology* (Cambridge, Mass.: Harvard University Press, 1951), 104. Raymond Grew gives a different twist to this image in Chapter 10, when he remarks that the perception of global ecology "can be expected to affect our view of history as much as ideas of geology and evolution affected historical practice in the nineteenth century."

10. Arnold Toynbee, *The Industrial Revolution* (Boston: Beacon Press, 1956), 55 (originally published in 1884).

11. See the exciting new book by Liah Greenfeld, *Nationalism: Five Roads to Modernity* (Cambridge, Mass.: Harvard University Press, 1993).

12. Benedict Anderson, *Imagined Communities* (London: Verso, 1983). Incidentally, it should be noted that some protagonists of nationalism in the eighteenth and nineteenth centuries envisioned it in the service of humanity at large, that is, as universalism.

13. Eric Hobsbawm, *Nations and Nationalism Since 1780* (Cambridge: Cambridge University Press, 1990), 163.

14. *The Economist*, June 23, 1990, 12.

15. Quoted in Greenfeld, *Nationalism*, 85.

16. Amartya Sen, *New York Review of Books*, June 14, 1990, 51. Sen also noted that the situation is changing slowly.

17. T. H. Huxley, "Administrative Nihilism," in Alburey Castell, ed., *Selections from the Essays of Thomas Henry Huxley* (New York: Appleton-Century-Crofts, 1948), 35.

18. Shevardnadze's quote is from the *New York Times*, December 6, 1989, A31, and Lin Binyan's is from the *New York Times*, "News of the Week in Review," February 19, 1989, 1.

19. Quoted in William Luers, "Czechoslovakia: Road to Revolution," *Foreign Affairs* 69 (Spring 1990), 86.

20. Fred C. Schapiro, "A Reporter At Large," *The New Yorker*, January 20, 1992, 40.

21. See, for example, the works of Erik Erikson, especially *Childhood and Society* (New York: W. W. Norton, 1950).

22. Ferdinand Tönnies, *Community and Society* (in German, *Gemeinschaft und Gesellschaft*), trans. and ed. Charles P. Loomis (Harper & Row: New York, 1963). For my own views on Tönnies and this general problem, see *A New Science: The Breakdown of Connections and the Birth of Sociology* (New York: Oxford University Press, 1989; paperback ed., Penn State Press, 1993) and "The Breakdown of Connections and Modern Development," *World Development* 19, no. 1 (January 1991), 31-44.

23. Allan Hoben and Robert Hefner, "The Integrative Revolution Revisited," *World Development* 19, no. 1 (January 1991), 22. This entire article is very much worth reading, especially with thoughts about global history in mind. For Geertz, see his "Integrative Revolution: Primordial Sentiments and Civil Politics in New States," in *Old Societies and New States: The Quest for Modernity in Asia and Africa* (London: The Free Press of Glencoe, 1963). The other essential article is Edward Shils, "Primordial, Personal, Sacred and Civil Ties," *The British Journal of Sociology*, 8, no. 2 (June 1957), 130-145.

24. Moses Finley, *The Use and Abuse of History* (London: Chatto & Windus, 1975), 132.

25. Lucien Febvre and Henri-Jean Martin, *The Coming of the Book*, trans. David Gerard (London: Verso, 1990).

26. George Eliot, *The Mill on the Floss*, ed. A. Byatt (London: Penguin Books, 1985), 15 and 81.

27. Quoted in *The Economist*, August 10, 1991, 80.

28. David Harvey, "Between Space and Time: Reflections on the Geographical Imagination," *Annals of the Association of American Geographers* 80, no. 3 (1990), 424.

29. Marshall G.S. Hodgson, *The Venture of Islam: Conscience and History in a World Civilization*, vol. 1, *The Classical Age of Islam* (Chicago: University of Chicago Press, 1974), 55-56.

30. David Ludden, "Orientalist Empiricism," unpub. ms., 6.

31. Harvey, "Between Space and Time," 426-428.

32. Thomas Babington Macaulay, *Critical and Historical Essays*, 2 vols. (London: J.M. Dent & Sons, 1946), II, 389.

33. David Harvey, *Money, Time, Space, and the City: The Denman Lecture 1985* (Cambridge: Granta Editions, 1985), 10-11.

34. A wonderful article on this subject is Masayuki Sato's, "Comparative Ideas of Chronology," *History and Theory* 30, no. 3 (1991), 275-301.

35. There is a *Journal of World History*. That is not, however, the same thing as a journal of global history, although there undoubtedly would be overlaps.

PART ONE

The Theory
of Global History

1

The Rounding of the Earth: Ecology and Global History

Neva R. Goodwin

Introduction: Some Prerequisites for a New Subfield

Several books that I read a number of years ago had stuck in my mind as belonging to a special category but one for which I knew of no name. Recently, I have come to believe that the reason I did not know the name for this category was that it did not yet exist. But the right label has now been hit upon, and it is *global history*.

The first books I noted as belonging to this hitherto unnamed category were C. D. Darlington's *The Evolution of Man and Society*, Hans Zinsser's *Rats, Lice and History*, and William McNeill's *Plagues and Peoples*. If there was a common theme that linked these, it was the interweaving (if not, as in Sigmund Freud's dictum, the identity) of biology with human destiny.

More recently, a cluster of books has appeared, still coming from the special perspective that can now be recognized as the earmark of global history but ringing in changes on a different theme, that of human ecology or the interaction between humans and the environment. Examples in this area are *Out of the Earth: Civilization and the Life of the Soil* by Daniel J. Hillel, *Changing the Face of the Earth: Culture, Environment, History* by I. G. Simmons, *Seed to Civilization: The Story of Food* by Charles B. Heiser, Jr., and *Biohistory: The Interplay Between Human Society and the Biosphere Past and Present* by S. Boyden.

The common theme of these latter examples is the interaction of humanity and earth; the four authors are united in believing that our relation with the earth—the soil—is a reflection and a warning regarding the even larger issue of humanity's relation to our home planet, earth. I will discuss how this subject might fit under the name *global ecological history*, but first, it is necessary to put into its proper context the idea that is being suggested here: that there are recognizably different sorts of history and that it is legitimate for new ones to arise from time to time.

When one thinks of the different sorts of history that have been written recently—feminist history, for example, or the new social history (sometimes called history from below)—there seem to be four prerequisites for their legitimate appearance as history:

1. The subject matter must actually exist or have existed.
2. It must be consciously recognized as a subject unto itself.
3. It must be regarded as a fit subject for history.
4. There must be a perception that this subject is not adequately treated in the sorts of history that are already being written.

The writing of feminist history, for example, began with a combination of all these factors. Regarding requisite 1, females had always existed as approximately half of the human species. What had not existed in any widespread form was requisite—a defined recognition of feminist issues as such. Those could, however, be discovered with hindsight; history could be reframed in their terms as requisite 2 came into being with a modern definition of feminist issues. Requisite 3 was fulfilled only as a result of gradual (and, even at the present time, only partial) success in winning the bitter battle over requisite 4. This last issue was the real crux of the matter: to persuade a sufficient number of historians and readers and students of history that the subject matter—females and feminist issues—was not being adequately represented in standard historical treatments.

In the case of the new social history, again the subject matter—most generally, "the common people"—had always existed and had been known to exist. Here, there may have been more awareness of the subject *as* a subject, at least in the minds of politicians who had to sway these people; of social commentators (such as Aristotle and Niccolò Machiavelli) who perceived their role in the fabric of society; and of many religious leaders, clergy, and activists who, over the centuries, devoted themselves to bringing the common people to one form of salvation or another. The sticking point with the new social history appears to have been requisite 3. Unlike the situation with feminist history, once the case had been made that the common people were a fit subject for history, there was not much effort to argue against requisite 4, which would claim that the common people were not being adequately treated in standard approaches.

In the light of these other new sorts of history and parallel to the prerequisites for their emergence, some questions arise with respect to the new category of global history, of which I claim to have descried some examples:

1. What is its subject matter?
2. What is the basis for a conscious awareness of it?
3. Why is it a fit subject for history?
4. Is it reasonable to claim that the subject matter of global history is not adequately treated in the sorts of history that are already being written?

In the following sections, these questions will be taken up one by one. In answering the second question, I will come to the ecological writings wherein a major contemporary movement toward global history may be found.

What Is the Subject Matter of Global History?

Most broadly, global history is the story—or perhaps more realistically, a collection of stories—about the human race as a whole. The global historian presents stories with which all humans are invited to identify, rather than stories aimed to arouse the group consciousness of some.[1]

By the definition just given, feminist history would not be global history: It seeks to stir the group consciousness of one part of humanity, not the whole. Traditional history has also been intended to arouse group consciousness but on a geographical basis; it is disqualified as global history on both gender and geographical grounds.[2] Another interesting comparison to something that is *not* global history would be the history of the Jews. That is clearly not limited geographically, but equally clearly, it is not a story with which everyone is invited to identify: Indeed, the "insider—outsider" qualities of this story are part of its intrinsic character.

These three examples suggest some of what global history is *not*. It is not geographically localized; it is not gender specific; it is not the history of a particular ethnic or religious group. These could well be among the *themes* of global history but only when they emerge as part of some larger issue that is defined in the first instance as global. For example, the story of the Jews might play an important part in a history that looked at human migration from a global perspective. Similarly, feminist historians would have contributions to make to a global history of changing patterns of nurturance in the twentieth century. And the geographical boundaries of states and other groupings could, in themselves, be a topic for a global historical exploration of, for instance, the changing role of the state since 1648.

One aspect of the two recent movements in historiography that have been cited here will help shed additional light on what global history *is*. Feminist history and the new social history both proceed from a particular point of view, a particular *perspective*; in doing so, they illuminate the perspectives that had been left out of the standard histories in existence before their consciousness-raising introduction. Feminist history, with its perspective of the female half of the species, makes us aware that old standard histories had been written very largely from a male point of view. The new social history, with its common-people perspective, makes us aware that the old histories had been written mostly from an elite point of view or, one might say, from the viewpoint of the people in power.

For global history (by analogy with the phrase *sub specie aeternitatis*, meaning "with the perspective of the whole of time"), we may propose the phrase *sub specie speciis*, meaning "with the perspective of the whole species."[3] But what does it mean to take the perspective of the human race as a whole? Again, it is easiest to understand this newly proposed historical point of view by contrasting it with the dominant viewpoint that it challenges. The outstanding contrast is to the nationalist or local point of view that has been the predominant historical perspective not only since the rise of the nation-state in the sixteenth century but even back to the time of Plutarch or Julius Caesar. Most histories have had good guys and bad guys. If history as written until the last two decades has revolved around a single, outstanding topic, it has been wars, and their outcomes, which have been characterized as "victory" or "defeat," depending upon whether the nation or similar grouping whose point was represented in the history won or lost.

Those are very sweeping statements, only true if looked at from the most general kind of perspective—the kind of perspective, in fact, that is afforded by global history. I will now defer further consideration of what else we can expect to have imposed upon the adherents of this sort of history by its perspective. Instead, I will take up the second question posed earlier, regarding the appropriateness of establishing this proposed new kind of history.

What Is the Basis for a Conscious Awareness of Global History?

This question may be rephrased in this way: "What historical changes have created the global consciousness that is necessary to global history?" Among the answers to this question, one would include trade; technologies that, for example, permit rapid travel; the sharing of cultural and religious elements; and a system of values or ethics that defines the sphere of what matters to an individual as encompassing the whole human race or perhaps the whole biosphere (which, by definition, includes the whole human race).

Such an ethical system may arise in a variety of ways and has, indeed, done so in various times and places. At present, it is taking on a new form and a new strength in response to one additional source of global consciousness. This historical change is a process by which the human impact upon the environment has been continually and ever more rapidly extended—a process, I will argue, whose cumulative effects are such that, in the twentieth century, they differ not only in degree but also in kind from human experience before the nineteenth century.

To grasp the enormity of this change, try to imagine yourself as a member of a small community in a land perceived as having limitless scope. Here, individuals or bands or societies of human beings are insignificant in the vastness of the world that swallows them. Now compare that image with the reality that has emerged within the present century. It is not just that our technologies of transportation have altered our perceptions of distance, allowing us to fly across any ocean in a few hours. More to the point, we have invaded and altered all parts of this world; we have proven the limits of the earth by filling it up.

Ten or twelve thousand years ago, our species survived almost wholly on food collected from the "natural" state of the world, as yet unaffected by agriculture (though some speculate that human predation had already significantly affected the composition of species on most of the continents). Today, of a total terrestrial surface area of 147×10^6 square kilometers, 18×10^6 square kilometers (or a little more than one-eighth of the dry land of the earth) is under direct human use for habitation, cultivation, or other production (Simmons 1989, p. 14). A much larger fraction, as I will show, is indirectly employed to human ends. Human activities have eradicated two-thirds of the earth's forest cover. We have tunneled through the Alps (followed by migrating birds that found the new passage within days of its opening); we have created the Arctic haze and the ozone holes; and we are probably increasing the temperature of the whole system—the ecosystem of the earth—on which we are dependent.

Perhaps the most dramatic statement of this new reality has been made by the economist Herman Daly, in his description of what he called the "full world hypothesis." In a paper whose title is particularly appropriate to our subject—"From Empty World Economics to Full World Economics: Recognizing an Historical Turning Point in Economic Development"— Daly began with a calculation made by Peter Vitousek et al. (1986, pp. 368-373):

"If we take the percent appropriation by human beings of the net product of land-based photosynthesis as an index of how full the world is of humans and their furniture, then we can say that it is 40% full because we use, directly and indirectly, about 40% of the net primary product of land-based photosynthesis (Daly 1991, p. 18).

Daly noted that the calculation of the doubling time for the human use of resources should be based not only on the growth of the human population but also on population times per capita resource use. On this basis, the doubling time for the rate at which humanity is taking over the earth is thirty-five years. Looking backward, Daly calculated that in an average human lifetime of seventy years, we have doubled our filling of the earth twice, increasing from approximately 10% full in the 1920s to 40% full now. The rapidity of this shift is one of the reasons why people are only just beginning to understand its implications. Daly warned that

> 100% human preemption of net photosynthetic product . . . would seem to be ecologically quite unlikely and socially undesirable (only the most recalcitrant species would remain wild—all others would be managed for human benefit). In other words, effective fullness occurs at less than 100% human preemption of net photosynthetic product, and there is much evidence that long run human carrying capacity is reached at less than the existing 40% . . . Although 40% is less than half it makes sense to think of it as indicating relative fullness because it is only one doubling time away from 80%, a figure which represents excessive fullness (Daly 1991, p. 18).

The further implications that Daly drew from this include: (1) the need to shift from a mindset that sees man-made capital as always able to substitute for natural resources ("natural capital") to a recognition of the degree to which the two are complementary ("what good is a saw mill without a forest? a refinery without petroleum deposits? a fishing boat without populations of fish?" [Daly 1991, p. 19]), and (2) the necessity of recognizing that "the productivity of manmade capital is more and more limited by the decreasing supply of complementary natural capital" (Daly 1991, p. 19). The latter includes both the productive and the absorptive capabilities of the natural world.

A number of policy conclusions arise from this chain of logic. One example is a cluster of observations about investment, e.g., that "investment must shift from manmade capital accumulation towards natural capital preservation and restoration" (Daly 1991, p. 22). Also, because it is critical to cease artificially inflating returns on investment by ignoring the drawdown of complementary natural capital that has underpinned the apparently high returns of the past, it will be necessary to shift to an expectation of lower overall returns in the future.

The broader conclusions drawn by Daly were these:

Perhaps the clearest policy implication of the full-world thesis is that the level of per capita resource use of the rich countries cannot be generalized to the poor, given the current world population. Present total resource use levels are already unsustainable, and multiplying them by a factor of 5 to 10 as envisaged in the Brundtland report, albeit with considerable qualification, is ecologically impossible. As a policy of growth becomes less possible the importance of redistribution and population control as measures to combat poverty increase correspondingly (Daly 1991, p. 23.).

All this is very dramatic and of critical import. However, our material effect on the earth, as just described, is not the starting point for global consciousness. This consciousness, a psychological issue, begins, I believe, with our sense of the spatial relationship we have with our habitat. Ten thousand years ago, our species was a drop in the bucket, a little frog in a big pond; today, it is the species that has explored all of the territory, made some kind of a mark on every part and aspect of the biosphere, and eliminated every frontier. Our identity as the filler of the world, the rounder of the globe, may be said to have started with explorers such as the Portuguese in the fifteenth century; or perhaps even earlier with the Polynesian rafters (if, in fact, the latter were also motivated by the perception that, if they sailed far enough, they could go around the earth and come back where they started).

A modern expression of what it means to live on an earth that has been rounded and closed up was given by a beloved writer of children's books, Dr. Seuss. In *The Big Brag*, the boasting of a rabbit that could hear for miles and of a bear that could pick up odors from a great distance was topped by a little worm that bore through the air with his farseeing eyes and finally reported:

I looked 'cross the ocean, 'way out to Japan.
For I can see farther than anyone can . . .
I looked across Egypt; then took a quick glance
Across the two countries of Holland and France.
Then I looked across England and, also, Brazil.
But I didn't stop there. I looked much further still.
And I kept right on looking and looking until
I'd looked 'round the world and right back to this hill!
And I saw on this hill, since my eyesight's so keen,
The two biggest fools that have ever been seen! (Seuss, 1986.)

We may find a similar scenario in a different kind of source:

Imagine that in a space-ship we can rove among the stars and find points where our remote sensing technology can pick up the light reflected from earth about 2 million years ago and then zoom in, capturing images of the land surface every century or so until the very recent past. These images could be made into maps of the cover of the land surfaces and the conditions of shallow waters.... For example, in c. 8000 BC there is little land devoted to food production, rather than food collection, by humans; now there are 1472 million ha of cropland. In AD 1800 the area under urban use held 2.5 per cent of humans and now it houses 42 per cent. This book is about the history of such changes, and its basis is the gathering of empirical facts about the changes of the sort that our space-derived images would provide, were they not imaginary. But a unique feature of *Homo sapiens* is that observed facts also have meaning so we must provide a framework in which this information can escape from its status as mere isolated words or numbers and become a pattern. This pattern may be a clue to the kind of underlying regularities in nature and human activity that we call theory; equally it may lead to a set of tools for discussing the future, the more so since we may to a large extent choose the type of future we want (Simmons 1989, p. 1.).

It is perhaps not natural for humankind to start thinking about that whole of our environment until we have filled up the whole and been forced to turn back upon ourselves. In general, though, we know the boundaries between fact and fantasy; we know exactly how far we can go on the earth's surface before we come back to our starting point; and we know that nowhere on earth is there an ecosystem completely free of the effects of our own species.

These conditions make it almost impossible to avoid thinking globally. The whole globe swims into view as a single system when we have pushed the last frontier to the edge of the next town. It *demands* to be thought of as a single system when we can leave it and look back at it in space, to see Spaceship Earth from the outside. Systems analysis, as a discipline, confirms our global consciousness. We have a list of categories of systems, and we know just what kind this one is. We live in a quasi-closed system; that is, it is closed with the following exceptions:

- There is a quantifiable daily income of solar energy (the most important part, from our point of view, being that fraction transformed by plants into usable or "available" energy. (According to Daly and Vitousek, humanity is now appropriating 40 percent of that fraction on the land masses of earth.)
- There is a quantifiable daily loss of energy in the form of (mostly "unavailable") heat escaping from the atmosphere.
- A negligibly small amount of matter enters the system in the form of meteorites and other cosmic debris captured by Earth's gravity.

- A (thus far) negligibly small amount of matter is sent off the earth by humans in the process of exploring other parts of the universe.
- There are forces (most obviously, gravity) that operate across space and whose influence upon our planet also reduce the degree of "closedness" of our system.
- Those are all the exceptions. For the rest, we know, by and large, what we have; this is what we must make do with for the rest of our existence on earth.

This is the situation in which we find ourselves. It is not new (except for the small exception to closedness, whereby humans send material off this planet), but it is newly perceived and felt. The relatively recent knowledge and understanding of what it means to live in a quasi-closed system is well expressed in the book by Simmons:

Living tissue . . . comprises a number of chemical elements which combine with carbon to constitute organic matter. Of these, only oxygen and hydrogen are normally freely available in large quantities, and the others circulate between reservoirs ("pools") on varying scales. The pools usually include a non-living stage so the circulation of these elements is called a biogeochemical cycle. . . . The quantities and fluxes involved in many biogeochemical cycles are known at the world scale, and much research has elucidated the fine details for individual ecosystems. But we will note that the flow of such mineral nutrients (the overall term for these elements) is genuinely cyclic, unlike energy, even though the time-scale is geological rather than anthropocentric in some parts of a biogeochemical cycle (Simmons 1989, p. 13).

It is, I contend, this new consciousness, more than anything else, that makes us ready to consider that global history might be something real and interesting and of relevance to other contemporary issues of pressing importance.

The Brundtland Report, *Our Common Future* (1987),[4] has projected this same global consciousness forward, to force us to inquire about the future: *Are the patterns of development of the Western, industrialized nations sustainable into the foreseeable future? Can these same patterns safely and sustainably be followed by the rest of the world?*

It is becoming widely accepted that the answer to the second of these questions is "no." We hear that there are not enough trees to allow every citizen of the world to read the Sunday *New York Times*; not enough dumping space on earth's land or in the oceans to allow everyone to generate as much garbage as the average U.S. citizen does; and not enough tolerance in the ozone layer for the Third World to imitate the industrialized world's intensity of automobile use. If this is so, what implications can be drawn when we start thinking about the sustainability of modern patterns of development?

One of the implications is that *the pattern of change and development of any single country does not occur in a vacuum but must be understood as part of a global pattern of resource use.* Everything that has happened up to this very moment in time is history, and all of that (now unchangeable) history has its implications. The most obvious natural resources of our global environment—air, water, ocean habitats, genetic reservoirs—exist, at this moment, under levels of stress that are the result of past history. These stress levels are felt by different peoples in different ways. And incremental additions will be felt increasingly, in skin cancers, forests killed by acid rain, collapsed fish populations, and so forth.

Looked at historically, each nation's past development or nondevelopment fits into this overall picture and is a part of the explanation for where we are now: Each nation has had a certain impact upon the tolerance or the availability of certain resources. Looked at futuristically or with the eye of a planner, every additional movement in each nation's development will be a step—forward or backward or to the side—in the dance between the total global population of humans, on the one hand, and the carrying capacity of the earth, on the other.

It is particularly interesting, when thinking in this way, to consider patterns of agricultural development. Here, recognition of broadly *un*sustainable patterns has started in the most recently developing areas (as they adopt a scattering of farming techniques ranging from high to low tech) and is only gradually spreading to the leaders of the technological revolution in agriculture. Thus, it is well known that many changes in African farming techniques are headed for disaster; it is quite apparent that Indonesian farmers have been overstressing their soil and water resources; there are warnings on the sustainability of the advanced techniques that have been used for several decades in India; and unrest has been sparked among a small group of "low-input farming" advocates in Hungary. What about the United States? Would advice be likely to flow from this country to, say, Argentina, suggesting that its best path into the future may *not* follow the tracks laid down in the past in North America? (See Goodwin 1991.)

There are ethical and political issues involved here, as well as economic and technological ones. It is an untenable position for the world's largest resource user to tell other nations, "Now that we've gotten the lion's share, you should go easy on the rest for the sake of global humanity." The past is history, but it strongly shapes the future, including how various nations feel about the options they face. And how they feel about the options will, in turn, influence how they choose to act. Global history is concerned, among other things, with the events that constrict or enlarge the options that are open to mankind as a whole.

This is the context for an inevitable interdependence between the answers to the two questions posed above: "Are the patterns of development of the Western, industrialized nations sustainable into the foreseeable future?" and "Can these same patterns safely and sustainably be followed by the rest of the world?" It turns out that they cannot be answered separately. In asking how a country like Argentina should develop its agriculture, another question is implicitly raised: How should the United States (and, by extension, Canada, Australia, and New Zealand) *have* developed agriculturally? In charting an optimal course for the less developed countries, important issues are raised on whether it might be desirable for the more developed countries to veer in their course.

The four works of global ecological history that I cited near the beginning of this chapter share some characteristics with the foregoing discussion. Their concern with the past, with history, is closely—even agonizingly—linked to a concern for the trajectory into the future that may be inferred from that history.

Why Are These Global Subjects
a Fit Topic for History?

Probing the idea of history as a prelude to the future, we might inquire whether the books that are written from this motivation can be best understood as works of history or whether they should be placed in some other category. The following quotations, from the four works of global ecological history mentioned earlier, give the feel of the kind of work being discussed here:

> Traditionally, most agrarian societies have had annual birth and death rates in balance at about 40 per thousand. In the last forty years, however, death rates have dropped in many developing countries to below 15 per thousand, while birth rates have remained close to traditional levels. The imbalance is most notable in Africa, where population growth rates in some countries are over 3 percent per annum. They were almost this high in Asia two decades ago, but most Asian countries are now undergoing a slow decline of birth rates that eventually will bring births and deaths into balance (Hillel 1991, p. 262).

Between 1850 and 1960—the great period of voluntary European migration—60 million people left the continent to settle in far-away lands. This figure represents about a fifth of the population of Europe at the beginning of this period.

Largely as a consequence of these developments, the Caucasian population of the world increased 5.4 times between the years 1750 and 1930, while in the same period the Asian population increased 2.3 times and the African population less than 2 times (Boyden 1992, p. 113).

> Most of the important domesticated animals came from the Near East, a few from southeast Asia. After they were domesticated, use of these animals spread around the world. The ancient Egyptians kept a large number of animals, but with the exception of the cat, none became truly domesticated. A few animals were domesticated in the New World, but with the exception of the turkey they did not become widely used outside of their homeland. Columbus brought cattle and sheep with him on his second voyage and these Old World animals soon became widespread in the Americas (Heiser 1991, p. 34).[5]

Energy use per head in an industrial world can usefully be compared with past times. Hunter-gatherers can only tap solar energy and nearly all of this comes in the form of food and fire. Their energy throughput as food is perhaps 2000 kcal per head per day. . . . Even without access to fossil fuels, agriculturalists nevertheless use draught animals, construct irrigation channels, use wind and water power and may produce surpluses: They can be responsible for throughputs of 10-20,000 kcal per head per day. . . . Members of today's full industrialized societies are at the level of 120,000 kcal per head per day (Simmons 1989, p. 212).

Perhaps the first reaction to the passages just quoted will be, Is this really history? That is a valid question: One reason to have quoted at such length was to raise it for discussion. These passages do not sound like the kind of history we are used to. By way of comparison, it is worthwhile to offer some companion examples of a more familiar type of history. Here are three fairly typical passages:

> [In the 1396 Crusade of Nicopolis] knights assembled with great pomp at Buda and proceeded along the Danube of Nicopolis, pillaging and slaying. On Sept. 25 they met the Turks about four miles south of Nicopolis. The knights ignored all advice and pressed forward; after an initial success they were completely overwhelmed and many captured. Forces were about 20,000 on each side (*An Encyclopedia of World History* 1948, p. 326).

> The Chalukya ruler, Jayasimha Siddharaja, a patron of letters, although himself a Saiva, organized disputations on philosophy and religion, and favored a Jain monk, Hemachandra, who converted and dominated Kumarapala. As a good Jain, he decreed respect for life (*ahimsa*), prohibited alcohol, dice, and animal fights, and rescinded a law for confiscation of property of widows without sons. He also built (c. 1169) a new edifice about

the Saiva temple of Somanatha, which had been reconstructed by Bhimadeva I (1022-1062) after destruction by the Moslems (*An Encyclopedia of World History* 1948, p. 332).

William the Conqueror, whose cause was favored by the Pope, was soon submitted to by the English, who wanted leaders, and had been of late much accustomed to usurpation and conquest. Edwin and Morcar, the earls of Mercia and Northumbria, declared for him: and even Stigand, the patriotic archbishop of Canterbury, found it advisable to go with Edgar Atheling to meet William and offer him the crown (Carroll 1977, pp. 32-33).[6]

There is a level of detail here that is part of the fascination of such histories. Individuals are named: Jayasimha Siddharaja; the good Jain, Hemachandra; William the Conqueror; and Stigand, the patriotic archbishop of Canterbury. The numbers given are generally on a comprehensible scale: We can imagine 20,000 Christian knights arrayed against as many Turks. If the old standard histories were written from the point of view of the people in power (as I claimed earlier), still we are invited to see power from the inside and thus to identify with the story. We are shown how power can be used to protect widows and rebuild temples, how it can influence popes and patriots.

In global history, if the books cited in this chapter are any guide, the doings of individuals and groups like those named here will no longer claim center stage. A few counterexamples that come to mind are the exceptions that prove the rule. In *The Evolution of Man and Society*, there was a vivid encounter with Nesta, the daughter of Rhus ap Tewdwr and the "patroness of all Norman hybridization," who, according to C. D. Darlington (1969, p. 442), made a unique contribution to the genetic pool of the British Isles by producing nearly twenty children from at least half a dozen different fathers.[7] In the three quotations from ecological histories, the only individual mentioned was Christopher Columbus. As I see it, global history, by and large, will not be about individuals.[8]

In place of the details of the old standard histories, which portray local incidents and individual actors, global history will depend upon generalizations about the effects of (or on) human beings in groups or as a species. Unlike histories that gain their coherence from a geographic, gender, or ethnic definition, global history will depend upon *themes*. The theme of the book by Hillel, for example, is the human/soil interaction. The story line follows the recurring, expectable results of agriculture, where cycles of success are followed by collapse due to silt and salt buildup. Some of the details of the stories of global ecological history are geographically localized, as in Hillel's descriptions of the fall of Greece and Rome (each related to declining soil fertility) or in Heiser's brief review of the locus for animal domestications. Often, however, the details are given in the form of global statistics, like Hillel's figures on the demographic transition, on the loss of forest cover, and on the amounts of water withdrawn by humans from the natural hydrological cycle.

Themes, generalizations, statistics—do these make up history? One of the four books on ecological subjects has the word in its title: Simmons's *Changing the Face of the Earth: Culture, Environment, History*. The quotation from that book given earlier could equally well appear in a work on energy economics or energy policy. Moreover, the major headings of the book are "Primitive Man and His Surroundings"; "Advanced Hunters"; "Agriculture and Its Impact"; "Industrialists"; and "The Nuclear Age" (a relatively short section). A large part of the "historical" material, in fact, comes from prehistory. One point illustrated by this is that, if one is looking for a story that will be relevant to all people, the further back in time one goes (at least within the life span of our species), the easier it is to find it. This is because after a certain number of generations (eight is the number I have heard), virtually any civilization contains individuals who were one's own genetic ancestors. Thus, global history, in addition to taking in a broad geographical sweep, may often encompass a longer than usual sweep of time, as well.

This observation raises the question of identity again. In eschewing geography as the source for identification, does global history offer genes instead? What does it, in fact, offer that is not to be found in other, existing kinds of history? This brings me to the last of the four original questions.

Is It Reasonable to Claim That the Subject Matter of Global History Is Not Adequately Treated in the Sorts of History That Are Already Being Written?

To answer this, I will assume that global history has been accepted and ask the inverse of the question just posed: Will global history—along with the two other new sorts of history that have been discussed here (new social history and feminist history)—completely replace the old? Consider first the new types that already exist. I would guess that there will always be some interest in the histories of power offered by the elitist, old standard histories. The new social history will not replace these, but while coexisting with them, it may become the more popular type.

It seems harder to justify histories that explicitly give only a male point of view. If that statement is accepted, then its corollary may also be accepted: It is hard to justify histories that explicitly give only a female point of view. This leads to the conclusion that, if or when it is truly successful, feminist history will be so well incorporated into a new standard history that, as a separate strain, it will be virtually eliminated—

except as a watchdog function that will probably be needed to keep that history from reverting to the view point of one sex *or* the other.

I am suggesting that some form of the standard history will probably continue as a complement to the new social history. Furthermore, both will likely adapt under the pressure of the feminist challenge by changing quite radically, to incorporate the half of humanity that had earlier been excluded from full representation. Do either of these projected forms (a gender-equal elite history or a gender-equal history of "the people") include all that is proposed in global history? The answer seems to be no because of the nationalist or local point of view that characterizes most existing history books.

Conclusions: Global History for the Future

This is not to suggest that global history will answer to all needs, just as new social history does not. There will always be interest in the particular—the local and the national. At the same time, global history has a niche of its own: It is relevant when we truly want to see the human race *sub specie speciis*, as though we are looking at the whole earth and its inhabitants from another spaceship—for example, in studies of the human impact on the global environment. Perhaps the most difficult issue—which I will raise here, but not attempt to resolve—is how global history will cope with the fact that the more human beings recognize their global identity, the more they simultaneously cherish their specific local identities. In the real world, globalism and localism are mutually reinforcing trends (though not without tension). The institutional and intellectual niche for global history will somehow have to take account of this reality.

We are most apt to seek a global point of view when we want to think about the future. The four ecologically oriented books cited in this chapter are very evidently related to the kinds of policy required to preserve reasonable options for future human beings. They suggest the types of behavior changes and policy shifts that will be necessary to make our patterns of development sustainable. In contrast to the old standard histories, which identified good guys and bad guys in terms of groups at war against one another, the bad guy in the ecological histories is the human race in its present mode of destroying the world on which it depends. To be a good guy, according to a species survival criteria, one must learn to establish a sustainable balance.

The way we write history influences the way we think about policy and vice versa. In the title to his article quoted earlier in this chapter, Daly cited "an historical turning point in economic development." His sense that history had come to a new place in the human/environment relationship impelled him to point out several new policy directions. These, in turn, suggest new ways of looking at the history of growth and distribution: Surely, history must be written differently if we come to regard as a disaster, rather than a triumph, the scale of our population growth and the speed and manner of our appropriation of earth's resources. The sense of what the most important subjects are will also shift with new policy positions. For example, there appears to be reason for a heightened interest in a history of investment that would look, over time and space, at what investment means and who will reap what benefits from it.

Though less obviously, the three books cited at the beginning of this chapter, which linked human destiny with biology, also had messages for policy and for the future. For instance, valuable lessons can be drawn for our understanding of AIDS from Zinsser and, even more, from McNeill. Perhaps the deepest lesson in all of these books, however, is a rather general one regarding the place of a single individual (e.g., the individual reader). Whether in looking at the long sweep of genetic evolution—with the coadaptation of humans, the microorganisms they carry, and the animals they hunt, domesticate, or unintentionally harbor—or in looking at the changes we have wrought, from the time we first learned to use fire and metal, upon the planet earth, we see ourselves as just one member of a long progression. In perceiving our relative unimportance, it may be hoped that we will also come to value a way of life that preserves something larger and longer lasting with which we can identify. Perhaps that is the human race, past and present; perhaps it is that even more abstract concept, the biosphere.

Is this not what history has always been about, at least in part? Have not the sensitive readers of Pliny or Edward Gibbon or Macaulay come away humbled by their exposure to vast panoramas, in which their own time is but an instant? If this is so, it is an argument for including global studies, as described in this chapter, within a tradition that would call them history—even though their use of themes, generalizations, and statistics has a different feeling from the local and individual particulars we are more used to seeing in history books.

Notes

A number of friends and colleagues have responded in useful ways to this chapter; the following is but a partial list of those to whom I am indebted. Mary Midgley has not only discussed the chapter with me, but has written out her comments at several stages. Miriam Campanella and Boris Mironov also kindly supplied me with written comments. Sudhir Kakar especially drew my attention to the centrality of the concept of identity throughout the chapter. Ralph Buultjens and Bruce Mazlish have also made especially helpful suggestions.

1. As Mary Midgley rightly noted, "There can't be a single, comprehensive global story: all stories are partial" (personal communication, August 1991). Sudhir Kakar probed the concepts in the preceding paragraph with some penetrating questions: What psychology of identification is assumed here? Is it on an individual or a group basis that humans are invited to identify with the stories of global history? Is it possible, as implied here, to identify with a group as large as our species? My own assumption is that the answer to the last question is yes. But I recognize that if this definition is to be used in work that is more specifically applied than this chapter, questions such as those posed by Kakar will require more informed reflection than I am able to give.

2. Feminists, claiming that traditional history largely left out happenings of concern to women, see that genre as defined both geographically and by gender. It is worth noting, however, that traditional history was not overtly *intended* to consolidate a male consciousness. To the extent that it excluded women, it did so because the writers (men) did not notice them; many women, presented with no alternative, accepted these stories as their own and did their best to identify with them. I remember studying Greek history in fifth grade with an uneasy awareness that it was hard to identify with those people. I also recall an uncomfortable, unexpressed feeling that to insist upon knowing more about the women of the time would simply result in humiliation (by identification), caused by confronting the inferiority of their position.

3. Mary Midgley made an impassioned objection to this, citing the inadequacy of the concept:

> I have to say, *this simply is not half global enough*. It is not possible to stop at the species boundary. Nobody, not even people who would willingly ditch all the whales and the elephants and the albatrosses and the battery chickens and the arthritic, cross-eyed transgenic pigs, can now consider our species in isolation from the others. Its fate simply is not separate in the way that people used to believe. What is happening in the rainforests and the Sahel and Polynesia and the Antarctic and Lake Baikel is happening to everything and everybody. It will increasingly happen to them everywhere (personal communication, August 1991).

Here, again, we have the issue of identity: Whose stories are my story? Moreover, can we feel that something matters or act as if it matters if we do not identify with it?

Competing with identification as bases for action are self-interest and aesthetics, as well as other motives that can be subsumed under the term *morality*.

4. The principal author of this report, Jim MacNeill, is, coincidentally, a cousin of William McNeill, who was mentioned earlier. Although their last names are spelled differently, they share the same grandparents and a similar global outlook.

5. Heiser (1991, p. 34) defined a domesticated animal as "one that breeds under human control," adding that "if we accept this definition, it follows that human beings are not a fully domesticated species, for they have not yet succeeded in controlling their own breeding."

6. Devotees of *Alice in Wonderland* will recognize this as the passage offered by

the Mouse to the shivering creatures that came out of the pool of tears; he described it as "the driest thing I know." (I have always wondered why the Mouse considered this so especially dry; perhaps the reason is that so much of the passage is in the passive tense.)

7. One may question Darlington's accuracy; if it does not stand up to such questioning, then we cannot cite his book as representing "good" global history. All the same, that does not take it out of the global history category.

8. Several of those who are especially interested in global history—including Bruce Mazlish—have taken strong exception to this statement.

References

Boyden, S. *Biohistory: The Interplay Between Human Society and the Biosphere Past and Present*, vol. 8 in the Man and the Biosphere Series. Paris: UNESCO and Lancaster, England: Parthenon Publishing Group, 1992.

Brundtland Commission (World Commission on Environment and Development, Jim MacNeil, principal architect and chief author). *Our Common Future*. New York: Oxford University Press, 1987.

Carroll, Lewis. *Alice's Adventures in Wonderland*. New York: St. Martin's Press, 1977.

Daly, Herman. "From Empty World Economics to Full World Economics: Recognizing an Historical Turning Point in Economic Development." In *Environmentally Sustainable Development: Building on Brundtland*, edited by Robert Goodland, Herman Daly, and Selah El Serafy; World Bank Environmental Working Paper 46 and UNESCO series, "Man and Biosphere" 1991.

Darlington, C. D. *The Evolution of Man and Society*. New York: Simon and Schuster, 1969.

An Encyclopedia of World History. Compiled and edited by William L. Langer. Boston: Houghton Mifflin, 1948.

Goodwin, Neva R. "Lessons for the World from US Agriculture: Unbundling Technology." *Global Commons: Site of Peril, Source of Hope*, special issue of *World Development* 19, no. 1 (January 1991): 85-102.

Haskell, Thomas L. "Capitalism and the Origins of the Humanitarian Sensibility." *American Historical Review* 90, no. 2 (April 1985): 339-361, and 90, no. 3 (June 1985): 547-566.

Heiser, Charles B., Jr. *Seed to Civilization: The Story of Food*. Cambridge, Mass.: Harvard University Press, 1991.

Hillel, Daniel J. *Out of the Earth: Civilization and the Life of the Soil*. New York: Free Press, Macmillan, 1991.

McNeill, William H. *Plagues and Peoples*. New York: Anchor Books, Doubleday, 1989.

Seuss, Dr. Theodore. "The Big Brag," in *Yertle the Turtle and Other Stories*. New York: Random House, 1986.

Simmons, I. G. *Changing the Face of the Earth: Culture, Environment, History*. Oxford: Basil Blackwell, 1989.

Vitousek, Peter et al. "Human Appropriation of the Products of Photosynthesis."
  Bioscience 34, no. 6 (1986): 368-373.
Zinsser, Hans. *Rats, Lice and History*. Boston: Little, Brown, 1935.

2

Global History:
Historiographical Feasibility
and Environmental Reality

Wolf Schäfer

The history I should like to see written is one which probably cannot be written adequately yet: that of the world since the Second World War, and more particularly, during the third quarter of the twentieth century.
—Eric Hobsbawm, "The Missing History"

Global history is the unwritten history of the twentieth century, and we have to find out how it can be written. Yet this term *global history* is not only intriguing but also quite arrogant. It is intriguing because it captures an important part of what is going on in the world around us, and it is arrogant because it sounds so bombastic and seems to violate the guideline that small is beautiful and that first-rate historical work should be narrowly focused and based on original research.[1] The source of this ambivalent response to global history is not the emergence of global realities as produced by countless historical actors but rather an inflated concept of global history as produced by some historians and social scientists. Everybody recognizes the turn toward globalization in contemporary history, and we are ready to assume that global history works on the level of reality. However, on the level of historiography, we are not so sure and are inclined to be skeptical, if not worried. Neither the successful institutional implementation nor the "correct" conceptual construction of global history are matters that one can take for granted.

This chapter builds upon a research-oriented construction of global history. It identifies the set of global realities that could and should become the focus for vigorous research, and it takes a first cut at what is currently the most prominent global reality, the global environment. Of course, that is much too limited an approach for a full treatment of global history, but comprehensiveness is not my aim here. I want to explore the professional feasibility of writing global history, and I will be satisfied if I can make that point.

The first section distinguishes two types of global historiography: a capitalized Global History that I would want to avoid and topical global history studies that are not only very promising but also eminently possible, if they spring from firsthand empirical and/or interpretive research. I argue, moreover, that global history should not be identified with traditional world history. The terminology is in flux, and a clear-cut understanding of the conceptual differences between the approaches of world and global histories is warranted. Global history is not a twentieth-century supplement to world history but rather a new and distinctly different approach to the study of global processes in contemporary history. This does not mean that all work cataloged under the heading of world history is of little value. In fact, newer studies in world history are often valuable contributions to the prehistory of global studies (especially the work of Philip Curtin, Alfred Crosby, and Michael Adas). The growing literature about global issues in fields such as sociology, economics, and international relations is already playing a significant part in enhancing our understanding of current history.

To begin with, global history does not attempt to give a total account of ourselves, our world or times past, present, and future. Traditional world history, particularly in its totalizing form, tried to cover the whole world, the whole human past, and the whole of humanity. But these are no longer plausible conceptions due to the growth in knowledge and an increasing complexity. I object to grand syntheses of world history and endorse the writing of comparatively humble pieces of work. Studies in global history are likely to deal with "big structures, large processes and huge comparisons,"[2] but acceptable contributions must be of limited—that is, less than total—scope, and they have to be research oriented.

My own experience tells me that global history is a great teaching field; yet I hold that global history must prove its viability by becoming a productive research field first and foremost. World history tried to launch itself via teaching and a few outstanding contributions like McNeill's *Rise of the West* (1963),[3] but it never managed to overcome the doubts of the research historian who thought: If one does not read all the languages of the world—and who does?—and if one has not searched all the archives of the world—and who has?—how can one tell the story of world history professionally? Of course, total knowledge is an impossible standard, and even the most local historian would not want to subscribe to it.

There is nothing wrong with bold generalizations and high levels of abstraction. But it defeats the purpose of advancing historical knowledge if the specialists appreciate the stories in the globalist's account that they do not know much about and fault his or her scholarship in the fields of their particular expertise. In regard to devastating qualifications of this kind, my prescription emphasizes researchability and a drastic reduction in holistic weight. To overcome the skeptical attitude in the historical profession, which I happen to share, I propose to construct global history as a cross-cultural, multinational, interdisciplinary, but nevertheless completely ordinary research tool for historians and social scientists.

The second section of this chapter lists the realities of our global history world and claims that global history investigates the emergence and present character of self-conscious, multiple local activities with immediate worldwide range, consequence, and/or significance. Global historians study subjects interacting on a global plane—that is, human actors who are aware of and responsible for the evolution, interplay, and cross-fertilization of a global civilization with a global technoscience in a global environment. After these preliminary theoretical clarifications, I finally proceed to sketch the paradigmatic ecological reality of global history, namely, our continuous unveiling, changing, monitoring, and interpreting of the face of the earth.

I

The urge to understand it all is a universal condition. But the wish to understand it all by *seeing* it all in one sweeping glance has certainly become very strong in the tradition of Western "man."[4] Lucian's Icaromenippus improved on Daedalus and Icarus and securely attached the right wing of an eagle and the left wing of a vulture to his shoulders, and flew to the moon. He peered down from on high and saw

> the traders, the soldiers, the farmers, the litigants, the women, the animals and, in a word, all the life that the good green earth supports. . . . Whenever I looked at the country of the Getae I saw them fighting; whenever I transferred my gaze to the Scythians, they could be seen roving about on their wagons: and when I turned my eyes aside slightly, I beheld the Egyptians working the land. The Phoenicians were on trading-ventures, the Cilicians were engaged in piracy, the Spartans were whipping themselves and the Athenians were attending court. As all these things were going on at the same time, you can imagine what a hodge-podge it looked.[5]

The satirist from Samosata on the Euphrates who settled in Athens in the second century A.D. and Leften Stavrianos, the world historian from Vancouver who settled in Chicago in the twentieth century, both wanted to see it all and all at once. Lucian adopted a lunar point of view to mock the "comical little creatures" on earth. Stavrianos, however, called for a more serious view from the moon in 1964.[6] He proposed to adopt a lunar perspective in order to gain "a higher, unifying vision of the whole human past."[7] With Lucian, we can laugh about human vanity, but with Stavrianos, or, better, with the concept of a "unifying vision of the whole human past," we must struggle. It was meant well, but I believe that it was and is impossible and, as far as I am concerned, neither desirable nor acceptable as a goal.

In what follows, I will try to explain this opinion. I am against capitalizing global history. The goal of creating a unifying vision of the whole human past strikes me as very *alteuropäisch* ("old European"). A unifying vision is fine as long as it does not try to compute the sum total of everything. *Le grand récit a perdu sa crédibilité* ("The grand story has lost its credibility"), declared Jean-François Lyotard in 1979 in *La Condition Post-moderne*.[8] I would like to emphasize that for the scheme of global history. What must be resisted is the temptation to create a new grand narrative for our time, which lurks in deep ecology,[9] new wave holism,[10] the "comprehensive self-organization paradigm"[11] and other currents of thought.

The word for "too global" is *globaloney*, used in 1951 by the *Chicago Tribune* to ridicule the idea of using world history as a means to advance world peace.[12] I think one should try to avoid this epithet. Therefore, I would like to endorse the writing of *petits récits* ("little narratives") in an interdisciplinary, cross-cultural, and multinational research field, which would be thematically organized much like women's studies or science studies and which might, in turn, be called global history studies.

Global History (with capital letters) is most often called world history, sometimes universal history, and occasionally ecumenical history—historians are notorious for their terminological generosity. All these terms are functionally equivalent despite their semantic nuances and different conceptual histories. The idea that world history has to "unite the whole human past and be total, global, and universal in time and space"[13] captures in a nutshell, unfortunately with approval, what I mean by Global History with capital letters.

World history and global history are often used interchangeably. This can be seen best in the editorial statement in the first issue of the *Journal of World History*, which began publication in spring 1990. The editorial ran under the title "A New Forum for Global History."[14] The term *global history*, however, is not new. As early as 1962, Stavrianos coauthored a successful high school world history textbook under the classic prefeminist title *A Global History of Man*.[15] As Gilbert Allardyce wrote, "Stavrianos's ideas connected him with those advocating the 'global approach' to international education, and the work of his Global History Project at

Northwestern University largely coincided with the rise and decline of the globalism idea in American learning between 1957 and 1975."[16] According to Allardyce, "The term global history was simply a modish, space age name for world history."[17]

A new and more promising, i.e., less total, version of world history was implied in the editorial foreword to a series of "Essays on Global and Comparative History," published by the American Historical Association since 1987. Michael Adas, the editor of these pamphlets for college and secondary school teachers, remarked in his prefatory note:

> Though the current interest in global history reflects a continuing fascination with the broad patterns of human development across cultures that were the focus for earlier works on world history, the "new" global or world history differs in fundamental ways from its predecessors. Writers of the new global history are less concerned with comprehensiveness or with providing a total chronology of human events. Their works tend to be thematically focused on recurring processes like war and colonization or on cross-cultural patterns like the spread of disease, technology, and trading networks.[18]

I find two interesting points in this quote: The interchangeability of world and global history, on the one hand, and the support for a global history no longer written with capital letters, on the other.[19] Yet it is hard to appreciate fully the achievement that this inconspicuous arrival of a new global history constitutes without a fair deconstruction of the traditional approach to world history. If we want to promote a global history that is modest and small as well as epistemologically up to date, we must first discuss the lingering legacies cum fallacies of grand (old) world history.

The bequest of traditional world history that is most troubling is the anachronistic desire for totality. Old world history revolves around a false trinity of (1) the whole playground of historical action, (2) the whole span of historical time, and (3) the whole of humanity as the subject of history. How could anyone ever expect to cover this much? The answer must be historical or clinical. At least some sort of megalomania inspired the young Toynbee, who wrote in 1911, "As for Ambition with a great screaming A, I have got it pretty strong. . . . I want to be a great gigantic historian . . . and become a vast historical Gelehrte."[20] However let us try the historical answer.

The totality of the whole world started out conceptually large but comparatively small in square miles. The "world" of world history was nonglobal most of the time. The Greek historian Polybius, for instance, who became a voice of his masters after he was brought to Rome as a political hostage, wrote ecumenical history. Awed by what he had witnessed during his lifetime in the second century B.C., Polybius presented the violent transformation of a multipolar political arena into the *Orbis Romanus* as world history. He could do that because the circle of Roman power enclosed a whole world. The civilizational horizon of this world was local, however, and did not reach too far beyond the Mediterranean rim.

The egoistical Greek word for the "inhabited lands" of the known world—*oikumenê*—was used in the bilingual Greco-Roman period to distinguish between civilized and noncivilized parts. Toynbee adopted it later for the whole "habitat of mankind," noting that "the true extent of the Oikumenê is much larger than the area of the 'civilized' world known to the Greeks and Romans, but . . . this comprehensive Oikumenê is nevertheless much smaller than the biosphere."[21] McNeill, in his presidential address to the American Historical Association (1985), spoke of the need for world history to develop an "ecumenical history, with plenty of room for human diversity in all its complexity." He went beyond Toynbee and pointed out that any one person is a full member not only of the human race but also of the "wider DNA community of life on planet Earth."[22] World history after McNeill is completely ecumenical and ecological or "ecumenological" and covers the whole planet, with all its living beings in each and every niche of the globe, micro- and macroparasites as well as human beings.[23] That much input, however, is a mixed blessing. It changes the original equation between one particular world and "the" world and makes the task of writing world history very complicated if not impossible.

The ancient totality of world history was based on civilizational arrogance and geographical ignorance. It allowed the more or less undisturbed side-by-sidedness of numerous self-centered worlds, theoretically with a homegrown world historian for each one of them. All these Polybiuses could write local world history, but none of them could write global world history. Toynbee and McNeill tried to correct this. But they preserved the old concept of totality and tried to make world history coextensive with global history. They paid tribute to the advancement of knowledge in history, geography, ecology, medicine, and molecular biology, and other fields. But the world history that worked was not global, and the global history that might work will have to sacrifice totality. The fields of historical action have not only grown rather numerous with the unveiling of the face of the earth, they have become ever more complex due to other advances of knowledge. The world's geometry has become fractal; totality is a nonentity. We experience worlds within worlds within worlds—far too many for any grand narrative.

"It has been calculated," wrote F. R. Ankersmit in a recent article on historiography and postmodernism, "that at this moment there are more historians occupied with the past than the total number of historians from Herodotus up until 1960."[24] And well over 90 percent of these historians, I could add without much computing, are specialists. They may be classified as African, American, or Asian historians, for example, but the actual research work they do is much more narrowly focused. Professional expertise is limited in terms of historical approach, area, and period. Research historians understand what it means to know a field—it means to feel bold enough to identify the flaws and review the merits of new work in that field.

If it is our "great and solemn duty" to "construct the best possible portrait of the whole human adventure on earth," as McNeill affirmed with authority in his defense of world history,[25] then I am afraid we cannot but fail. Modern historiography constantly deconstructs by sheer cumulative effect any one portrait of the whole human past, even the best. Individual historians may not want to be iconoclasts, but their contributions add to the maze of history and are bound to offset other contributions; they function like the poor Christian sinner who is born to sin. We are no longer in the privileged position of Bishop Jacques-Bénigne Bossuet, who could proceed with blessed simplicity through a straightforward and lucid past. A Bossuet could tell his readers—the dauphin and his father, the Sun King—that history deals "only with the deeds that concern princes," that rulers can learn from history "without any risk,"[26] and that world history spares the royal mind the confusion that arises from "scrupulous attention to minutiae":[27]

> Universal history is to the history of every country and of every people what a world map is to particular maps. In a particular map you see all the details of a kingdom or a province as such. But a general map teaches you to place these parts of the world in their context; you see what Paris or the Ile-de-France is in the kingdom, what the kingdom is in Europe, and what Europe is in the world. In the same manner, particular histories show the sequence of events that have occurred in a nation in all their detail. But in order to understand everything, we must know what connection that history might have with others; and that can be done by a condensation in which we can perceive, as in one glance, the entire sequence of time. Such a condensation, Monseigneur, will afford you a grand view.[28]

This explanation about the understanding the whole has been continued by world historians ever since Bossuet with additional good words about the appropriate historical perspective, the parts and the whole,[29] the forest and the trees,[30] and so on. Bossuet, however, was in a much better position than we are to cover "the entire sequence of time." He started with Adam and quickly moved through the epochs of Noah, Abraham, Moses; continued with the fall of Troy, Solomon, Romulus, Cyrus, Scipio; and arrived in due time at the "last age of the world." That last age began with the birth of Jesus Christ in the year 1 A.D. and encompassed the epochs of Constantine, Charlemagne, and Louis XIV. The bishop's history of the world emerged not from secular darkness but from the Lord's almighty linguistic workshop: "The first epoch begins with a grand spectacle: God creating heaven and earth through his word and making man in his image (1 A.M., 4004 B.C.). This is where Moses, the first historian, the most sublime philosopher, and the wisest of legislators, begins."[31]

It is important to notice that this grand narrative commenced with the first "year of the world," year 1 *anno mundi* or 4004 B.C. Bossuet's *Discours sur l'histoire universelle* (1681) covered exactly 5,685 years (4,004 plus 1,681). For millenarian thinking, this was rather close to the end of the world. Indeed, the world was expected to last 6 world days (until ca. 1996); thereafter, on the seventh day, the kingdom of God would be erected.[32] The great Isaac Newton, who spent much of his time in the 1670s correlating biblical prophecies with historical data, was not the only one who tried to calculate the date for the end of the world.[33] Bossuet and his contemporaries thought that historical events were "already established and immutable and not the result of research and analysis by the historian."[34] The future, though hidden, was certain until the Enlightenment, not a multiplicity of possible futures but one written down in the book of destiny, preexistent and inflexible.

The concept of time has changed since the late seventeenth century and not in favor of world history. The "famous Bossuet" was removed from the Royal Library in Paris in *L'An 2440* (1771), Louis-Sébastian Mercier's futurist utopia. Mercier was among the first to cross the timeline drawn at the year 2000.[35] Many have followed him, and we are close now. Indeed, the tremendous growth of modern historical scholarship has turned the past into a plurality of worlds. Only semantic inertia allows us to speak of "the past" as if it could be grasped in one piece. The past has, in effect, become a welter of pasts, approached from different ideological perspectives and analyzed with the interpretive tools and gauges of over two dozen historiographical schools. All these pasts carry their own temporal horizons with futures past, presents past, and pasts past. And research historians are bound to complicate the already overcomplex picture by reconstructing these pasts within pasts.[36]

The fiction of the whole of humanity is a noble idea as long as it is understood as a regulative principle, i.e., as a safeguard against exclusive particularism. The whole of humanity is put to good use if, like Micah, we believe that everybody shall have the right to sit in peace "under his vine and under his fig tree."[37] But we enter treacherous ground when we begin to speak about the whole of humanity as if it were an existing entity. The whole of humanity is at best, a project, not a reality. As a project, it serves to criticize human affairs in which, for instance, only men are allowed to sit under vines and fig trees. The project version of humanity keeps one's eye on the fact that we are operating with a telos, if at all, and not an achievement. If, however, the utopian and critical function of the idea of the whole of humanity is replaced by a hypostatization of what we like to think about ourselves and all other human beings at the time, then we leave the open realm of critical historiography and enter the darker domains of metaphysical closure and "mythistory."

McNeill has taken the risk of redefining history as mythistory and the historian as a "truth-seeking mythographer."[38] Serious myth-history is, in McNeill's view, "a useful instrument for piloting human groups in their encounters with one another and with the natural environment."[39] The idea of humanity as a whole is certainly a prime candidate for modern myth-history. But we must ask, Which humanity? Do we refer to the one that is said to be a whole or the one that is but a promise? I read McNeill as coming close to saying that humanity is out there in the world as a whole.

> Humanity entire possesses a commonality which historians may hope to understand just as firmly as they can comprehend what unites any lesser group. Instead of enhancing conflicts, as parochial historiography inevitably does, an intelligible world history might be expected to diminish the lethality of group encounters by cultivating a sense of individual identification with the triumphs and tribulations of humanity as a whole.[40]

Oswald Spengler, rejected the whole idea of humanity as an empty category for world history.[41] McNeill, by contrast, regards the ideal supergroup of humanity as the moral gravity center of world history. He more than follows the lead of his teacher Carl Becker toward an affirmation of socially honorable ideologies; he speaks in favor of "collective self-flattery" i.e., a "flattering historiography," requesting "an appropriately idealized version of the past." He understands world history as an effort to "allow a group of human beings to come closer to living up to its noblest ideals."[42] Thus, McNeill puts the world historian in a very responsible position for the "right" course of history.

Living up to the universalist ideal of humanity as a whole, however, has already meant many things: Catholic theology, Christian mission, Enlightenment philosophy, Marxian emancipation, European imperialism, and so on. It is not an easy task to speak for the whole with legitimacy, especially when the whole is not a live subject but a compliant macroconcept of metahistory. Spengler ranted against the "West European scheme of history, in which the great Cultures are made to follow orbits round us" and rightly ridiculed it as the "Ptolemaic system of history."[43] Yet his own "Copernican discovery" of the morphological laws of world history could not identify more than eight world cultures, and that short list contained only two cultures of which he knew something: the Greco-Roman and West European (Faustian) ones. Stavrianos's world history "of man" was designed to speak for the whole of humanity but left half of it out.

Our situation might be different if the first decades of the "atomic age" had led to one all-encompassing world state or a new, truly unifying world order. Toynbee,[44] Jaspers,[45] and many other great thinkers about the big picture in the 1950s believed that they were experiencing an end of history and predicted some kind of world unity "either by force in a despotic world-empire or through mutual agreement in a world order based on the rule of law."[46] None of this has come true, but all of it can be a topic in the origins of global history. Today, the whole of humanity is no less a fiction than it was yesterday. To be sure, the universalist concept of one humanity can still be helpful, but only if it is applied to the abundant misery of human history in a deconstructive way, that is, as a radical critique à la Marx of all circumstances in which man is humiliated, enslaved, abandoned and despised.

II

The list of global realities is as profuse as it is confusing. It jumps from global economy and global ecology to global politics and global pollution, from global tourism and global terrorism to global communication and global diseases, from global warming and global social movements to global science and global technologies. No doubt, the preferred adjective of the current Zeitgeist is global. It crops up in everything, even in history. Leaving nothing out, the global perspective lives up to its name and generates more noise than information. We are inundated by global issues and swim around in global waters—but what is it exactly that we are swimming in and talking about?

I assume that our planet is the point of reference when we speak about global realities. The entire physical globe serves as the standard or bench mark by which the production of global realities is measured. Everything below this mark is nonglobal. We can say that global realities are produced by multiple local activities with worldwide range, consequence, and/or significance. Accordingly, the term *globalization* can be understood to indicate the spreading and interpenetration of multiple local activities with worldwide range, consequence, and/or significance.

For example, Mitsubishi Corporation, which has "13,629 employees working in 232 offices around the world, who send in more than 30,000 pieces of information every day,"[47] is engaged in numerous local activities of the defined kind; it coproduces the global economy and contributes to the globalization of trade. Electronic scholars who have instant access to libraries and data bases all over the world fit our definition as well. They can add their terminals to terminals everywhere via their local electronic networks and join electronic discussion groups (e-mail lists) in their fields of interest. They take part in an activity that coproduces the emerging global culture of ubiquitous information, babble, and discourse.[48]

To order our heterogeneous list of global realities, we start again with the planet itself. Global warming and pollution are realities that pertain to the whole earth. They globalize myriads of local activities that impinge on our natural habitat. It seems appropriate to collect them in a folder labeled *global environment*. Global communication, modern science, and high technologies, however, belong to another group. They globalize advanced Baconian activities and create an artificial environment populated with the realities of a virtual or second nature. I propose to place them in a category termed *global technoscience*. Global economy, politics, terrorism, and so on form a third cluster of realities. They globalize an expanding variety of socioeconomic, sociopolitical, and sociocultural activities that constitute critical elements of what might be called the first *global civilization*.[49] So, for the time being, we venture to say that multiple local activities with worldwide range, consequence, and/or significance produce a cluster of socially linked realities: a global environment, a global technoscience, and a global civilization.

As a hypothesis, we might suggest that global history will have to reconstruct the emergence and present character of these activities and study their evolution, interplay, and cross-fertilization. This, however, is not a task for one worker but for scores of social scientists cum historians, research teams, and institutes.

Tender loving care for the global environment has become the currency of political rhetoric in the late twentieth century. "If we don't address the issue of global ecology, we won't have to worry about the other issues," declared the president of Mexico, Carlos Salinas de Gortari, in a full-page advertisement in the *New York Times* recently. He announced that the Mexican government would host the United Nations World Environment Day on June 5, 1990, and that "a minimum of five million trees [would] be planted throughout Mexico" on that very day, "as many as possible planted by children."[50]

The rapid diffusion of environmental concerns in the last twenty years—real or apparent, inspired by political interests in one way or another, and articulated by schoolchildren and world leaders alike—is truly remarkable. The new environmentalism has succeeded in making the health of the global environment a local political issue in many places,[51] including the Soviet Union.[52] More and more people have come to understand that we have one physical environment only—that our environment is global and that it can be ruined. This knowledge was produced and is sustained by four multiple local activities with worldwide range, namely, the unveiling, the changing, the monitoring, and the interpretation of the face of the earth.

The unveiling of the face of the earth by human exploration revealed the physical particularities and gestalt of planet earth. Geographical discovery began long ago, but quite a bit of the unveiling occurred rather recently.The empirical rounding of the earth's imagined corners took all the 4,000 years from King Sargon of Akkad (ca. 2340 B.C.), who ruled over the four corners of a relatively small and flat world, to Louis XIV (1643-1715), who reigned over a much larger and rounder world—yet under a Catholic sun that was still circling around Aristotle.

Until lately, the world oscillated between spherical and flat, was walled in by forbidding oceans, and was severely limited by supposedly uninhabitable, fiery or icy hinterlands. Most ancient and medieval navigation was coastal. However, the horizons widened after Henry the Navigator (1394-1460), and "by the year 1600 the surface of the known earth was doubled."[53] George Sarton, the polyhistor of science, noted how recent the complete unveiling of the face of the earth, in fact, was:

> One of the most remarkable achievements of the beginning of the twentieth century was the tectonic synthesis of the Austrian geologist, Edward Suess (1831-1914), in *Das Antlitz der Erde*. This was an elaborate survey of the "face of the earth," the whole earth, a description of all the irregularities of its crust, the mountains, the seas and lakes, the valleys, the river beds and deltas—an attempt to explain the deformations and foldings which led to the earth's present appearance. . . . It is hard to realize that in the middle of the fifteenth century, at the time when the Renaissance is supposed to begin, man's knowledge of the "face of the earth" was still restricted to a very small portion of it, and even in that portion was very superficial. One of the great tasks to be accomplished was the discovery of the earth.[54]

This discovery was completed, I would add, when Johannes Kepler's "dream" came true in the late 1960s and human eyes looked up from the moon to see the earth in the sky.[55] "Earthrise"—the sublime Copernican spectacle of the earth rising above the rim of the moon—was seen first from lunar orbit by the crew of Apollo 8 in December 1968 and then, in July 1969, by the astronauts of Apollo 11 from a dusty base in the lunar Sea of Tranquility.[56] Neil Armstrong's "giant leap for mankind"—the famous line and actual footstep—made good sense. To gain an overall view of the face of the earth, one had to leap away from it. The observer had to distance himself considerably from the global environment in order to fully appreciate it. We now possess an accurate, as well as highly symbolical, image of our home in space. This image does not represent one country or nation: It is an image of Spaceship Earth, of the "cloud-whorled blue planet," of the "emerald globe in a black sea."

The poetic language underscores the fact that people want to express that they have changed their minds.[57] The age-old struggle of society against nature has lost its relevance and legitimacy.[58] People today tend to be more interested in maintaining and improving the well-being of their environment than in fighting nature. Society has become more of a challenge than nature. The unveiling of the face of the earth finally captured and dramatized our global interdependency with nature and with all fellow travelers on this planet.[59]

The changing of the face of the earth by modern civilization revealed the ecological vulnerability of the planet. The negative environmental impact of *Homo sapiens* reached an unprecedented magnitude in the second half of the twentieth century and triggered an equally unprecedented burst of novel knowledge about the global mosaic of ecological systems.[60] The enormous appetite of the industrial way of life for natural resources, combined with a significant increase of environmental degradation turned George Perkins Marsh's early warning that the earth might become "an unfit home for its noblest inhabitant" into a close call a hundred years later.[61] The widespread fears of deadly fallout and pollution were most effectively articulated in Rachel Carson's "fable," *Silent Spring*, in 1962.

> The roadsides, once so attractive, were now lined with browned and withered vegetation as though swept by fire. These, too, were silent, deserted by all living things. Even the streams were now lifeless. In the gutters under the eaves and between the shingles of the roofs, a white granular powder still showed a few patches; some weeks before it had fallen like snow upon the roofs and the lawns, the fields and streams. No witchcraft, no enemy action had silenced the rebirth of new life in this stricken world. The people had done it themselves.[62]

However, local environmental change with global consequences is not new. The determined use of fire or the agricultural and industrial revolutions were multiple local discoveries and inventions with vast consequences for the global environment. The difference between the mastering of fire or the domestication of plants and animals and, for instance, the development, introduction, and distribution of personal computers is not in range or importance but in diffusion-time. The spread of the neolithic revolution across the world took millennia. The industrial revolution is still reaching out. Yet the spread of innovations in our time is not only superfast but also inevitably self-conscious and reflexive.[63]

The epoch of global history was introduced by contaminated clouds, drifting with the winds and discharging radioactive ash, hailstones, and rain for days, weeks, and months. Fallout from atmospheric nuclear testing in the first rounds of the escalating nuclear arms race affected the entire earth and not just the United States, the USSR, Britain, or France. It changed the world instantly and—as far as the environment is concerned—for centuries and millennia to come. The graphite core of a nuclear power station has a half-life of 5,700 years.[64] Sure ways of ultimate disposal for high-level wastes are not known. But the existence of such waste *is* known, and that makes all the difference between global and preglobal history.

The development of radar in World War II, for example, was a military secret, to be sure, but for the people involved, it was clear from the very beginning that this was an extremely momentous innovation. No retrospective reconstruction by historians of science was needed to establish the importance of radio detecting and ranging (radar). In fact, the Radiation Laboratory at MIT, had its own historian of science writing the history of radar as it was being made.[65] As noted before, global history is the history of multiple and self-conscious local activities with immediate worldwide range, consequence, and/or significance.

The epoch of global history privileges synchronicity, that is, lateral relations in the present, as much as modernity privileged diachronic progress from the past into the future. The debate about global warming, however, reminds us that there are still time lags between related events, but either they can be anticipated and discussed long before or they tend to become shorter with the advances of technoscientific progress. Immediacy within global history means conscious local activities and expected worldwide results of local activities are linked within the strategic horizon of the present.

The monitoring of the changing face of the earth with scientific instruments, remote sensing by satellites, computer models, and other means of modern science and technology continuously reveals and projects current and approximate future states of the global environment. Worldwide and systematic monitoring of our global environment is a fairly new activity that leads to the production of potentially relevant information.

"Taking the earth's pulse," to use Daniel Botkin's phrase, records two sorts of change. There is evidence of both anthropogenic change (deforestation due to economic activities, for instance) and natural variability (for

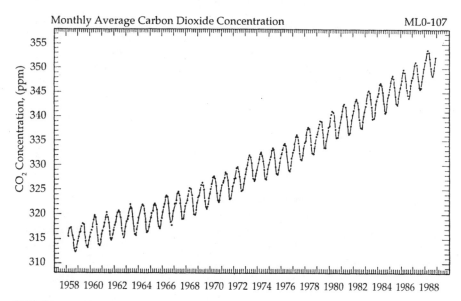

FIGURE 2.1 The rising concentration of carbon dioxide on Mauna Loa

instance, in the energy output of the sun). If natural and cultural types of change interact, both are linked in one data set. This complicates the tasks of identification and interpretation. The rising concentration of carbon dioxide (CO_2) in the atmosphere is such a mixed case. As Figure 2.1 shows, measurements of CO_2 on Mauna Loa, Hawaii, steadily taken since 1957, revealed

> two clear patterns: an annual oscillation, with a decline in summer followed by an increase in winter . . . and, imposed on this rising and falling, a steady annual increase like a rising tone. The summer decline is the result of photosynthesis on the land in the Northern Hemisphere. . . . The increase during the winter is the result of respiration without photosynthesis. . . . Our civilization is part of this invisible touch, reaching the slopes [of Mauna Loa] as the continual increase in the concentration of carbon dioxide in the atmosphere, which is a result of the burning of fossil fuels and the clearing of land.[66]

Each word about global history—a breath of CO_2 in and out—is faithfully recorded on Mauna Loa as a local contribution to all the inhalations and exhalations in the Northern Hemisphere. However, the current monthly average CO_2 concentration of about 350 ppm may be "excessive" or just "high"; the recent warming may be "momentous" or "within the limits of natural variability"—climatologists are divided, historians do not know yet, and global historians are not expected to find out.

Climatologists must distinguish between signal and noise; they must respond to the scientific challenge with "improved climate monitoring and reporting."[67] The challenge for global historians lies in the very nature of this response. They bracket the climatologists' problem and study the professional request for more and better global monitoring and reporting. They find themselves situated in a thoroughly reflexive context, registering the activities of global recorders and observing the problems of global observers. They respond to this challenge by adopting the role of "reflexivity minders."

Global historians keep track of the efforts and struggles to monitor, model, and manage global realities. They report about human behavior in the social and cultural climate of a global civilization that requires permanent investigation of itself and its environments. They write history in a time when people feel compelled to control the forces of global change, if not evolution, and to choose their own future history with as much foresight and understanding as possible.

The interpretation of scientific data about the changing face of the earth reveals the mischievous structure of ecological communication in the absence of hard or uncontroversial facts. The environmental discourse exhibits deep and persistent controversies not only about ecological problems and solutions but also about facts; not only among lay people but also—and most notably—among information-rich scientific experts. We would need an expert system to settle disagreements among experts, which, in turn, we could never agree upon, and so forth, leading to an infinite regress. We must conclude that the environmental issue is politicohistorical all the way down to the construction of the facts.

We know that we lack crucial pieces of information (like the geographical distribution of organisms or the number of global species) and that we do not have all the relevant data (1.4 million species have been identified worldwide, but current estimates of South American species alone range from 5 to 50 million, for instance). However, we have and prefer to have public debates about the rate of extinction and loss of species and the best measures to avoid mass extinctions in the next century.[68] But then, we must also face the problem that normative interpretations of even the most reliable environmental "facts" are unavoidable. The debates about our ecological options will not be decided by neutral data but by a synergy of facts, arguments, and power.

This may come as a disappointment to epistemological purists who want environmental politics to follow the facts and not the politics. They fear the social contamination of scientific objectivity and defend the old philosophical apartheid of is and ought, facts and norms. But the "ill-structured" and "messy" epistemological situation created by conflicting views about the state of the global environment is now, by default, the human context of our natural environment. Ecological communication is about possible alternative (different developments of nature) and, thus, is basically political. Scientists, social movements, subsystems of society (the economy, polity, judiciary), and international organizations conduct an ecopolitical discourse that accomplishes the normative construction of environmental facts. The making of environmental history and politics is, therefore, not just a scientific or technical issue but also a germane research topic for political scientists, sociologists, historians, and anthropologists.

If we look around, we will see that "untuneable problems are by no means rare."[69] They are especially "wicked" with regard to decision-making under global constraints, that is, when problems can no longer be solved "within the boundary of a single unity of command, decisional, institutional or systemic."

> Classical rationality states that global problems require global solutions, and that global solutions require a "global mind." Nothing is further from the truth, and nothing is more false then the hypostasis of a global mind. If there is evidence that acid rain is a typical global problem beyond the action of a single state, the implementation of the global solution, when it is achieved implies the capacity to act locally by a plurality of microactors. The global solutions, then, are chosen by a plurality of agents, and implemented (or not implemented) by a plurality of actors.[70]

In addition to the plurality of microactors who shape global history as much as macroactors do, there is a plurality of problems, "each one focused by the shared credibility it enjoys in the eyes of those who subscribe to it, and each held separate from the rest by the mutual incredibility that is the global corollary of locally focused (that is, tribal) credibilities."[71] The commendable "de-tribalization" of "decisionmaking under contradictory certainties," as Michael Thompson termed it, requires that we learn to deal with the legitimacy of conflicting certainties (multicertainties), the reality of the different worlds of micro- and macro-actors on the global scene (multirealities), and the competition of alternative ways to answer pressing problems (multisolutions). These are conspicuous, nonconventional elements of our postmodern condition and rich social resources of global history.

The history of the world since the Second World War forced a "genuinely global perspective upon us," observed Hobsbawm in 1989, adding that "'world history' is no longer the Western scholar's polite concession to

UNESCO, but the only history that can be written."[72] In this vein, I have tried to distinguish world history from global history and to present some compelling arguments in favor of the latter—which is, I suppose, the history Hobsbawm meant when he referred to "world history" with apt rhetorical overstatement as the "only" and most relevant history today. I have also tried to spell out what it means to write global history "adequately." The answer, I am afraid, has to address the paradox that global history must be big enough to capture the planetary processes of our time and small enough to satisfy the requirements of normal academic research, beginning with doctoral dissertations. Traditional world history easily meets the first but hardly the second condition and is, perhaps, more a calling than a craft. However, the issue is not world history *or* global history; rather, it is the distinction between the two and the understanding that global history is a piecemeal history for global processes in the twentieth century.

Notes

A first draft of this chapter was discussed at the Bellagio Conference on Global History, convened by Bruce Mazlish and Ralph Buultjens, on July 8-12, 1991. I am very grateful for the remarks of my eminent commentator, William McNeill, who gracefully disagreed with my irreverent agnosticism vis-à-vis grand world history. I would also like to express my gratitude to friends, colleagues, and students for many useful hints, comments, criticisms, and help, especially Liz Garber, Ian Roxborough, Fred Weinstein, John Williams, Paula Viterbo, Steve Wasay (all from Stony Brook), Seyla Benhabib, and Klaus Eder.

1. For an eloquent celebration of academic narrowness, see Eric H. Monkkonen, "The Dangers of Synthesis," *The American Historical Review* 91, no. 5 (1986): 1146-1157.

2. For a spirited and inspiring pleading for "historically grounded huge comparisons of big structures and large processes," see Charles Tilly, *Big Structures, Large Processes, Huge Comparisons* (New York: Russell Sage Foundation, 1984).

3. Gilbert Allardyce, "Toward World History: American Historians and the Coming of the World History Course," *Journal of World History* 1, no. 1 (Spring 1990): 23-76. On p. 26, Allardyce quoted McNeill—"Try to teach world history and you will find that it can be done"—and reported that it is the policy of the World History Association (WHA), formed in 1982, to prove the possibility of world history by teaching it.

4. For a feminist interpretation of the visual logic of Western thought, see Evelyn Fox Keller and Christine R. Grontkowski, "The Mind's Eye," in *Discovering Reality: Feminist Perspectives on Epistemology, Metaphysics, Methodology, and Philosophy of Science*, edited by Sandra Harding and Merril B. Hintikka (Dordrecht: D. Reidel, 1983), 207-224.

5. Lucian, *Icaromenippus, or the Sky-man*, in *Loeb Classical Library No. 54: Lucian*

in Eight Volumes, vol. 2, (Cambridge, Mass.: Harvard University Press; and London: William Heinemann, 1988), 289, 297.

6. Leften S. Stavrianos, "A Global Perspective in the Organization of World History," in *New Perspectives in World History,* edited by Shirley H. Engle (Washington, D.C.: National Council for the Social Studies, 1964), 616-620. On p. 617, he asked, "What does this new [global] perspective mean . . . ? It means the perspective of an observer perched on the moon rather than ensconced in London or Paris or Washington."

7. Allardyce, "Toward World History," 40.

8. Jean-François Lyotard, *La Condition postmoderne: Rapport sur le savoir* (Paris: Les Editions de Minuit, 1979), 63.

9. For a critical review of deep ecology and related works, see Alan Wolfe, "Up from Humanism," *The American Prospect,* no. 4 (Winter 1991): 112-127.

10. For a taste of this, see James Lovelock, *The Ages of Gaia: A Biography of Our Living Earth* (New York: Bantam, 1990). On p. xvi, he wrote, "Gaia theory forces a planetary perspective. It is the health of the planet that matters, not that of some individual species of organisms. This is where Gaia and the environmental movements, which are concerned first with the health of people, part company."

11. This is comprehensive, indeed; see Erich Jantsch, ed., *The Evolutionary Vision: Toward a Unifying Paradigm of Physical, Biological, and Sociocultural Evolution* (Boulder, Colo.: Westview Press, 1981). On p. v, we encounter the statement that autopoiesis "encompasses all levels of reality, from the cosmic or physical through the biological, ecological, and sociobiological to the sociocultural."

12. Allardyce, "Toward World History," 28.

13. Ibid., 67.

14. *Journal of World History* 1, no. 1 (Spring 1990), iii. The journal is published by the University of Hawaii Press.

15. Leften S. Stavrianos, Loretta K. Andrews, George I. Blanksten, Roger F. Hackett, Ella C. Leppert, Paul M. Murphy, and Lacey B. Smith, *A Global History of Man* (Boston: Allyn and Bacon, 1967).

16. Allardyce, "Toward World History," 43.

17. Ibid.

18. Michael Adas, "Foreword," in *The Columbian Voyages, the Columbian Exchange, and Their Historians,* by Alfred W. Crosby (Washington, D.C.: American Historical Association, 1987), v.

19. For some of the books that could count as "new" global history, mainly comparative and cross-cultural studies, see Philip D. Curtin, "Graduate Teaching in World History," *Journal of World History* 2, no. 1 (1991): 81-89.

20. William H. McNeill, *Arnold J. Toynbee: A Life* (New York and Oxford: Oxford University Press, 1989), 31.

21. Arnold Toynbee, *Mankind and Mother Earth: A Narrative History of the World* (New York and London: Oxford University Press, 1976), 28.

22. William H. McNeill, "Mythistory, or Truth, Myth, History, and Historians," *The American Historical Review* 91, no. 1 (1986): 7.

23. William H. McNeill, *The Human Condition: An Ecological and Historical View*

(Princeton, N.J.: Princeton University Press, 1980) and *Plagues and Peoples* (New York: Anchor Books, Doubleday, 1989).

24. F. R. Ankersmit, "Historiography and Postmodernism," *History and Theory* 28, no. 2 (1989): 138. The late Derek de Solla Price did a calculation of this kind in the 1960s for scientists, but who did it for historians? See his *Little Science, Big Science* (New York and London: Columbia University Press, 1963), where, on p. 1, he wrote, "We can say that 80 to 90 percent of all the scientists that have ever lived are alive now."

25. William H. McNeill, "A Defence of World History," *Transactions of the Royal Historical Society* 32 (1982): 86. The Prothero Lecture, read July 1, 1981, Royal Historical Society.

26. Jacques-Bénigne Bossuet, *Discourse on Universal History* (Chicago: University of Chicago Press, 1976), 3.

27. Ibid., 109.

28. Ibid., 4.

29. Stavrianos, "A Global Perspective," 618.

30. McNeill, "A Defence of World History," 82 ff.

31. Bossuet, *Discourse on Universal History*, 9.

32. G. J. Whitrow, *Time in History: Views of Time from Prehistory to the Present Day* (Oxford and New York: Oxford University Press, 1989). On p. 81, he noted, "Millenarian belief arose from combining the idea expressed in Psalm 89:4 that 'A day with the Lord is as a thousand years' with the interpretation of the Sabbath, or seventh day, as a symbol of heavenly rest in accordance with Hebrews 4:4-9." So, if 6 times 1,000 years are to be expected and 5,685 years of world history are gone by, 315 years are left. Adding these remaining 315 years to 1681, the publication date of Bossuet's *Discourse*, the year 1996 is the predetermined end of history.

33. Richard S. Westfall, *Never at Rest: A Biography of Isaac Newton* (Cambridge: Cambridge University Press, 1983), 319 ff.

34. Orest Ranum in his introduction to Bossuet, *Discourse on Universal History*, XIX.

35. Kant wrote in *Allgemeine Naturgeschichte und Theorie des Himmels* (1755): "Die Schöpfung ist nicht das Werk von einem Augenblicke. ... Es werden Millionen, und ganze Gebürge von Millionen Jahrhunderten verfließen, binnen welchen immer neue Welten und Weltordnungen nach einander, in denen entfernten Weiten von dem Mittelpunkte der Natur, sich bilden, und zur Vollkommenheit gelangen werden" (A 113). ("The creation is not the work of an instant ... millions, and whole mountains of millions of centuries, will elapse in which new worlds and world orders will form and come to perfection one after another in the remote distances from the center of nature.")

36. Reinhart Koselleck, *Futures Past: On the Semantics of Historical Time*, translated by Keith Tribe (Cambridge, Mass.: MIT Press, 1985).

37. Mic. 4:4-5.

38. William H. McNeill, *Mythistory and Other Essays* (Chicago and London: University of Chicago Press, 1986). I must admit that I am deeply troubled by McNeill's marriage of myth and history, not least because of my German back-

ground and my familiarity with the *Myth of the 20th Century* by Alfred Rosenberg. I know that McNeill advocates mythmaking for humanity and not for particularistic groups, but I also know that humanity is a lofty abstraction and that deadly competition among human groups is very real. Myth-history, I am afraid, is likely to serve the interests of real people more than the imagined community of the whole. This is not to say that the writing of history should only respect scholarly concerns—our trade serves all sorts of nonscholarly interests, to be sure. However, this is a question of the right proportions. "Mythistory" throws the doors wide open to all sorts of precritical interests in history. This, I think, is dangerous.

39. McNeill, "Mythistory, or Truth," 10.

40. Ibid.,.

41. Oswald Spengler, *The Decline of the West* (New York: Random House, 1965). On p. 17, he stated, "'Mankind' . . . has no aim, no idea, no plan, any more than the family of butterflies or orchids. 'Mankind' is a zoological expression, or an empty word."

42. McNeill, "Mythistory, or Truth," 6. For the strong influence that Becker's much debated relativism (as expressed in "Everyman His Own Historian") had on McNeill, see McNeill's *Mythhistory and Other Essays*, 162-165. However, there is an important difference between Becker and McNeill: Becker was content with myth-preservation as the function of history, whereas McNeill advocates myth-making.

43. Spengler, *The Decline of the West*, 13.

44. Pieter Geyl, *Debates with Historians* (Cleveland, Ohio, and New York: World Publishing, 1958), 185.

45. Karl Jaspers, *The Origin and Goal of History* (New Haven, Conn.: Yale University Press, 1953), 193 ff.

46. Ibid., 24.

47. *The Economist* 319, no. 7709 (June 1-7, 1991), 72.

48. His or her local electronic mail system is most likely connected to Internet, the global backbone network that was established in 1983 and links over 130,000 computing sites worldwide (universities, research institutes, national archives, and so on).

49. In a recent self-assessment of world-systems analysis, Wallerstein strongly questioned the usefulness of the distinction between economic, political, and cultural arenas of social action. Opposing this customary distinction from a "unidisciplinary" point of view, he asked scholars to look anew at the received tradition and work out the theoretical, methodological, and organizational implications of "a single arena with a single logic." Though I am not sure that Wallerstein's "mono-logic" is the answer, I, too, see a thorny and challenging problem here and would welcome a thorough epistemological discussion of this issue. See Immanuel Wallerstein, "World-Systems Analysis: The Second Phase," *Review* 13, no. 2 (Spring 1990): 287-293.

50. *New York Times*, May 30, 1990, A7.

51. The history of environmentalism is already well known and documented. For its prehistory, see Clarence J. Glacken, *Traces on the Rhodian Shore: Nature and*

Culture in Western Thought from Ancient Times to the End of the Eighteenth Century (Berkeley and Los Angeles: University of California Press, 1967). For the history of environmentalism in England between 1500 and 1800, see Keith Thomas, *Man and the Natural World: A History of the Modern Sensibility* (New York: Pantheon Books, 1983). For nature in Asia, see J. Baird Callicott and Roger T. Ames, eds., *Nature in Asian Traditions of Thought: Essays in Environmental Philosophy* (Albany: State University of New York Press, 1989). For American environmentalism in the last 200 years, see Roderick Frazier Nash, ed., *American Environmentalism: Readings in Conservation History*, 3d. ed. (New York: McGraw-Hill, 1990). A wealth of further reading can be found in Ian Gordon Simmons, *Changing the Face of the Earth: Culture, Environment, History* (Oxford and New York: Basil Blackwell, 1990), 397-445.

52. Barbara Welling Hall, "Soviet Perceptions of Global Ecological Problems: An Analysis of Three Patterns," *Political Psychology* 11, no. 4 (1990): 653-680.

53. George Sarton, *Six Wings: Men of Science in the Renaissance* (Bloomington: Indiana University Press, 1957), 5.

54. Ibid., 4 ff.

55. Edward Rosen, *Kepler's Somnium: The Dream, or Posthumous Work on Lunar Astronomy* (Madison and Milwaukee: University of Wisconsin Press, 1967). Kepler was probably the first to liken our planet to a spaceship (in the notes to his *Somnium*). Discussing the Galilean sunspots, he wondered: "Who could ever arrive at the idea that the spots on the sun are stationary, while that ship of ours, which is called the earth, carries us in so short an interval of time around the sun, revealing to our very selves the various parts of its surface and its spots in succession", p. 105, note 146.

56. Walter A. McDougall, *The Heavens and the Earth: A Political History of the Space Age* (New York: Basic Books, 1985). On p. 412, McDougall wrote that President Lyndon Johnson sent copies of "Earthrise" to "every head of state in the world, even Ho Chi Minh, while the luxuriant ecology movement gained an icon by grace of the very technology it denounced."

57. It is instructive to see how incredibly funny the new language of ecology must have sounded in its earlier days. The *American Scientist*, for example, printed a letter to the editor in 1960 that poked fun at H. T. Odum's "New Ecosystem Ecodynamics—with its attendant ecomixes, ecoforces, ecofarces, ecofluxes, eco-conductivities, ecopotentials, . . . and all that sort of ecojazz." See Bernard C. Patten, "Letter to the Editor," *American Scientist* 48, no. 2 (1960): 118A.

58. Serge Moscovici, *Society Against Nature: The Emergence of Human Societies* (Hassocks, Nr. Brighton, England: Harvester Press, 1976).

59. The evolution of ever more distant and accurate views of the earth moved from Leonardo da Vinci's first aerial sketches, Nadar's [the pseudonym of Felix Tournachon] aerial photograph (1859), to Willis T. Lee's *The Face of the Earth as Seen from the Air* (1922), to the "Landsat" pictures of the world.

60. The current knowledge about the human impact on the environment from the time of early man to the nuclear age has been masterfully reviewed by I. G. Simmons, *Changing the Face of the Earth*. The advancement of our ecological understanding can be studied by comparing Simmons's opus with·George Per-

kins Marsh's pioneering and influential work, *Man and Nature: Or, Physical Geography as Modified by Human Action* (Cambridge, Mass.: Harvard University Press, 1965); this work was first published in 1864.

61. Marsh, *Man and Nature*, 43. On pages xxiii and xxv, we learn that Marsh wanted to title his book "Man the Disturber of Nature's Harmonies," but Charles Scribner, his original publisher, objected and asked, "Is it true?" Scribner thought of man as part of nature; Marsh believed in man as the perennial opponent of nature who has "to make himself her master." Environmentalists today would side with Scribner.

62. Rachel Carson, *Silent Spring* (Boston: Houghton Mifflin, 1962), 3. The battle over DDT and *Silent Spring* is placed in historical perspective and scientific context in Thomas R. Dunlap, *DDT: Scientists, Citizens, and Public Policy* (Princeton, N.J.: Princeton University Press, 1981).

63. For an example of cultural self-reflexivity, see J. David Bolter, *Turing's Man: Western Culture in the Computer Age* (Chapel Hill: University of North Carolina Press, 1984).

64. Simmons, *Changing the Face of the Earth*, 351, figure 6.2.

65. Henry Guerlac (who later became an eminent scholar on Antoine-Laurent Lavoisier and eighteenth-century science) was recruited in 1943 "to prepare an official history of the Laboratory, intended to justify, should there be a congressional investigation, the large amount of money spent by the country's preeminent radar development operation"; see the foreword by Dale Corson in Henry E. Guerlac, *Radar in World War II* (New York: Tomash/American Institute of Physics, 1987), xv.

66. Daniel B. Botkin, *Discordant Harmonies: A New Ecology for the Twenty-first Century* (New York and Oxford: Oxford University Press, 1990), 172/74 and the figure on 173.

67. Fred B. Wood, "Monitoring Global Climate Change: The Case of Greenhouse Warming," *Bulletin of the American Meteorological Society* 71, no. 1 (1990): 42. In that article, the author presented "a concept for improved climate monitoring and reporting that can be implemented rapidly at modest expense, and can be utilized by scientists and policy analysts until more complete monitoring systems become available."

68. William K. Stevens, "Species Loss: Crisis or False Alarm?" *New York Times*, August 20, 1991, C1 and C8.

69. For an illuminating and witty analysis of three contradictory scenarios on energy policy put forward by the "energy tribes" (based on four years of participant observation at the International Institute for Applied Systems Analysis in Laxenburg, Austria), see Michael Thompson, "Among the Energy Tribes: A Cultural Framework for the Analysis and Design of Energy Policy," *Policy Sciences* 17 (1984): 321-339.

70. Miriam L. Campanella, "Globalization: Processes and Interpretations," *World Futures* 30 (1990): 7.

71. Thompson, "Among the Energy Tribes," 336.

72. Eric Hobsbawm, "The Missing History," *Times Literary Supplement*, 23-29 June, 1989.

3

Global History
and the Third World

Ralph Buultjens

For cultures of the West the existence of Athens, Florence or Paris is more important than that of Lo-Yang or Pataliputra. But, is it permissible to found a scheme of world history on estimates of such a sort? . . . The most appropriate designation for this current West-European scheme of history, in which the great Cultures are made to follow orbits round us as the presumed center of all world-happenings, is the Ptolemaic system of history. The system that [should be] put forward in place of it I regard as the Copernican discovery in the historical sphere, in that it admits no sort of privileged position to the Classical or Western Culture as against the Cultures of India, Babylon, China, Egypt, the Arabs, Mexico—separate worlds of dynamic being which count just as much in the general picture of history. . . . How immensely far . . . one must look . . . before one dare assert the pretension to understand world-history, the world-as-history.
—Oswald Spengler, *The Decline of the West*

Global Consciousness and Global History

Globalization is uniquely human. No other species has demonstrated the capacity to embrace and enact a global vision. We have come slowly to this capability: In the past, only a few segments of human activity inspired universal perceptions and planetary actions. Among them were religion and exploration—the missionary impulse and the challenge of physical adventure. The Bible, long a sacred text for so many believers, contains numerous statements indicative of a world outreach:

The Voice of God: I will give you as a light to the nations, that my salvation shall reach to the ends of the earth (Isa. 49:6).

The Injunction of Jesus: Go therefore and make disciples of all nations (Matt. 28:14).

The Prophecy of Zechariah [about Jesus]: He shall command peace to the
nations; his dominion shall be from sea to sea, and from the River to the
ends of the earth (Zech. 9:9).

Other major religions have similar worldviews. The Buddha, early in
his ministry, exhorted his followers: "Go ye forth . . . out of compassion
for the world, for the welfare, the profit, the bliss, of Gods and all mankind."[1] Hinduism evolved the concept of *Chakravartin,* a righteous world
ruler who would spread *Dharma* (universal moral law). And the Koran,
the sacred text of Islam, proclaims: "To Allah belongs the kingdom of the
heavens and the earth and all that they contain . . . when Allah's help and
victory come . . . you see men embrace His faith in multitudes" (5:120 and
110:1). These global visions were supported with vast spiritual and physical energy. Yet while they underwrote a vigorous outreach, they failed to
create a unified world system.

The global concept contained in the thrust for exploration was no more
successful in sustaining globalization. The great adventurer Richard Francis Burton, trying to explain his thirst to reach and know every corner of
the world ruminated: "I ask myself Why? And the only echo is—damned
fool—the devil drives."[2] Other intrepid explorers had visions that took
them to the ends of the earth. These planetary voyagers left no part of the
world undiscovered, but their global impulses were confined to limited
areas of endeavor and did not have a universal, integrating effect.

In contrast to these sporadic efforts, globalization is the leitmotiv of our
age. The earth is increasingly functioning as one society, the result of
rapid developments in a variety of technologies, primarily transportation
and communications. In historical significance, the invention of the satellite transmission—television link may be as important as the invention of
agriculture. More than any other occurrence or development, it brings the
world together through powerful visual images from all over the globe.
This focus forces a realization that all parts of the planet are interrelated.
For the first time in the human record, we are instantly globalized in a
revolution of expanding horizons.

These innovations have underwritten the globalization of economics
and politics. Finance, manufacturing, and trade have few national boundaries. The knitting of these sectors has to a large extent destroyed ambitions of economic autarky. The last holdouts of importance, China and
Burma, are now seeking ways to participate in the worldwide economic
system instead of withdrawing from it. The thrust toward free enterprise
and more open economies reinforces this trend, and the era of exiting
from the world system appears to have ended with the retreat of socialism.

Much of the same can be observed in politics. As Kenyan scholar Ali

Mazrui put it: "Almost every country in existence seems to have accepted entry into the global political system and is not seeking an exit therefrom ... political absorption into the international arena in terms of exchanging ambassadors, voting at the United Nations, expressing opinions on diplomatic issues of the day, is almost universal."[3] Isolation, unless enforced by the world community, is neither desired nor an option today.

The emerging global economic and political systems have become vehicles for expressions of conscience. The speed with which ecological interest and human rights issues have been globalized, for example, is dramatic. The spread of these two movements does more than create international concern; it implies recognition and application of universal standards and values. All this suggests that distinct patterns of globalization are being established, despite existing national, ideological, ethnic, and religious divisions.

There is, however, a danger in this development. If globalization is to contribute to a positive new civilization, there must be a comparable development on a spiritual level—a global consciousness that touches the human mind and spirit. Without such an evolution in attitudes—changes that require a growing appreciation of the fraternity of humankind and the universal value of life—globalization may, in fact, promote and disperse negative trends, including global economic exploitation and a proliferation of high-technology weapons. Unaccompanied by a redeeming consciousness, the globalization of technology and systems may simply advance the worldwide spread of *anything*, positive as well as negative. Global consciousness, then, is the agent needed to point globalization in the direction of higher civilization.

A consciousness gap between the world of fact and attitudes of mind is one of the alarming features of the contemporary world. Although there have been serious setbacks and humanity's story is uneven, history frequently records the triumph of better people, better things, and better values. But in large measure, this seems to be the consequence of chance and fortune: There is no known master mechanism that eventually ordains the victory of good over evil.

How can we improve our chances in this era of globalization? Historian Michael Howard indicated that, unless there is a global consciousness building on the knowledge of the past, the prospect is dismal.

There is no assurance of a happy ending. All may disintegrate into ruin and chaos on a scale never before seen. The future depends not on any abstract concept of historical development, not on the random play of chance, nor on the providence of an almighty God. It depends on our skill in using that capacity for reason and judgement which has already brought us so far; reason and judgement both educated and created by historical experience.

On the whole we have done quite well in avoiding or recovering from
catastrophe, but we have no justification for looking forward to a time
when we can sit back and say "That is it. Now we are safe." ... The
historical process, through the very challenges it poses and the responses it
evokes, itself creates the morality of mankind.[4]

If history is to contribute to global consciousness and help create this
morality for humans, it must be a global history. Indeed, apart from
history, there are few other disciplines or instruments that can encourage
development of a global perspective. The record of religion does not
inspire great confidence; philosophy, on its own, does not have sufficient
impact; and institutional structures, including the United Nations and an
assortment of voluntary agencies, have had notably little success in creating a broad-based ethic of globalism. It is surely history's turn.

Global consciousness or the ethic of globalism cannot, of course, be
introduced or achieved at a uniform level. At all times, there will be
different levels of awareness among different peoples in different societies. Consequently, plural global consciousnesses are perhaps more likely to result, and historians will need to be sensitive to this diversity. Since
they almost inevitably speak from their own time, historians will probably
come to address the question of globalism at some point. The task is to
accelerate this process.

In this context, global history will require, among other things, two
important components—major Third World content and new ways to
evaluate this content in relation to its global value. The size of the Third
World (encompassing over 70 percent of the earth's population and over
50 percent of its land area) gives it considerable significance. Beyond the
weight of statistics, this significance is substantially enhanced by the
Third World's history. The long and rich experiences of these regions,
especially their contribution to planetary progress, have largely been
neglected. Thus, the development of a new cosmology of history requires
uncovering much of the Third World's history and integrating it into a
global history. In doing this and evaluating the result, we will likely
develop the consciousness that our new globalized civilization needs.

The Third World in Global History

I will now examine a few selected areas that are essential for the
construction of global history, drawing on elements of Third World history to demonstrate that conventional perceptions will change significantly when the experiences of the Third World are incorporated. The
areas selected and the examples used are random choices—instances of

trying to make specific what Alfred North Whitehead described as being "provincial in time, as well as in place."

Area I: The Concept of Time

The single greatest human invention may well be time. The Western/ Christian perception of time carries with it a number of social connotations. Time puts things in order and prevents chaos in life; timekeeping and punctuality are important for an individual's personal integrity; and the cosmology derived from science largely rests on the measurement and observation of time. In this world, time is in control of human action—a fact that has increasingly influenced, if not dominated, all of contemporary society.

In doing so, Western/Christian time is driving out another concept of time, a concept that has governed the view of the majority of the world's people for most of history. The Asian/African/Middle Eastern tradition has a much more open-ended understanding of time. Precision in its observance has not been tied to the maintenance of order, integrity, or progress. And because the worldview of Asians, Africans, and Middle Easterners in the past—and of many today—is not intimately linked with time, historical measurement takes on another dimension in these cultures.

Whether these differences in attitudes toward time flow from religion (with the Christian concept being linear, and the Hindu/Buddhist concept cyclical), from geography (as in Middle East), or from social structure (as in African tribal societies) has been the subject of much study. Global history will need to relate these various perspectives of time in balancing the past and present. It will ask whether societies that are less tyrannized by time are more liberated or less disciplined and what urgencies are produced by a preoccupation with time. In sum, one of the first tasks of global history is to evaluate the importance of the element of time.

Area II: Cultural Boundaries Versus the Nation-State

To many Third World thinkers, the system of nation-states is an unreal and meaningless method of organizing units of government. At the root of their worldview are race, culture, and religion, boundaries that are much more real. Modern ethnic and ethnoreligious nationalism—both as a dividing and a unifying force—validates this belief. Three centuries ago, the Western liberal concept of the nation-state, a concept downplaying the importance of racial, cultural, and religious differences, evolved as the organizing principle of global political consolidation. The development of national markets and national economies was expected to ensure cohesion. And in several regions of the world, they did and still do serve the ideal of a multilingual, multicultural, and multireligious state.

Yet the call of race and culture and religion, or combinations of these factors, is strong today. This is not particularly confined to the Third World, although some of their strongest expressions are evident there. In the next generation, the focus of much political conflict is likely to be a struggle between old loyalties and the Westphalian world order. Several pertinent questions arise. Will global history treat the Westphalian era (1648-1985) as a historical aberration? Has the amazing speed and relative ease with which the nation-state concept became established in the world during the three centuries after 1648 obscured its unnatural essence? Will we now live in a world only partly Westphalian and largely delineated by more basic definitions? Will this accelerate or retard the rise of nationalism? And even assuming a world of nation-states, is examining the nation-state the most meaningful way in which to approach global history?

Do attacks and pressures on the nation-state indicate a further fragmentation in the human community? In the Western tradition, there is often a straight-line progression from local unity to national unity to global community. A disruption will set back this continuity. Yet in some Third World heritages, the fragmentation of society has no relation to the unity or disunity of the world. Thus, we have the ancient Hindu concept of *Vasudhaiva Kutumbakam* ("the world is one family")—a world with a common ancestry and a common ecology but not necessarily a common destiny. Servepalli Radhakrishnan expressed this Hindu sentiment: "The present organization of the world is inconsistent with the zeitgeist shining on the distant horizon."[5]

Area III: Politics

In the area of politics, Third World perspectives are markedly different from those of the West. Global history will have to balance the relative importance of these experiences and viewpoints—a difficult agenda because of the intensity with which political beliefs are held. Here are five examples:

- In the Third World, the great struggles for liberation in the twentieth century were the anticolonial upheavals. World War I and World War II are much less important. Communists, for the most part, were consistently anticolonialist in the Third World, and Western democracies have had a very mixed record.
- From the Third World perspective, the political universe has recently been divided into three groupings: The Northwest countries

with democratic-capitalist systems, the Northeast countries with state control of politics and economies, and the once-colonized remainder of the world. The battle between Marxism and democracy is essentially a civil war in the West (or should we call it the North?). Having defeated the Marxists, the anti-Marxists are now in conflict with the Third World.

- Fouad Ajami extended this notion further: "With the end of this civil war there is a return to that older frontier between Islam and Christendom. We know the feud by a modern term—the North-South conflict. But the modern international order of stratification rests, in good measure, on that old frontier between the Christian West and the World of Islam."[6] Ali Mazrui argued that Islam has potent weapons in this conflict—economics against the West, demographics against the former Soviet Union, and Pan-Islam everywhere.[7]

- The Third World disproved Marxist theories well before they were exploded elsewhere. Karl Marx argued that development preceded revolution and that the most mature links in the capitalist chain would break first. Instead, however, revolution has preceded development—as evidenced in the Third World. What is more, poverty and injustice have rarely brought revolution. Ideology has been defeated by tradition, e.g., in India and in several Islamic and African countries.

- Proponents of the food-freedom nexus (people require food before they can even think of freedom) believe that development precedes democracy. Yet many poor and deprived peoples have consistently affirmed their commitment to democracy, e.g., in India and Sri Lanka. Recent trends demonstrate that democracy is frequently contagious, spreading independently of levels of development in Third World nations.

There are other valued contributions that the Third World experience can make to an understanding of global politics. The Third World is, for example, the most recent reminder that empires are not everlasting and that decolonization is traumatic, if not ruinous, for imperial states— lessons from which the Soviet Union might well have profited.

Many Third World cultures have a multidimensional way of looking at things. Happenings can be good and bad, past and present, being and nonbeing, repetitious and unique at one and the same time. How else can we explain that the Soviet Union was an imperialist force in Europe and a liberating force in parts of the Third World? (The reverse may be argued for the United States.) Dualities and multiple personalities in policy are far more easily accepted in the Third World than in the West, where the virtues of consistency are so highly esteemed. Global history will be required to address these Third World contributions, attitudes, and issues, weaving them into a cohesive global pattern.

Area IV: The Politics of Gender

Conventional world history tells us that the most important political figures at the start of the twentieth century were major European leaders—the kaiser of Germany, the czar of Russia, the queen of Britain and her prime minister, the leader of France; perhaps the president of the United States should also be listed. Yet global history must surely include a little-mentioned woman, the Dowager Empress Tzu-hsi of China, who was the real ruler of over one-quarter of the world's population at the turn of the century. In a candid self-appraisal, Tzu-hsi wrote:

> Do you know I have often thought that I am the cleverest women who ever lived and that others cannot compare with me. Although I have heard much about Queen Victoria and read a part of her life . . . still I don't think her life is half as interesting and eventful as mine. Now look at me, I have 400 million people all dependent on my judgement.[8]

Given her modest beginnings, her rise to power against great odds, and her control of China for over forty years, Tzu-hsi's comments may not be incorrect! Although she is much neglected by both women's history and general history, any scholarship that perceives the world as a whole will accord the dowager empress much higher recognition.

Global history of more contemporary times, examining the role of women in politics, will also have to note an extraordinary geocapsule of progress. Every significant nation in South Asia has elected a woman as head of government (prime minister) at some time in the past three decades: The world's first woman prime minister, Sirimavo Bandaranaike, in Sri Lanka in 1960; the world's second prime minister, Indira Gandhi, in India in 1966; the Islamic world's first woman leader, Prime Minister Benazir Bhutto, in Pakistan in 1988; and the Islamic world's second woman leader, Prime Minister Khaleda Zia, in Bangladesh in 1991.[9]

At a time when there is considerable interest in and scholarship on women's political roles, this regional development, in an area that contains 20 percent of the world's population, has largely gone unnoticed. Global history and globally oriented women's studies need to give more attention to this remarkable constellation—to analyze how traditional societies can evolve in this way. Far more modern regions, with pioneering records in women's rights, have made no comparable advances.

Area V: Science

Many volumes have been written about advanced science in the ancient Third World. China, the Indian subcontinent, Cambodia, parts of the Middle East, and Egypt have received primary attention. Perhaps because of their visibility, engineering achievements from the Great Wall to the Great Pyramid have been closely examined. Yet with all this study, if classical Western and modern history are reviewed from a global perspective, certain interesting omissions are evident.

For example, several Greek writers, beginning around 100 B.C. with Antipatros of Sidon, prepared lists of the Seven Wonders of the World— the most amazing feats of engineering that they had heard described or seen.[10] Indeed, the Seven Wonders have become an enduring bench mark of excellence in the record of construction technology. But missing from their lists and from the ranking they bequeathed to posterity are the Great Wall of China, the huge dam at Ma'rib in Arabia, the Canal of Nikau II that connected the Red Sea to the Mediterranean (and on which large ships sailed 2,500 years before the Suez Canal was built), and the enormous Buddhist stupas of Sri Lanka. All these existed at the time the Greeks wrote of the Seven Wonders.

Another example relates to paper. Despite the importance of paper in human life, its inventor has been largely ignored by history; his name rarely merits inclusion in major encyclopedias or standard textbooks. However, an official history of China, prepared around the fifth century A.D., described how Tsai Lun, a privy councillor of the Emperor Ho-di and later his public works inspector, invented paper:

> In ancient times writing was generally on bamboo or on pieces of silk, which were then called *ji*. But silk being expensive and bamboo heavy, these two materials were not convenient. Then Tsai Lun thought of using tree bark, hemp, rags and fish nets. In [105 A.D.] he made a report to the emperor on the process of paper-making and received high praise for his ability. From this time, paper has been in use everywhere in our Celestial Kingdom and is called the "paper of Marquis Tsai."[11]

Tsai Lun's process was not very different from that used in modern papermaking, but it was ten centuries after Tsai Lun that the art of manufacturing paper reached Europe. (A recent ranking of the most influential persons in history now lists Tsai Lun as seventh in importance.[12]) A somewhat similar situation took place with printing. Although the *Chronicle of Cologne* for 1499 hailed Johannes Gutenberg as "the inventor of printing," an unknown Chinese had preceded him in this endeavor around the ninth century A.D.[13]

Many historians have sought to explain the decline of science in the Third World.[14] Various theories attribute this to geography, epidemics, colonization, intellectual exhaustion, social disorder, population growth, and other causes, and there is probably some evidence to support each of these contentions. However, it may also be that science in the Third World has gone through a period comparable to the Dark Ages in Europe—a period from which it is just beginning to emerge. In this perspective, the "dark ages of science" in the Third World would have lasted six centuries versus nine or ten centuries for the European Dark Ages.

Area VI: Religion

All the major world religions were nurtured in non-Western cultures. Of these, Christianity and Judaism later spread to Western countries. The Islamic, Hindu, Buddhist, and Confucian faiths remain essentially sheltered in the Third World—although significant Western outcroppings are beginning to appear. Religion was an early entrant into the field of globalization, yet despite successful missionary enterprises (particularly those by Christianity and Islam), religions failed to fully globalize their vision. Nonetheless, their impact on history has been powerful and often disturbing.

In the context of global history, religion evokes questions that have a special interest for the Third World. These include:

- the reasons why the West has not produced any major religion of its own;
- the processes by which Christianity was able to dominate the West while other religions failed to do so;
- the ways in which chain reactions and waves of fundamentalism spread, as well as their recurrent cycles; and
- the extent to which fear and loathing of non-Christian religions inspired historic Western interaction with the Third World.

The relationship between Islam and the West has been particularly long and forceful. For about 1,000 years, from the late seventh to the late seventeenth centuries A.D., the Christo-Islamic border was the most contentious faultline in world politics. Now, after more than 300 years of muted conflict, the tensions are again surfacing.

This time, however, the role of Islam is somewhat different. Its own objectives are ill defined because its large constituency is fragmented. Yet Islam could be on the cutting edge of future Third World hostility toward the West. It also has a unique capacity to evoke Pan-Islamic fervor—for the most part, symbolic spasms but sufficiently disturbing to upset many in the West. Another new feature is the presence of about twenty million Moslems in Western countries today. For the first time, an Islamic constituency has evolved as part of Western society. Is this a kind of global history in the making?

Area VII: Migration

The dramatic increase in migration and refugee flows, both legal and illegal, in recent years brings an important and dynamic segment of the Third World into the West. Indeed, except for the forced transportation of African slaves, there has never been a similar movement of this size. Migration as global history is in its opening chapter.

It is difficult to anticipate the cultural results of this population shift, variously estimated at between five and fifteen million individuals each year. However, in one unpleasant way, the global impact is already highly visible. Several expatriate groups in the West (the Sikhs and Tamils, for example) help to sustain violent political action in the countries of their origin. Two other observations are in order: first, that Third World migrants come to stay (and most of them retain unusually close links with their former homelands) and second, that the flow is totally in one direction—there is no countermovement from the West to the Third World.

Migration is as old as time. However, the present thrust, which shows every sign of expanding, is without precedent. As Third World peoples settle in the West and benefit from expanded educational opportunities, they may well become an important voice for global history.

Area VIII: Exploration

The Age of Exploration, the period around the fifteenth and sixteenth centuries A.D., is usually depicted as a major bench mark in the Western experience,[15] and the extraordinary physical feats of the explorers of this era are rightly applauded. The conventional understanding is that exploration was essentially a European enterprise and testimony to the inventiveness, vision, and daring of Europe. However, this assumption is not totally correct.

Global history will have to focus on at least two other exploration heritages. The Arabs were trading vigorously across the Indian Ocean and down the East African coast well before Europeans arrived there. And in the early fifteenth century, the Chinese Age of Exploration was in full bloom. In nineteen years, between 1414 and 1433, the Chinese launched seven huge operations, activities fully backed by the state. In each of these grand voyages, extending beyond India to the Gulf of Aden and the African coast, the Chinese fleet covered a larger extent of ocean than anyone had traversed before.

Zheng He, grand eunuch of the three treasurers, organized and commanded several of these big expeditions and certainly deserves as much recognition as Christopher Columbus. Seven decades before Columbus first crossed the Atlantic, this Ming dynasty admiral sailed with a fleet of stupendous size. Columbus had 3 ships with 1 deck each, together weighing a total of 415 tons. He had about 100 men, whose diet included dirty drinking water and flour baked with seawater. Zheng He's first fleet had 62 galleons supported by more than 100 auxiliary vessels. His larger galleons had 3 decks, and each weighed about 1,500 tons. Over 3,000 men accompanied Zheng He; they were fed grain, soya sauce, and other foods stored in his supply ships, and they drank tea and fresh water from the water tankers.[16]

What is important is not only the scale of these voyages but also the behavior of the Chinese. In most ways, they behaved much better than Western explorers. They were not aggressive, conquered no land, and did not plunder. They made no effort to impose their religion on Africans. They negotiated and traded but left no settlers. And apparently, they sired no children by local women, although they were not accompanied by women from their homeland. As Philip Snow put it, "For once in African history an armada of foreigners came, did their business and went away."[17]

While Western Europeans did discover the Americas and succeeded in circumnavigating the globe, the Chinese (as of the early fifteenth century A.D.) were far better poised to undertake these ventures. Why they did not do so is a subject for another study. However, the fact is that the Age of Exploration was not *only* a European epoch, a fact that any global history will have to record and discuss.

These fragments in eight areas of history have been detailed to demonstrate one of the tasks of global history—to establish a fair balance of the record. This will require both extensive research and a willingness to challenge existing analysis, correcting and expanding current world history as well as creating a new global approach. What is perhaps more important is that any meaningful global history will also have to confront established notions and preconceptions that are deeply lodged in the historical consciousness of both Western and Third World societies. In doing so, major questions of historiography and technique arise. Some of these will now be considered.

Preparing for Global History:
Questions from the Third World

Western History and Global History

In preparing for a global history, in which the Third World experience is an essential element, two primary questions arise about sources and attitudes. The first concerns Western historical traditions. Until well into the twentieth century, Western history treated the non-Western world as secondary and primitive. This view was colorfully expressed in a line from Alfred Tennyson's poem *Locksley Hall* (1843): "Better fifty years of Europe than a cycle of Cathay." And in his encyclical *Immortale Dei* (1885), Pope Leo XIII, one of the most learned pontiffs, congratulated Christian Europe on having "tamed the barbarous nations and brought them from savagery to civilization."

This perception was also reflected in serious scholarly efforts. Between 1758 and 1766, a famous compilation of fifty-eight volumes known as *Universal History* (its full title was *The Modern Part of a Universal History*) was produced in London. This celebrated work contained four volumes on the Biblical Middle East, eleven volumes on Greece and Rome, twenty-seven volumes on Europe and European activities abroad, and only fifteen volumes on the remaining portion of the world.

At the end of the nineteenth century, another major European historiographic effort was published—the celebrated *Histoire générale*, edited by Ernest Lavisse and Alfred Rambaud (published in Paris between 1892 and 1901 in twelve volumes). In its 291 chapters, little attention was paid to the non-Western world. There was some moderately good coverage of the ancient Middle East as a source of European heritage in the first volume. Thereafter, the medieval Arabs and the Ottoman Empire got four chapters, India got two chapters, the Far East got six chapters (about the same as Holland), the rest of Asia including Iran got three chapters, North Africa got one chapter, and the rest of Africa got another one (largely focused on the European partition of the "Dark Continent"). In all, the non-Western world accounted for less than 10 percent of the contents of the *Histoire générale*.

Since then, there has been some change in the "Cycle of Cathay syndrome." World history now accords much more significance to the non-Western story. Yet knowledge and attitude problems persist. In many ways, this is symbolized in the conventional use of the phrase *Third World*. For most people and many scholars in the West, the Third World covers almost all countries in Asia (excluding Japan), Africa, the Middle East, and Latin America. The phrase has three widely accepted connotations:

- It is the lowest ranking in the hierarchy of modernization, well behind the industrial West and the previously Socialist countries in Eastern Europe.
- It implies societies in which there is little specific differentiation of social roles, e.g., where there is no clear separation of church and state and where an intermingling of religious and political groups exists.
- It portrays societies in which individuals function within collective structures (castes, tribes, extended families), rather than as separate persons.

The image that emerges depicts a somewhat inert and backward area, mostly populated by premodern peoples—with the term *modernization* as the distinguishing marker. However, modernization is largely defined by the West to describe Western approaches, ideas, and processes. At the heart of this definition is the notion of progress. Many Western thinkers, such as Robert Nisbet, see it as essentially a Western concept that "has been a benign intellectual influence—inseparable from the crucial motivations, impulses, desires and incentives behind the extraordinary accomplishments of Western civilization. . . . This idea has done more good over a twenty-five hundred-year period . . . than any single idea in Western history."[18] Nisbet has such faith in progress and its beneficence that he sees its erosion or decline as a signal weakness in Western civilization.[19]

"Progress," however, does not march on even ground. The expectations are higher and the rules easier for Western societies than for non-Western cultures. As Fouad Ajami pointed out, for centuries the law of nations presumed that the rules stopped at the edge of Western civilization. Thus, use of the crossbow was forbidden in conflicts between Christian knights in the early years of the twelfth century A.D. But the rules of engagement with heathens were less benign—they were rules for a wilder territory.[20]

This dualism persists. The old controversy about dropping the atom bomb on Japan in 1945 has resonances of it. Persistent surprise that democracy functions effectively in India and Sri Lanka betrays a similar outlook. So does widespread amazement that East Asian economic modernization is so successful and that non-Western migrants can flourish in Western societies. Jeane J. Kirkpatrick, the Reagan administration's ambassador to the United Nations, gave a sanctimonious twist to the concept of progress as a Western notion: "Our moral standards are so much higher than everybody else's."[21]

Both Nisbet and Kirkpatrick ignored or underplayed a basic fact of history. At times, there was far more progress in non-Western societies than in Western areas. Moreover, non-Western societies have been able to sustain progress for long periods, as demonstrated in ancient China and modern Japan. Yet the unidimensional attitude is widespread. As Ross Dunn noted: "A major drawback of traditional Western civilization [studies] is [their] common presumption that the rise of Europe and the United States to world economic and military dominance in the twentieth century can be adequately explained simply by looking back over the history of the West, neglecting the world context into which each age of Western history was born."[22]

As for the expectation of continued beneficence from progress (and fears that a growing antagonism to progress will undermine Western civilization), an ancient Hindu legend is instructive. It is the myth of *Samudra Manthanam* ("the churning of the oceans"), a warning given some twenty centuries ago in the age of the *Devas* ("gods") and *Asuras* ("demons"). The Devas and the Asuras were said to have collaborated and coordinated a huge churning of the oceans. After a while, valuable gifts began to emerge from this process. The more they churned, the more gifts surfaced—treasures that they joyfully divided. But their excessive disturbance of the waters released a deadly poison, a *Garala* that they had not expected. When the poison began to gush, the Devas and Asuras had no answers. They fled, leaving the universe in danger of extinction. Then, the great god Shiva appeared and swallowed the poison, enabling evolution to continue and the universe to survive excessive exploitation by its residents. The essence of this myth is that the divine power of Shiva is in the heart of every person, regardless of race, culture, religion, or nationality. As our consciousness awakens, we realize that we all belong to a world family—a family that cannot exploit its environment heedlessly without expecting the toxic agents of cosmic destruction to emerge. The hubris of progress brings the nemesis of regress.

In this context, conventional Western historiography, with built-in assumptions about and applause for modernization and progress, provokes several questions. Can a historiography that is, consciously or unconsciously, so rooted in these traditions provide the raw material for a global history? How can it readjust its internal compass before making a balanced contribution? Are the inputs of those Western historians and philosophers of history who try to stay outside this stream (Spengler, Toynbee) sufficiently strong to provide a Western countertradition? The answers to these questions are fundamental to an assessment of the contributions Western history can make to global history.

Third World History and Global History

The second major question that concerns a global history in which Third World experiences are an essential element is the historiography of the Third World. A further note of clarification regarding the scope implied in the term *Third World* is necessary here. Its conventional definition embraces the two segments of the non-Western world—areas in which historical populations remain and areas in which historical populations have been displaced (i.e., Latin America and the Caribbean). This definition is essentially a socioeconomic description.

For purposes of this chapter, the term *Third World* is used *culturally*. It refers to areas in which the bulk of people are descendants of ancestors who have long lived in these regions—most of Asia, Africa, and the Middle East. Thus, Latin America and the Caribbean are excluded. Japan is an ambiguity: Its culture remains lodged in the Far Eastern heritage, but its enormous economic modernization makes it very different. It has become an advanced industrial economy within a Third World cultural setting.

A word about the future of this terminology is also necessary. Although used in this text in the way defined earlier, the very phrase *Third World* is incongruous in the context of global history. As a more globalized approach evolves, it will probably be necessary to bury the concept of separated Western history, Third World history, continental history, and the like. For purposes of global historiography in the future, such distinctions would have little meaning. Today, their value lies largely in descriptions of the ways in which our current knowledge has been constructed and arranged.

How useful is the historiography of the Third World as I have defined it? Two relevant points attend this question. First, Third World societies have made very few attempts to study areas and cultures outside their own; indeed, traditions of comparative scholarship are uncommon there. Middle Eastern scholar Bernard Lewis explained that:

> [the countries of the Third World] did not study Europe. They did not even study each other, unless the way for such study was prepared either by conquest or conversion or both. The kind of intellectual curiosity that leads to the study of a language, the deciphering of ancient texts [beyond one's own culture] without any such preparation or motivation is still peculiar to Western Europe, to its daughters such as America, and to its disciples such as Russia and Japan. Those who do not share this curiosity are puzzled by it and naturally respond with incomprehension and suspicion.[23]

At times, this leads to a certain scholastic nationalism and resentment. Suspicious Third World natives ask what right outsiders have to study their history. It is, in this view, their property, and the study of it is an intrusion, especially because the goal of such study is often what it was in the past: to subjugate, dominate, denigrate, and exploit. This perception of external involvement being an invasion, perhaps with larcenous intent, into local cultural territory is partly the heritage of colonialism and partly resentment at earlier Western interpretations of the Third World. Care and confidence-building will be required in order to assure that a global history effort is not seen in this way by many in the Third World.

A second point concerning the contribution of Third World historiography to global history relates to the nature of the Third World's history. In the Far East, especially in China, historians have an unbroken series of comprehensive records at their disposal. Sometimes, these are laced with a particularly local flavor. For example, to the Chinese way of thinking, the existence of trade between China and a foreign country was evidence of friendly ties, even if an exchange of goods was indirect, not on equal terms, and involved no human encounter. Yet a core of facts has been preserved.

Islamic societies have also frequently maintained continuous records, and often, when Islamic influence strengthened in non-Islamic areas, this heritage was enhanced. Thus, the Mughal dynasty maintained diligent accounts or memoirs from the time it established itself in India. The founder of Mughal rule, the Emperor Babur, set the pattern with *The Babur Nama*, an autobiographical writing that combined history, a description of his kingdom, biography, and personal reflections; it was initially compiled around 1530 A.D. In the Middle East itself, the tradition is strong. Thus, we have Ibn Khaldun's early fifteenth century *Introduction to History* or *The Muqaddimah*,[24] an effort that Arnold Toynbee regarded as the greatest work of its kind that has ever been created by any mind in any time or place.

However, the tradition of writing history is not so well established in large parts of the Third World, especially in India and Africa. India has a large body of neohistorical literature, but most of it is hagiographic or mythological. In addition, much epigraphical evidence is not easily connected to specific historical periods. The Mauryan Emperor Asoka (ca 274-232 B.C.) left records inscribed on stone, which he hoped would endure forever. These rock edicts are among the most important exhibits of Indian history. They did not, however, refer to Asoka by his name but by the title King Priyadarsi. Most of the edicts were written in Prakrit; a few in the north were in Greek and Aramaic. When the Prakrit script was deciphered in 1837, no supporting history was available to identify King Priyadarsi. It is only through references in the *Great Chronicle* of Sri Lanka, *The Mahavamsa*, that Priyadarsi was confirmed as being Asoka.[25] Thus,

Indian sources, if they existed at all, were a poor guide because they were
so fragmentary and because so much history was transmitted orally.

R. C. Majumdar, one of modern India's eminent scholars, commented:

> For the longest period of Indian history, namely from the earliest time
> down to the Muslim conquest in the thirteenth century A.D., a period of
> about 4000 years, we possess no historical text of any kind, much less such a
> detailed narrative as we possess in the case of Greece, Rome and China. . . .
> The shortcoming is certainly not due to the absence of the raw material of
> history, since India provides data in unsurpassed abundance. But this
> abundance, found in the myths recorded in the Vedas, epics and Puranas,
> belongs to the realm of poetry, mythology and cosmology rather than
> history.[26]

Yet in more recent times, Indian history has been well developed.
Generations of scholars have constructed a fairly detailed picture of the
past. In this effort, the literacy of the Indian tradition—languages of
record such as Prakrit and Sanskrit—has helped immensely. It is also
important that much of Indian history has been recovered by Indian
scholars themselves. Among those who labored to make this history
better known was Jawarharlal Nehru. "The chief virtue of his historical
writings was to correct the distortion caused by the Europe-centered view
of Western scholars, and to reestablish the importance of Asia in world
history and world culture. When it came to history this was his passion
and he wanted Indian scholars to join in it."[27]

This situation is markedly different from that in Africa. The peoples of
Africa and, indeed, the majority of black people everywhere are heirs of
an oral tradition—the transmission of records and wisdom by song and
poetry and speech. Ali Mazrui noted: "In the absence of the written word
in most African cultures, many tentative innovations or experiments of a
previous era were not transmitted to the next generation . . . an oral
tradition transmits mainly what is accepted and respected [it] is a tradition of conformity, rather than heresy, a transmission of consensus rather
than dissidence."[28] In addition, Mazrui pointed to the absence of numer-
acy, or mathematics at a more elaborate level, as a feature of the African
past.

The lack of voluminous records forces African historians to reconstruct
their history from oral memories, inscribed genealogies, and old ruins. As
Philip Snow commented: "Their concern is rather to clarify the past than
to justify the present; rather to discover their ancestors than to explore a
possible encounter between their ancestors and others. . . . They are wary
of such an encounter."[29]

How, then, can scholars incorporate African history and engage African scholarship in global history? Perhaps those in quest of a global history will initially need to collaborate with Africans in the quest for African history. Accommodation and appreciation of the oral tradition will also have to be discussed in this context. It certainly cannot be ignored in any study or preparation of history.

Subsumed in all this is the question of values. History, after all, is not only a record of things, people, cultures, and happenings. It also evaluates. Yet differences in value systems are so profound that it is possible to arrive at vastly different conclusions from a single set of facts—conflicting conclusions that may all be correct in light of the values used to distill them. Those who attempt a global history then have four options:

- to construct global history from the same value base that has been used for other histories in the past;
- to attempt a value-free approach;
- to attempt a global history that presents several values viewpoints, each labeled accordingly;
- to construct a new global value base before or while writing global history.

Given these circumstances, other concerns emerge. Can global history be written by any single individual, or does its very nature demand a collaborative effort? Is such a task too daunting? Historian Steven Runciman thinks it is difficult even at a regional level, despite his conviction that it has value:

> What I would like to see is a great work that would cover the history not only of the Ottoman Sultans and their Turkish subjects but also of their subjects of other races, Arabs and Jews and the Christian minorities, Greek, Slav and Armenian. It is, I know, a work that demands too much of any author. He would have to be at home not only in Ottoman Turkish and Arabic, and preferably Persian as well, but also in Greek, in the Slavonic languages and Armenian, and it would take the greater part of a lifetime to collect, study and correlate the sources. He might well feel it necessary to employ collaborators; but a book to which many scholars have contributed is seldom satisfactory, unless it is firmly controlled by one master-mind. So this is a work that I shall never see: which is to be regretted, as it could do so much to explain to our statesmen the problems that confront them in Eastern Europe and Western Asia.[30]

However, in the context of today's globalization, it is an effort that must be undertaken, whatever the result. William McNeill, in his biography of Arnold Toynbee, reminded us that there is inspiration to be obtained from that scholar's approach: "Toynbee, more than any other single person, was able to introduce to a large portion of the world's reading public the simple truth that Asians, Africans, Amerindians and even specialized peoples like the Eskimo had a history that was independent of and analogous to the history of Europeans. The vision of a human past cast, as he said, not just in Western terms was, therefore, a great and central contribution."[31]

In a way, our efforts to create global history reach beyond Toynbee. As McNeill put it in another context, "Much depends on how the discipline of history develops, and whether historians and other intellectuals persevere in trying to reduce humankind's manifold adventures on planet earth to an intelligible whole."[32] In this time of globalization, much more depends on its human counterpart—a global history that gives the Third World its place in history and thereby advances global consciousness. If only for these reasons, we must begin.

Notes

1. F. L. Woodward, ed., *Some Sayings of the Buddha* (London: Oxford University Press, 1939), 30.

2. Letter to Monckton Miles (Lord Houghton), 1863. See J. R. L. Anderson, *The Ulysses Factor* (New York: Harcourt Brace Jovanovich, 1970), 18-19.

3. Ali A. Mazrui, *Cultural Forces in World Politics* (London: James Currey, 1990), 239.

4. Michael Howard, "Structure and Process in History," *Times Literary Supplement*, June 23-29, 1989, 689.

5. Sarvepalli Radhakrishnan, *Eastern Religions and Western Thought* (New York: Oxford University Press, 1959), VII.

6. Fouad Ajami, "Islam and the West: A Cultural Duel," *Times Literary Supplement*, February 1991.

7. Mazrui, *Cultural Forces*, 224-225.

8. Letter by Tzu-Hsi (1835-1908), quoted in the introduction to Marina Warner, *The Dragon Empress* (New York: Athenium, 1986).

9. Sirimavo Bandaranaike was prime minister of Sri Lanka from 1960 to 1965 and again from 1970 to 1977. Indira Gandhi was prime minister of India from 1966 to 1977 and again from 1980 to 1984. Benazir Bhutto was prime minister of Pakistan from 1988 to 1990. Khaleda Zia was elected prime minister of Bangladesh in 1991. All were democratically elected.

10. The Seven Wonders of the World listed by Antipatros of Sidon were the Pyramids of Egypt, the Hanging Gardens of Babylon, the Statue of Zeus at Olympia, the Temple of Artemis at Ephesos, the Tomb of King Mausolos at Halikarnassos, the Colossus of Rhodes, and the Pharos Lighthouse of Alexandria. Later lists substituted the Walls of Babylon or the Temple of Jupiter in Rome for some items on the original list.

11. Quoted in Thomas Frances Carter, *The Invention of Printing in China (and Its Spread Westward)* (New York: Columbia University Press, 1925), 3.

12. Michael A. Hart, *The 100—A Ranking of the Most Influential Persons in History* (New York: Hart Publishing, 1978).

13. L. Sprague de Camp, *The Ancient Engineers* (New York: Ballentine Books, 1962), 323-327.

14. The classic study of ancient science and technology in China is, of course, Joseph Needham's *Science and Civilization in China*, published by Cambridge University Press. In almost three decades, Needham has authored fifteen of a projected twenty-five-volume work. The most recent is *Science and Civilization in China—Military Technology: The Gunpower Epic*, published in 1988.

15. See Philip Snow, *The Star Raft—China's Encounter with Africa* (Ithaca, N.Y.: Cornell University Press, 1988), 21-29.

16. Ibid., 21-22.

17. Ibid., 33.

18. Robert Nisbet, *History of the Idea of Progress* (New York: Basic Books, 1980), 8.

19. Ibid., 9 and 357.

20. Ajami, "Islam and the West."

21. Jeane J. Kirkpatrick, *New York Times*, April 15, 1989.

22. Ross Dunn, "Central Themes for World History," in Paul Gagon, ed., *Historical Literary—The Case for History in American Education* (Boston: Houghton Mifflin, 1989), 222.

23. Bernard Lewis, inaugural lecture at the Center for Non-Western Studies at the University of Leiden, 1990. A similar theme is reflected in Lewis's book, *The Political Language of Islam* (Chicago: University of Chicago Press, 1988).

24. Ibn Khaldun, *The Muqaddimah*, translated from the Arabic by Franz Rosenthal, Bollingen Series XLIII (New York: Parthenon Books, 1958).

25. Of the old cultures in South Asia, only Sri Lanka has a strong tradition of written history. *The Mahavamsa* (early sixth century A.D.) is the best known, but other histories, such as *The Dipavamsa* (fourth century A.D.), *The Culavamsa*, and *The Pujavalia* (both from the thirteenth century A.D.), provide valuable records of a quality not found elsewhere in the region.

26. R. C. Majumdar, quoted in Benjamin Walker, *Hindu World—An Encyclopedic Survey* (London: Allen and Unwin, 1968), 453.

27. Statement made to the author by Nehru's daughter, Indira Gandhi, New Delhi, December 24, 1982.

28. Mazrui, *Cultural Forces*, 140-141.

29. Snow, *The Star Raft*, 2.

30. Steven Runciman, "The Missing History—A Symposium," *Times Literary Supplement*, June 23-29, 1989, 701.

31. William H. McNeill, *Arnold J. Toynbee—A Life* (New York: Oxford University Press, 1989), 285.

32. Ibid., 288.

4

From Universal History to Global History

Manfred Kossok

I

"The concept of 'universal history' or 'world history' elicits the most contradictory opinions in response." This opening sentence of the introduction to the anthology *Universalgeschichte* ("Universal History"), written by Ernst Schulin (1974), could and should stand as a motto for every debate on the subject of universal, world, and global history. Yet one peculiar contradiction exists: The wish and necessity to grasp the world as a whole from a historical perspective, to know "what holds the world together at the core" (*Faust* I), i.e., to acknowledge the totality of history, ultimately runs up against insurmountable objective and subjective obstacles. The sheer volume of material threatens to overwhelm the individual historian, while groups of scholars working together rarely achieve more than what Ernst Troeltsch long ago dismissed as a "book binder's synthesis." The very concept of "world history" contains an internal contradiction. The question is not only how one ought to judge history and its potential for transmitting knowledge or its cognitive possibilities and limits; the definition of the term *world* must also be subjected to critical analysis. Changes in the meaning of the term over time are revealed at once if one compares the worldviews of ancient (Greco-Roman), Islamic-Arab, Chinese, and medieval Christian societies. The historical relativization of the concept "world" represents a challenge, above all, to those historians who view human history *a priori* as world history, in contrast to those who apply it only from about the year 1500 on (in some cases 1300). The fundamental nature of the debate was recently made evident once

Translated from the German by Deborah L. Schneider. The unfortunate death of Professor Kossok on February 27, 1993, prevented him from arranging his citations more formally.

again in Andre Gunder Frank's polemics against Immanuel Wallerstein
· (*Journal of World History* I, 1). For Frank, world history starts about 5,000
years before the beginning of the present era, i.e., with the emergence of
classical high cultures in the ancient Orient. Imanuel Geiss's *"World History"—Die global-historische Perspective* ("The Global Historical Perspective"), based on Lefton S. Stavrianos (1970) and William H. McNeill
(1963), argued for a similarly extensive conception of world history, with
the result that processes after 1500 would receive an almost "reductionist
interpretation": "World history is then [i.e., from 1492-1498 on] reduced
[!] in fact to primarily the history of Europe, the internal development of
which becomes indispensable for an understanding of its revolutionary
effect on the entire world (Geiss 1988). It is not my intention to pursue
here the variety of interpretations given to the term; for this, I refer the
reader to Schulin's anthology, although a review of the lively discussion
that has taken place since 1974-1975 is, in fact, urgently needed. The
Journal of World History, founded in 1990, and the affiliated World History
Association might provide the necessary forum for this.

As a rule, the concepts of universal history and world history are
treated as identical. However, in German historiography at least, one
significant attempt to distinguish between the two was made. This effort
was associated with Karl Lamprecht, *spiritus rector* of the Institute for
Cultural and Universal History, established at the University of Leipzig in
1909. This institute represented the most comprehensive academic under-
taking to that time to treat world history as a whole, including its geographical dimensions and structural complexity (economics, government,
law, culture, and mentality), and it has remained unique in German
historiography. Lamprecht's approach to the study of history in its totality, based on interdisciplinary and comparative studies, aroused considerable controversy in his day since it challenged the basic fixation of prior
German historical studies on nation-states and individuals. Indirectly, this
controversy represented an extension of the bitter "methodological quarrel" carried on in the 1890s between Lamprecht and established historians, who accused him of excessive liberalism and even Marxism (due to
his emphasis on economic factors).

In 1910, Lamprecht advocated making a distinction between universal
history and world history, and it is significant that the context he referred
to was European expansion. Lamprecht argued:

> We Germans have the two terms *Universalgeschichte* ["universal history"]
> and *Weltgeschichte* ["world history"], and we should accustom ourselves to
> refer to the new circumstances created by the most recent European ex-
> pansion, which naturally requires new concepts and thus new technical
> terms, i.e., to the history of European expansion and the Western Asian and

Mediterranean cultures on which this is historically based, as world history, in essence continuing the usage that has existed up to now for all practical purposes; the history of humankind as a whole, however, should be designated as universal history (*Weltgeschichte*, ed. by J. von Pfluck-Hartung, vol. 6).

This distinction between universal history and world history failed to become generally accepted. Nevertheless, certain aspects of Lamprecht's use of the term *world history* remain noteworthy:

1. His clear limitation of the term to a particular historical epoch, against a background of imperialism in full flower. This connection reminds one of William H. McNeill's confession (*JWH* 1, 1 [1990]) about the degree to which the imperial policies of the United States after World War II left their stamp on his work *The Rise of the West*. One could pursue much further the chain linking the term *world history* to a particular epoch: Are Voltaire's excursions into world history imaginable, for example, without the military and cultural expansionism of France under Louis XIV?
2. His assumption that world history can be understood as the history of European hegemony, as if this were self-evident.
3. His view of different cultures: He not only differentiated between "primary" and "secondary" cultures but also—since Europe received such special emphasis—made further subdivisions within the primary cultures themselves. Lamprecht's theory of cultures, which anticipated central aspects of Arnold Toynbee's thinking, was outlined in historical, geographical, and political terms by the Orientalist André Wedemeyer in *Die großen Kulturkreise der Menschheit* ("The Great Cultures of Human History," 1910).
4. His association of world history with (imperialist) world politics—a view that presupposed a clear relation between world history and the aims and strategies of power politics.

Theories that use the term *universal* or *world history* to refer to the time before 1500 automatically take parts of the world (or world history) for the whole. But though the premodern cultures of the Eurasian region—from the ancient Oriental societies to the dominance of China (1000-1500)—unquestionably represented the center of historical dynamics in their particular epoch, they were at no time truly universal phenomena, that is, phenomena that spanned the whole earth (the world). As long as certain continents or parts of continents remained isolated or were affected only peripherally, one could not speak of world history in the sense of a single, universal historical system. The fundamentally new qualities of modern history were determined by bourgeois society, with its claim to universal hegemony. Consequently, use of the term *world history* for the time before 1500 demands a more precise definition of the particular quality of premodern world history in its temporal, geographic, and structural dimensions. This is necessary to prevent all historical continuity from seeming totally random.

As early as 1845-1846, in his essay *"Die deutsche Ideologie"* ("German Ideology") Karl Marx addressed the question of how history became world history ("this transformation of history into world history"), and he formulated answers that are not only of interest for the definition of world history but also relevant for an understanding of global history (M. Kossok, *Karl Marx und der Begriff der Weltgeschichte*, 1984). In the passage on the "production of consciousness," he wrote of "the broadening of [individuals'] activity into world-historical activity" or "the measure in which history becomes transformed into world history" (55). Then he spoke of the two decisive theses. "The further the separate spheres, which interact on one another, extend in the course of this development," he wrote, "the more the original isolation of the separate nationalities is destroyed by the developed mode of production and intercourse and the division of labour between various nations naturally brought forth by these, the more history becomes world history" (58). Further, he stated that "big industry . . . produced world history for the first time, insofar as it made all civilised nations and every individual member of them dependent for the satisfaction of their wants on the whole world, thus destroying the former natural exclusiveness of separate nations" (77-78). Marx returned to this idea in 1857 in almost apodictic form in the *Einleitung zur Kritik der politischen ökonomie* ("Introduction to a Critique of Political Economy"): "World history did not always exist; history as world history is a result" (149). In essence, this represented the aim of understanding world history as a global historical system, a chain of historical thinking whose most recent links include the works of Immanuel Wallerstein on the "modern world system" (1974, 1988).

From a heuristic perspective, it is necessary to make several distinctions in dealing with the term *world history*; the *concept* of world history; world history as a *process*; world history as the *result* of human history; and world history in the *broader* and *narrower* sense.

II

Universal or world history encompasses a certain stage, quality, and dimension of human history. Consequently, there is a decisive difference between world history and the history of the world. Universal history in the *broader* sense of the concept can be understood as the total temporal, spatial, and structural process of human development. This process at first consisted of the quantitative sum of autonomous and autochthonous processes in their different geographic dimensions. The fact that no universal systemic framework exists (as yet) prohibits one from speaking in terms of partial processes. Despite the enormous geographical dimensions of major premodern cultures, they represented not universal but rather regional cultures in the last analysis, even though some of them covered an entire continent.

Universal history in the *narrower* sense means the "compression" of human history into a worldwide *system* of reciprocal communication (of both a dominant and a nondominant nature), penetrations, influences, and dependencies. Through these, historical and geographic regions that had been relatively or entirely autochthonous now entered into direct or indirect relations with one another. This had fundamental consequences for their further development, and a process of qualitative cumulation took place. Existing economic worlds (*économie-mondes*) began to merge into a world economy (*économie monde mondiale*) in the sense of Fernand Braudel's categories. Of course, this does not mean that the concept of world history is reduced to a process of merging economies, although both the power of economics and the economics of power no doubt played a decisive role in the transformation of history into world history. Therefore, the levels of "process" and "result" cannot be schematically separated from one another.

According to the primary criterion for the growth of (relatively isolated) *économie-mondes* into an *économie monde mondiale*, the definitive shift from human history to world history commenced in the late fifteenth and early sixteenth centuries. The years 1492 (the "discovery" of America) and 1498 (the Portuguese exploration of the Indian Ocean) functioned as a kind of prism, focusing the various lines of development within the framework of a process of *longue durée*, of continuity and break: caesura, turning point, point of intersection, and departure. At the same time, those years marked a date midway along the path to the modern world; they encompassed the end and the beginning of an upheaval in the "long farewell to the Middle Ages" (Jacques Le Goff). The era was rooted, on the one hand, far back in time, before the Western migration or expansion of the Mediterranean economy that began in the thirteenth century. (In this, not only the secular contrast of Venice and Genoa was decisive but also the changes on the Iberian peninsula as a result of the almost completed *reconquista*.) On the other hand, the effects of the years 1492 and 1498 continue to be felt in the present.

A prerequisite for the pivotal or threshold era denoted by these years was the shift of the dynamic center of historical development from Asia and the Near East to Europe. In concrete terms, however, this initially meant southern Europe and then (after considerable delay) also northern and western Europe. The historical world axis rotated 180 degrees; the "age of the east" was followed by the "age of the west." This not only involved a geographical shift of the time axis but also included a completely new quality of historical time. Europe—previously the geographic, economic, and cultural periphery of Asia—now began establishing its hegemony economically, technically, militarily, politically, institutionally, socially, and intellectually. The question Braudel posed in 1964 remains relevant today: "But why Europe" (instead of China or Islam)? If we give our imaginations free rein for a moment (for why should historians not be permitted an imagination?), we might ask, what course would world history have taken if the mighty Chinese trading and expedition fleets that reached East Africa at the latitude of Sofala early in the fifteenth century had continued around the southern tip of Africa? What if a successor of the eunuch admiral [Zheng He] had encountered the tiny caravels of Bartolomeu Dias and Vasco da Gama or even approached the coast of Portugal? Instead, as we know, the land party defeated the sea party in China around 1440 to 1450, i.e., at a time when the Portuguese had just approached Cape Bojador. The possible answers to the question "why Europe and not the others?" were pursued further in the anthology by Schulin, mentioned earlier. One of the more recent attempts at an answer to that question is Imanuel Geiss's theory concerning the "Latinity of Europe" (1991). The French historian Jean Piel has tried to identify all the possible factors in a work clearly based on Braudel, Wallerstein, and Pierre Chaunu, *Esquisse d'une histoire comparée* (1989).

To explain the emergence of Europe and its advance to the center of modern history, a causal trio can be identified, at the cost of a certain schematization and simplification. First, Europe had the scientific and technical ability to exploit nature and its resources in entirely new directions. For the first time in history, with the transition to a bourgeois society, a civilization arose that was in a position to exploit the natural resources of nature to the verge of total exhaustion within a historically short period—namely, from 1500 to 2000. Second, in a parallel development, a process of physical self-exploitation occurred, unlike any that premodern cultures and civilizations had known in terms of intensity; it reached its first great peak at the time of the industrial revolution, in combination with the scientific and technical advances. Finally, there was an almost total subjugation of the rest of the world to European domination, that is, the inclusion of Africa, Asia, and Latin America in a process of accumulation that had an entirely new quality.

At the same time, universal history in the narrower sense meant the Europeanization of the world in a direct or indirect manner. The hegemony of Europe—or to put it more generally, of the West—advanced through various stages until the era of late capitalist imperialism, thus representing a new historical dimension and quality of hegemony. The concept of hegemony also requires historical relativization, in a double sense. In one sense, it relates to changes in time and form. In another, it relates to the fact that neither Europe nor the West practiced hegemony in the same way; instead, this hegemony was always exercised by regional, partial sectors. For example, eastern and southern Europe were excluded to a considerable extent, a factor of great significance for the question of the continuing Asiatic heritage of this area (which has acquired a new relevance through recent events). Migration or displacement of the historical center *to* Europe always meant migration or displacement *within* Europe, as well. With the rise of northwestern Europe since the sixteenth and seventeenth centuries, the once dominant Mediterranean south and Iberian west have been pushed into the (European) periphery.

With regard to the new dimension and quality of European hegemony, several aspects deserve particular attention. Going beyond the boundaries and structures of the great premodern empires, Europe's hegemony embodied the first truly worldwide (universal) system of hegemony. The world and its history began to become indivisible. Furthermore, with European hegemony, the relationship of center and periphery took on a new historical quality, as Wallerstein argued in a comprehensive if controversial manner. Regional and structural developmental differences became institutionalized in the phenomenon of a perpetuated underdevelopment. The "development of underdevelopment" began, as A. G. Frank accurately described its. The coexistence of what had previously belonged to different times was no longer only the normal consequence and the "natural" expression of processes of regional and structural differentiation; it was also one of the decisive prerequisites for the spread and consolidation of European hegemony.

Only in Europe did the process of capital accumulation proceed in a comprehensive and "classic" manner—a process that unleashed the economic and social conditions needed to replace the Middle Ages with the modern period, giving this development a potentially global dimension. The place of capital accumulation as a critical structural element in the transformation of history into world history (on the basis of forming a "world system") is not uncontroversial, however, as the polemics of Frank against Wallerstein, mentioned earlier, demonstrate do. Frank stressed that premodern cultures also depended upon accumulation and that the ancient Oriental societies had at their disposal a variety of highly efficient means for this—for example, in tax collection or supply systems. In the last analysis, this debate was about fundamentally different views of accumulation: accumulation based on demand tribute in the form of added product (payment as work, goods, or money) *or* accumulation based on producing added value.

Since, in the broadest sense of the term, all premodern cultures (civilizations) represented, in different ways, forms of ancient Oriental and feudal society, including a variety of mixed and transitional forms, the problem of the structural prefiguration for the beginning of the modern era arises. That concerns the concrete situation after 1500 and the specifics of (primarily western) European feudalism (with peasants' property and free cities in the process of individualization being key factors), as well as feudalism's particular dynamic potential for forming capital. The wealth of variations, forms, and paths that resulted was pointed up by the CRM debate *"Sur le feudalisme"* (Paris, 1968), especially in the contributions by Charles Parain and Pierre Vilar. To determine more precisely the "change of scene" and "pulsation of progress" (Charlotte Welskopf, 1967) on the threshold of the modern era, it is necessary to point out that Oriental and Asiatic cultures were not overtaken by Europe in a single great leap but remained superior to it in a number of respects for a considerable time. Even the conquistadors, who invaded America as the knights of the original movement to accumulate capital, were unable to resist the fascination of the artistic, architectural, and scientific achievements of the Aztecs or Incas. For those non-European societies that were not totally destroyed or subjected to deformative acculturation, a period of stagnation at a high level of culture in comparison to the creatively destructive dynamics of European and western society remained characteristic. The manner in which Europe surpassed the East can, indeed, be characterized as an instance of "overtaking without equaling" in world history; the path did not follow the Oriental path but rather took a dynamic and creative detour around it.

The universalization of history under European hegemony ultimately meant the division of the world into subject and object regions (states, nations). The institutional expression of this development of a structural hierarchy was the *rise of the modern colonial system*, whose growth was clearly dependent on the advancing stages and consolidation of bourgeois society. The internal shift of emphasis within Europe can be traced in the changes to the European colonial system: the feudal-mercantile phase in the fifteenth and sixteenth centuries, with the major colonial powers being Portugal and Spain; the trade capitalism phase in the sixteenth and seventeenth centuries, with the major colonial power being the Netherlands; the trade and manufacturing capitalism phase, in the seventeenth and eighteenth centuries, with the major colonial powers being England and France; and the imperialist phase of the nineteenth and early twentieth centuries, with the major colonial powers being England, France, and

Germany. The division of the world was the goal of the global institutionalization of European/Western hegemony. From 1898 on, Western
hegemony also included the United States, with its formal and informal
empire in Latin America and its "open door" policy toward Asia.)

Relatively independent of the degree of direct subjugation or indirect
dependency, the relationship of non-European/non-Western regions to
Europe was characterized by an increasing functional marginalization.
(Latin America, for example, was directly subjugated; China was indirectly dependent.) All these regions became partial systems of the periphery on various levels, and clear gradations existed within the periphery
system, which the so-called CHP model (core-hinterland-periphery) attempts to describe. Functional marginalization meant being "pushed to
the edge of world history" in a literal as well as a metaphorical sense. This
new constellation of peripheral lands, which came into being about 1500
and achieved its final contours about 1900, was, in part,the consequence
of external (exogenous) factors (with invasion used as a means to establish
the supremacy of Europe). However, there were also specific internal
(endogenous) factors at work, the influence of which could not be recognized without a historical/systematic comparison. The first attempts at
doing this through a study of the fifteenth century have now appeared
(Eric R. Wolf, *Europe and the People Without History*, 1982; Guy Martinière
and Consuelo Varcla, *L'Etat du monde en 1492*, 1992; M. Kossok, *1492: Die
Welt an der Schwelle zur Neuzeit*, 1992).

A glance at the web of internal factors in the non-European world
reveals an extremely contradictory picture. At the moment of *"Europe's
Awakening"* (Franco Cardini, 1989), i.e., before the great expansion movement, China turned its gaze inward under the Ming emperors, a reversal
that resulted in the stagnation of the Middle Kingdom at its then current
level (which up to that time had been superior to that of Europe). Only
much later did Japan follow suit and close its own doors, a step that
occurred under the influence of its contact with Portugal (Sakoku 1636/
39).

The former giant empire of the Mongols was only a shadow of its
former self, despite a brief revitalization under Dajan Khan in the fifteenth
century, and it succumbed to increasing feudal fragmentation. Islam continued to spread by invasion and to form empires of the old (i.e., premodern) type: the Ottoman Empire, the Safavid dynasty in Persia, and the
Mogul empire in India. After the final defeat of Arab/Islamic forces in
western Europe (in the conquest of Granada, 1492), the Ottomans in
southeastern Europe represented the sole serious challenge until the seventeenth century.

In the pre-Columbian cultures of the Americas, Mayan culture had
reached its zenith long before the arrival of the Spaniards. The natural

and/or social causes for this remain controversial to the present day. The two other pre-Columbian high cultures fell victim to the almost total historical break in development resulting from the Spanish conquest (Max Zeuske, *Die Conquista*, 1992). At least in the case of the Aztec Empire, according to the research of Friedrich Katz (1969), this marked the end of an independent dynamic process or what was essentially still "open" development in a society based on slavery as well as elements of the early feudal state. The chief features of Inca culture, on the other hand, seemed to have been (quite contrary to the theories of Louis Boudin in *L'Empire socialiste des Inka*, 1928) a despotic, tributary method of production and a form of government that suggests comparisons—with all due caution— with ancient Oriental/Asiatic society.

The historical marginalization of Africa since the beginning of the sixteenth century, which brought the end of its notable "self-determined dynamic" (D. T. Niane, 1980), stemmed from an entire complex of causes. There was the undermining and collapse of the Asiatic/Arabic/East African économie-monde as a result of expanding Portuguese trade and trading-station colonization, as well as the decline of trans-Saharan trade (including the secret trade of the Wangara tribes) as a result of sub-Saharan West Africa's loss of importance as a provider of gold to Mediterranean Europe. Moreover, the instability of numerous autochthonous states resulted from invasions and migrations. Finally, the population declined due to the intensified European slave trade (especially in West and Central Africa), which, in contrast to the Arab/Islamic trade along the East African coast, had a far more catastrophic effect on African societies. Robert and Marianne Cornevin (1964) placed the number of Africans deported or killed in the slave trade between 1441 and 1880 at approximately fifty million; this merely quantitative and biological number also indicates the (re)productive, economic, and cultural potential that was lost to Africa's own development. "The effect of the slave trade was negative, and nothing but negative."

In comparison to the relative peace and quiet of the Middle Ages and the equally relative, but in some areas also absolute stagnation of nonEuropean cultures and civilizations, the entrance of Europe into the Modern Age meant the beginning of a permanent and multidimensional revolution. It was permanent in the sense of an increasing acceleration of social development, which shifted into a geometric time progression. And it was multidimensional in that this transformation encompassed all levels of social existence. No previous epoch had brought about such an increasingly radical shift of value systems in shorter and shorter periods of time as the world history of the modern era, shaped by Europe.

III

The beginning of the end of a universal history in the sense of a history of western (European) hegemony set in with the Second World War. This fundamental turning point had both a positive and a negative aspect. The positive aspect was the onset of decolonization. A system of hegemony ended—a system that had developed over almost 500 years and had determined the course of non-European history, with the exception of most of North, Central, and South America. (These areas achieved emancipation between 1775 and 1830, although political and national emancipation was affected at first by economic dependency.) How little the western, Eurocentric hierarchization of history was affected by this— despite the dissolution of traditional hegemonic constellations whose rise and fall after 1500 has been charted in equally classic and polemical manner by Paul Kennedy (1987)—is indicated by the ease with which the "decolonized" world was incorporated into the historical picture as the Third World. This classification, which corresponds to a specific and by no means positive value system, has remained unchanged in spite of the partial disappearance of the Second World after the crisis and downfall of state socialism. A process of hegemonic metamorphosis has been set in motion.

The negative aspect, which inevitably led to a crisis in traditional notions of politics and history, was the now obvious capacity of human-kind to destroy itself, which, for the first time in its historical devel-opment, brought the species to the point of no return. Knowing "how it actually was," which was the aim of the historical research of Leopold von Ranke, is no longer sufficient to point the way to the future, beyond the linear extrapolation of experience.

Since then, the chain of positive and negative elements that exert pressure toward a globalization of human development and its solutions has been constantly growing. These include changes in terms of: commu-nication and information, transnational and transcontinental economies, population explosion and new migrations, an ecological crisis of global dimensions, the potential exhaustion of natural resources, and the life-threatening consequences of the arms race. Furthermore, the East-West conflict has been replaced by an East-West economic gap that poses virtually as many risks in its economic, social, and political consequences, with the potential for reducing large regions of Eastern and Southern Europe to developing countries within the foreseeable future. At the same time, a North-South contrast (First versus Third World) may become the fundamental contradiction of the future, and it has a decisive potential for conflict; indeed, the contrast between North and South has long since ceased to be an external problem for the North in view of the expanding

Third World islands *within* Western societies. The explosive energies inherent in this became evident in the Los Angeles riots of April 1992. In the technical sphere, we now confront issues regarding the control and direction of high technology and gene technology in particular, and there are also new dimensions of the gender question to be considered. Ultimately, there is a general crisis of civilization. Today, we must ask to what extent human beings are still the subject of history in the sense of self-determining further development.

The objective globalization of human development in both its positive (creative) and negative (destructive) aspects has unquestionably proceeded faster than the subjective globalization, i.e., the ability to perceive this process and react rationally to it. "Our values are in a profound crisis; the human being of today is decisively shaped by alienation" (Gino Galasso). The most recent example of the inability to react rationally was offered by the UN environmental conference in Rio de Janeiro in June 1992. Thinking in terms of global history, which requires an interdisciplinary and truly global approach (especially by including scholars from different "worlds" and intellectual cultures), can make essential contributions to the creation, establishment, and spread of a global consciousness as a prerequisite for global action. Meanwhile, the elements of real global history that are already present should not be underestimated: multi- and transcultural conference centers, Greenpeace, Amnesty International, ongoing research on peace and conflict resolution, the ecumenical movement, and so on. Historians are not the first to think globally, and in no case should they be the last.

IV

Various possibilities exist for determining the relationship of universal and global history. Global history may be viewed as a continuation, as the extension of universal history up to the present time. Or global history may represent a qualitatively new phase of universal history. Finally, global history may be a successor to traditional universal history. Since all three elements obviously overlap, a quarrel over definitions would seem to make little sense. (The chapters by Mazlish, Goodwin, and Grew offer a good basis for reflection on the subject of definitions.)

From a methodological point of view, it is necessary to distinguish between three levels of universal and global history: the concept, the actual historical process, and universal and global history as the product (or result) of history.

In discussion, these three levels are frequently mixed; this is true, above all, of the relationship between the objective universalization or globalization of history and its subjective comprehension. Metaphorically speaking, Columbus realized how immense and infinite the world is, and herein lay a precondition for an understanding of historical universality. Conversely, the cosmonauts realized how small and finite the world is, and this helped us to grasp the globalization ("planetization") of our existence more rapidly. In this sense, global history can be comprehended as the search for the common survival of humankind. Universal history implied a history that was open, expansive, and infinite in its progressivity; global history implies a closed or (relatively) finite development, with the terms *finite* and *infinite* used in the sense described by Robert Havemann (*Dialektik ohne Dogma* ["Dialectics Without Dogma"], 1963-64). At the same time, global history implies the end of history—not, however, in the teleological-neoliberal sense used by Francis Fukuyama (1989, 1991), in defense of the system, but rather as an expression of the fact that the future developmental process will no longer be controllable solely through reasoning by analogy or by extrapolating of the experience of previous generations. It is not history per se that has come to an end but rather a certain *concept* of history. In my view, global history is more, after all, than one of the many fields of history (See the chapter by Grew); above all, it is much too serious a matter to be left to historians. First and foremost, global history means a new kind of thinking in view of the existential threat to humanity (which lies not in the distant future but in the immediate present). This task is linked to the combination of the most varied disciplines in the humanities, social and natural sciences, and technology. The globalization of objective reality requires scientific and scholarly globalization in the form of a division of labor. The partial "dehistoricization" of global history is a *conditio sine qua non*, and it becomes—in a merely superficial paradox—the foundation for a new understanding of history.

V

Global history as subject history presupposes a consensus on political and social human rights. But is a "universal" (that is, global) system of values conceivable—one that goes beyond the most general present norms of international law? Is it not rather a case of a consensus on the smallest common denominator? How is it possible to "harmonize" the value systems of different civilizations, and would it even be desirable? Toynbee's ecumenical model, which was based on the idea of a future world religion and which preached the reconciliation of world civilizations (*Mankind and Mother Earth*, 1976) can be regarded as a failure. And Karl Popper has now reduced his "open society" to the "fortress of Europe," which must be defended against attack from the poorhouse of the world (1992); this is nothing more than a neoliberal reinterpretation of

Mao Tse-tung's theory concerning the global conflict between "world city" and "world village." On the other hand, universal human rights cannot rest solely on the globalization of Western values. But what ways and possibilities exist to reconcile (or bring closer) Western and Eastern (or Southern) values and outlooks, which now confront one another both practically and theoretically as two more and more mutually exclusive forms of fundamentalism? To what extent is the "hard" fundamentalism of the Islamic East the natural reaction to the "soft" fundamentalism of the West (Christoph Türke, *Die Zeit* 16, 1992)? If, as Thomas Hughes said in *Unfinished History* (2d ed. 1981), the experience of Christianity is defined as a prerequisite for personal freedom (Imanuel Geiss's theory of Latinity would be related to this), then this means nothing less than denying to non-Christian (non-Western) cultures and civilizations the perspective of individualization. In other words, it means conceiving of Eastern collectivism as merely the negation of Western individualism. The discovery of the individual belongs, without doubt, to the great historical achievements of the modern era in the West. Humanism, the Renaissance, the Reformation, the Enlightenment, and liberalism all proved to be decisive stages of individualization and emancipation for the West. The unity of religion, hegemony, and society was shattered. The nation and the national state offered the optimal institutional, ethnic, geographic, political, and cultural framework for the dynamization of social life. The most radical stages of this process were expressed in the modern cycle of revolutions (from the sixteenth to the nineteenth centuries), in particular the "double revolution" at the turn of the nineteenth century (which was a combination of a political and social revolution in France with the industrial revolution in England). But is it not time to assess the price of this discovery and its consequent effects much more critically? The responsibility for the general crisis of civilization does not lie with the "collective" societies of Asia and Africa and the agricultural Indian communities of Latin America; rather, it rests with the extreme individualism of Western and European society. Global history must help to overcome the traditional notion that the West has a monopoly on dynamism and the East on stagnant contemplation. This stereotype is contradicted by Japan and the "young tigers" of Asia, but so far, they have been regarded as exceptions to the rule. No metasystem is currently in sight that could overcome or at least bridge these opposites on a global scale; clearly, it lies beyond our present mental horizons.

VI

In contrast to traditional universal history, global history can no longer be determined by hegemony; unlike traditional universal history, global history recognizes manifold forms of humanity, with all peoples having equal rights. This means, however (in total contrast to Fukuyama's universal liberalism model) nothing less than the potential "de-Westernization" of history, not in the sense of moving history backward but as a progressive opening for other kinds of historical experience and outlook: transculturation instead of acculturation (J. Maestre Alfonso, 1974). The concepts for a new world leadership developed by UN agencies (1991) prove how extreme Western domination has been at decisionmaking levels of the organization; the agencies consequently argue for de-Westernization in order to dissolve both formal and informal hegemonic structures. Given the existence of a *de facto* Group of Seven world government, realizing this expectation remains a utopian ideal in Ernst Bloch's sense of a *"Noch-Nichtsein-erwartbarer Art"* ("a 'not yet' of an expectable kind") for the foreseeable future. Nonetheless, it is a concrete utopia, on whose future configuration the solutions for the general crisis of civilization will depend, in the sense of making use of alternative possibilities for development.

If we follow Bruce Mazlish in conceiving of global history as a characteristic feature of the postmodern era, then we must nonetheless remain aware of the comprehensive and complex ways in which a renaissance of antiglobal, essentially premodern currents and phenomena is occurring. A main example of this is unquestionably the revitalization of regional, national, religious, and ethnic conflicts, combined with enormous migratory movements as elements of permanent destabilization. The truly antiglobal feature of the present is in the tendency of the first world to increasingly disengage itself from the Third World, thereby preparing the ground for fundamentalist reactions. Different historical epochs are now colliding. What place, then, does the "simultaneity of the nonsimultaneous" have in a concept of global history?

VII

One of the main difficulties for global history has proven to be a deeply rooted Eurocentrism. As the chapter by Ralph Buultjens shows, there are two sides to the difficulties: the limits of European (Western) historiography in understanding and mediating non-European (non-Western) history and the virtually equal difficulties inherent in the Third World's viewpoint toward Europe (and the West). Political and geographical frontiers can be crossed more easily than historical and cultural ones. This adds even greater significance to the new scholarly discourse, which requires new generations of scholars and new schools of thought. Individuals who embodied a cultural symbiosis in intellectual and political life have been rare—José Carlos Mariàtegui in Latin America, Leopold Sédar

Senghor in Africa, Jawaharlal Nehru in India. Arnold Toynbee's gigantic attempt to globalize history was shunted off into the philosophical and religious sphere, and Oswald Spengler (1919) could conceive of the end of European hegemony only as the decline of the West. And in spite of the Second World War, Hans Freyer (*Weltgeschichte Europas* ["World History of Europe,"] 2d ed. 1954), upheld the internal unity of world history and Europeanization.

In Europe, the prospects for a global history that might become more than a mere intellectual pastime are not favorable. The dominant school of empirical social history gives scant respect to the attempt at a universal history based on comparative methods, which was associated, above all, with the name of Karl Lamprecht; and carried on in Germany after 1945 (by Walter Markov in Leipzig) with a new theoretical approach, strongly oriented toward non-European history. Indeed, a criticism of "historical metaphysics" has even been raised. In contrast, the rapidly growing interest in comparative analysis of processes of social transformation in recent world history has confirmed the fruitfulness of the comparative approaches of universal history, which offer genuine foundations for a global history. Nevertheless, one should not overlook the degree to which the view of history has been renationalized as a result of the upheavals of 1989—not only in Eastern and Southern Europe but in Germany, as well. Even the ideology of Europe proves to be a form of nationalism raised to a continental level when seen in conjunction with the Third World: The concept of supranation yields supranationalism.

Certain political factors have incomparably greater weight, however. The demise of state socialism in Eastern and Southeastern Europe has led to the outbreak of traditional ethnic, cultural, and national conflicts, making it difficult to see the integrative elements of present and future historical processes. And as the economic and political unification of Europe progresses, the call for a European history is growing louder. This striving toward a European historical consciousness has the advantage of a potentially postnational character, at least in the sense of relativizing the individual existence of nations. The contradictory debates on the problem of refugees seeking asylum and the clear tendencies to prevent large-scale immigration reveal that behind the notion of Europeanization lies an intention of erecting a new wall to exclude the rest of the world. At the same time, plans are being discussed, using the same logic, to establish mobile intervention troops of the Western European Union (WEU) or the Conference on Security and Cooperation in Europe (CSCE) in order to pacify areas of political unrest on the European periphery or, in conjunction with the North Atlantic Treaty Organization (NATO), outside of Europe. Karl Popper openly advocated war when it was a matter of defending European interests against the Third World, which, in his view, had been granted independence "prematurely." Will traditional hegemony now be replaced by the primacy of military high technology, according to the model of the Gulf War? The Pentagon's policy of defending its military primacy with respect to Europe and Japan has already been clearly formulated. Such a policy would represent precisely the unfortunate balance, already recognizable in an early stage, of a global history that protects established interests rather than offering new definitions.

"Centrist" thinking is hardly limited to European and Western history and culture. This attitude is found in every great civilization. China always viewed itself as the Middle Kingdom and other peoples as barbarians, just as the Romans did. Other empires defined other centers of the world, from the Incas through the Mongols to the Mogul empire. Even modern historical and political debates are overlaid with centrist ideas. The *indigenismo* movement in Latin America, for example, contains a strong element of Americocentrism (just as Afrocentrist tendencies exist elsewhere). Similarly, to detach themselves from the schematic adoption of European categories, certain Latin American historians, sociologists, and economists argue that a Mexican or Peruvian method of production existed as an autochthonous form of social organization in pre-Columbian times.

Global history cannot, then, begin with the existence of a new, comprehensive world culture (even as a distant goal) nor with the conformity of historical development. But a global history with a comparative orientation must help explain the multidimensional nature of a humanity that is united in its essential interests. Global history is linked to global thinking and global consciousness, but in the political reality of the present, it is not global history but global strategy that plays the dominant role: Given the increasing dissolution of the old bipolar system constellation (the end of the East-West conflict), strategists are now beginning to think in terms of a unipolar (*pax americana*) or tripolar constellation (United States-Europe-Japan) in world politics. In fact, these represent merely new variations on the old centrist thinking dominated by ideas of hegemony, which, in the last analysis, are always based on the model of the European and Western social and value systems. (Western) Europe is already entering the phase of postnational development, thereby taking final leave of the nineteenth century as the classic era of nation-state. And most non-European peoples have not gone through a "normal" phase of national statehood and probably will not do so. Thus, there is a weighty argument for concentrating our attention on the integrative function of regions, in the framework of which multicultural and interethnic encounters (not necessary fusion) can take place.

VIII

Can global history exist without globalization and a simultaneous redefinition of the concept of progress? Without doubt, the crisis of human civilization—in the sense of an increasing existential threat to human survival—also implies a crisis in the traditional definition of progress in terms corresponding to the specific experiences of Europe. Whether the project of modernity is still open-ended and incomplete and we have entered a period of *"neue Unübersichtlichkeit"* ("new complexity"), as Jürgen Habermas claimed, or whether we have already overcome modernity in a postmodern manner or are even standing on the far side of postmodernity is of secondary importance in the end. We must be far more concerned with the fact that intellectual discourse is proving less and less able to reflect the dramatic realities in a manner that indicates the optimal course of action. The distance between interpreting (analyzing) reality and altering it is greater than ever before. Operating in parallel with this is the failure of the political classes—total in the East, potentially so in the West.

Even before the Brundtland Report was issued in 1987, confirmation existed for the Club of Rome's warning that the limits of growth have been reached in this sense—that it has become impossible to globalize the Western model of growth and consumption as a way of increasing development in the Third World to equal or even approach that of the most advanced industrial countries. In other words, the desire or intention to globalize the Western value system is not matched by the possibility or capability for an economic or social globalization. Who is prepared to draw the correct conclusions from this fundamental contradiction, which from the current perspective appears to be insoluble? What are the real chances that a new economic world order (which has set for itself the goal of overcoming the disadvantages and injustices of an international division of labor developed over centuries)—can serve as the material basis of *real* global history? How long can this situation continue to exist—a situation that increasingly prompts comparison with that of ancient Rome and its dependent provinces and allies?

The dynamics of the European concept of progress are also entirely foreign to non-European cultures and civilizations. And conversely, despite the almost naively teleological thinking of Fukuyama and his intellectual forebear, Georg Friedrich Wilhelm Hegel, European and Western thought has also long since begun to move beyond the Enlightenment idea of infinite human progress. The resulting skepticism and corresponding awareness of conflict have become constituents of the postmodern period. Until the present, however, these only took the form of ideas not actions, in Western societies, which continue to place the finite resources of nature at risk. With the downfall of state socialism in Eastern and Southeastern Europe, what appeared to be an alternative model of progress and development has come to an end, highlighting all the more clearly the weak points of the "victorious" society.

There is a consensus in negation, namely, that a linear continuation of previously existing developmental tendencies and experiences has become impossible. At the same time, there is an obvious vacuum with regard to a new definition for development ("progress"). In the end, all models are reduced to a continuation of previous experience, except that many people advocate that Western-like development should become "more sensible," "more equitable," "more united," "more democratic," "more ecological," "more humane." The vicious circle is evident, as is the difficulty (or perhaps inability) of formulating as yet unthought-of alternatives. How does it happen that we have limited the alternatives for "reasonable" development, i.e., development that can guarantee the survival of humanity under livable conditions, to the two possibilities of capitalism and socialism? Have we any idea how many alternatives world history under Western and European hegemony has lost through the destruction or deformation of other cultures and civilizations? How great is the danger that, to the long chain of "lost moments of history" (Hugh Trevor-Roper, 1988), there will be added another—the last one? If global history creates more awareness of this threat, it will have achieved one of its most important tasks. And if global history is to have any deeper meaning, it will lie in its ability to lead to practical action through a new consciousness.

5

Global History
in a Postmodernist Era?

Bruce Mazlish

I

At a time when many voices are proclaiming the dominance of local knowledge and cultural relativism, of privileged otherness and ironic deconstruction, and when local conflicts and cries for particular ethnic or religious communities hover over the lands, it may seem an ill-considered moment to assert claims for a global history. Yet as I argue in the introduction to this book, signs of the emergence of global history are all about us, needing only to be interpreted, clarified, and brought into conjunction and dialogue with these other claims.

Does globalism—the claim to be entering a global epoch—compete as a periodization with modernism and postmodernism, or does it exist in consonance with them? Initially, this requires addressing more specific questions about the relation of modernism to postmodernism and to the theme of progress and about the relation of all three of these terms to globalism and thence to global history. In addition, I intend to examine the role of the city—urban life—as the site of both modernism and postmodernism and then to ask about its status in regard to globalism and global history.

II

I will start with the claim, advanced in many quarters, that modernism has given way in the last decade or so to something called postmodernism. Ought we, therefore, to include the emergence of postmodernism among the new developments of the last few decades that foster the growth of global history? To evaluate this claim requires a brief discussion of the complicated origins and nature of modernism itself.

A beginning discussion would note that the word *modern* basically means "just now" and suggests the reflective awareness that we are looking from a present position backward to a dividing line of sorts. (In principle, therefore, every reflective period can be modern.) That dividing line in the West was, at first, the separation from the declining Roman Empire; hence, the Regius Professorship in Modern History at Oxford started around 500 A.D. But few scholars go so far back in seeking the advent of modernism; instead, some date it from the Renaissance, others from the Reformation or the seventeenth-century scientific revolution, and many others from the Enlightenment and the French Revolution.[1]

The late eighteenth century's claim to witnessing the birth of modernism rests on its assertion of a decisive break with the past, economically, politically, socially, and philosophically. On the cusp of the move from commercial to industrial capitalism, the Enlightenment period introduced the notion of unlimited expansion, of ceaseless change in the economic area. Symbolized by the year 1789, the period saw the declaration of universal sovereignty by the citizens of nation-states and the abolition of the "old regime." Socially, the epoch of bourgeois-class domination began, and the aristocratic order collapsed. And philosophically, it was a time when universal reason formed the basis for the assumption of unlimited progress toward human rights and individual as well as social perfectibility.

All these points can be argued, refined, and expanded upon. Here, I will note only that what Jürgen Habermas, the German philosopher, termed the "project of modernity," which he equated with the Enlightenment and its advocacy of universal reason and rights, has been challenged and called into question by critics such as Max Horkheimer and Theodore Adorno, for example, in their book *The Dialectic of Enlightenment*. In their view, the Enlightenment project of modernity is doomed to turn against itself and to transform the quest for human emancipation into a system of universal oppression, albeit in the name of human liberation. We are on our way to a Foucaultian view of modernity, wherein, for instance, Enlightenment practices in regard to the treatment of madness or the penal system are viewed not as steps forward but as tightenings of the disciplinary screw. At the end of this track, we arrive at a preliminary definition of postmodernism as the abandonment of the Enlightenment project.

Before we come to this conclusion, let us backtrack to a fuller consideration of modernism itself. For some present-day students, 1848 seems to be the axial date, the first phase of modernism's extended existence. Thus, Marshall Berman described the *Communist Manifesto* as "the first great modernist work of art" and called Charles Baudelaire the "first modernist."[2] It was Baudelaire who, for Berman as well as other critics before him (such as Walter Benjamin), exemplified and defined modern life. "Modernity," wrote Baudelaire in his seminal essay "The Painter of Modern Life" (published in 1863), "is the transient, the fleeting, the contingent; it is the one half of art, the other being the eternal and the immutable."[3] In this somewhat enigmatic statement, Baudelaire captured the tension in modernism, caught as it is between its character of ceaseless change and expansionism and its commitment to universal, eternal reason.

I have used the term *phase of modernism* to describe the period around 1848. Other students of the subject have identified the period between 1910 and 1915 as yet another phase, or stage, in the development of modernism. According to one scholar's definition, "Provisionally, 'modernism' may be understood in terms of what I take to be the central project of the intellectual generation entering the European cultural scene between 1900 and 1914: that of a 'cultural regeneration' through the secular-religious quest for 'new values.'"[4] Another scholar called this phase "heroic modernism" and identified it as a qualitative transformation, in which the impossibility of representing the world in a single language is now accepted: Multiple perspectivism and relativism are taken as the epistemological premises for revealing what is still, however, assumed to be a "true" reality that can be accessed.[5]

III

Even given the shadowy and shifting nature of modernism, as suggested by the preceding brief remarks, we should have a sufficient idea of its shape to contrast it with what is being called postmodernism. Oddly enough, where modernism seems mainly to be a European mode of thinking and feeling, postmodernism seems to have manifested itself first in either the so-called Third World or in America, North and South—or perhaps in both areas at about the same time.[6]

If one sees its origins in the Third World, an implicit conclusion is that postmodernism is a product, more or less, of globalization. Thus, the anthropologist Michael M. J. Fischer declared that "the trendy labels 'postmodernism' and 'postmodernity' are part of the aftermath of the Algerian Revolution. The theorists of postmodernity in France come from a generation of people who were born in Algeria, who taught as young academics there, and who were politically formed by the experience of the Algerian struggle for independence: Helen Cixous, Jacques Derrida, Jean-François Lyotard, Pierre Bourdieu." As Fischer concluded, "Postmodern theorizing originated historically in the Muslim world of North Africa, then ... rapidly [was] recognized and carried out into the world by migrants from India—Homi Bhabha, Salman Rushdie, Gayatri Spivak—and other parts of the former colonized world."[7]

The argument for postmodernism's American origins follows. The term *postmodern* was first used by an Englishman, Arnold Toynbee, in his *Study of History*. He described the postmodern as a new and final age of Western civilization when, beginning in the 1870s, that civilization slipped into a repudiation of rationality and an embrace of the irrational. Nevertheless, scholars are quick to point out, Toynbee was acclaimed in America, not Europe. The next link in the argument is that the term was used by the U.S. poet and critic Randell Jarrell in 1946, in regard to the poetry of Robert Lowell. At this point, it is asserted, the transition to postmodernism as a primarily aesthetic term came into being.

According to Thomas Bender, however, postmodernism should be looked upon as a "Creole" invention for he had in mind writers such as Jorge Borges. On this reading, South America rather than North America is the cradle of the new aesthetics.

Whatever its actual origin, the overall argument made by almost all postmodernists—and I shall simply state it in summary terms—is that a major shift has occurred in the "structure of feeling." We have moved away from universal modernism's vision of the world as fundamentally positivistic, technocratic, and rationalistic, with an accompanying belief in linear progress, absolute truths, rational planning, and standardization of knowledge and production (though I shall argue later that this is a one-sided view of modernism, ignoring its antimodern component). Simultaneously, we have moved toward postmodernism's privileging of heterogenity, fragmentation, and indeterminacy, with an accompanying distrust of universal or "totalizing" discourse and a concern for the validity and dignity of the "other."

In light of this definition, it should be noted that one possible consequence of the displacement of modernism by postmodernism, assuming it has occurred, is the disappearance of nationalism. Liah Greenfeld summed up this possibility when she wrote, "Nationalism is an historical phenomenon. It appeared in one age and it can disappear in another. But if it does, the world in which we live will be no more, and another world, as distinct from the one we know as was the society of orders that it replaced, will replace it. This post-national world will be truly postmodern, for nationality is the constitutive principle of modernity."[8]

Before consigning nationalism and modernism to the dustbin of history, however, I should note that many peoples are still trying to jump on the train of modernity, while much of the West presumably is trying to jump off. There is little evidence of postmodernism in East Central Europe and in the lands of the former Soviet Union, to cite only a few examples.[9] The desire of these peoples, by and large, is for modernity and modernization.

In any event, some critics and observers, while accepting the definition of postmodernism given previously, judge it as simply another phase of modernism: After all, modernism itself is characterized by fragmentation, Nietzschean relativism, ceaseless change, and so forth. In contrast, those who uphold the uniqueness of postmodernism answer that, while fragmentation is deplored and challenges to reality are fought off in modernism, these are celebrated as positive goods in postmodernism. Thus, in this view, postmodernism goes beyond modernism and takes us into a new cultural epoch.[10]

IV

Where in all of this debate are we to situate globalism and global history? Is postmodernism, for example, a factor helping to create the conditions for global history? Is it itself primarily a result of other global factors? Or is it some combination of the two possibilities? We must still look at other features of our present situation before hazarding answers.

Before doing so, however, we must retreat again and note that the whole debate about modernism and postmodernism (in spite of the latter's possible Third World origin) is largely a Western debate—or it has been until now.[11] The fact is that modern history itself (like modern science and industrialism) has been primarily a Western development since about the seventeenth or eighteenth centuries. By and large, the Western historian has been the only one to write the history of other peoples in "scientific" form. (Western anthropologists, similarly, have studied "other" cultures, but these cultures have not, in turn, sent anthropologists to study the West; this situation, however, may be on the point of rapidly changing.) Thus, it is the Western historian who structures history in terms of modernism and postmodernism and imposes it on the rest of the world. In a dark mood, one might argue that the export of modernism (which is much greater than any alleged import) and now postmodernism is the other face of colonial "appropriation," with its plundering of "native" art and ethnographic identity.

One need only read Max Weber's 1920 introduction to his *Protestant Ethic and the Spirit of Capitalism* (1904-1905) for a typical statement: "A product of modern European civilization, studying any problem of universal history, is bound to ask himself to what combination of circumstances the fact should be attributed that in Western civilization, and in Western civilization only, cultural phenomena have appeared which (as we like to think) lie in a line of development having *universal* significance and value."[12] Weber then went on to list such features as science, history, art, architecture, printing and the press, representative democratic states, and capitalism—"the most fateful force in our modern life"—all of which he claimed were not unique to the West but were uniquely and simultaneously developed in the West. This unique development adds up to modernity.

It also adds up to modernization, i.e., the idea that, once developed, "modern" society can and will spread elsewhere.[13] According to this claim, although local features may be different, the major features of the Western model will be duplicated in other countries. Before Weber, Karl Marx had had the same idea, though with a different end in view. After Weber, development economists often discussed the idea further in terms of convergence theory.[14] Whatever its particular form, the notion that the future shape of the world could already be discerned in the industrializing experience of the West has exercised a powerful hold over minds everywhere.

In the tangle of discussion on these complicated issues, it may be said that Weber was right about the expansion of industrialism but wrong in stating that it would merely be an extension of the Western model. Although its origin is Eurocentric, industrialization has subsequently arisen in non-Western form in other parts of the world as well.

Nevertheless, such industrialization has carried with it differing elements of modernism, defined here as a Western aesthetic and cultural attitude (which includes antimodern feelings). It should be acknowledged, however, that individuals in various parts of the world may be rejecting the Enlightenment component of modernism more vigorously than people in its original Western homeland. For example, while often accepting aspects of modernization, i.e., industrialization, fundamentalist movements have vehemently opposed "poisonous" values, such as human rights or the skeptical, objective, empirical orientation of modern science.[15]

With this said, I must repeat that modernism has traveled widely to non-Western countries. But has postmodernism succeeded modernism? If so, can elements of it, too, then be expected to eventually manifest themselves worldwide? In this context, I will pose anew the question of whether global history is simply an aspect of modernism or postmodernism or, instead, a way of conceptualizing history that goes beyond them and in the process transcends their basic Eurocentrism?

At the risk of trying the reader's patience, I shall again postpone answers, as I attempt to paint in other parts of the problem. I do this while recognizing the danger pointed out by Sherlock Holmes when he told his client in "The Naval Treaty" that "the principal difficulty of your case lay in the fact of their being too much evidence. What was vital was overlaid and hidden by what was irrelevant." We shall see in the end whether there is "too much evidence" or whether vital parts of the puzzle exist that cannot be left out if the complete solution—the picture as a whole—is to emerge. To test the applicability of Holmes's statement, I wish to add yet another topic to my discussion of modernism and postmodernism.

V

That topic is the idea of progress. Much has been written on that subject, and more will be; certainly, a separate article and even a book could be in order here.[16] However, since my concern now is solely with the idea's relation to global history, I shall deal with the concept of progress in the briefest of terms.

All societies need a way of organizing time and their view of the past. Most ancient and primitive societies opted for a cyclical view: Time was believed to repeat itself. Christianity, in contrast, introduced a linear view: A unique event—Christ's birth—divided before and after, once and for all.[17] The idea of progress gives a special direction to that linear view, continually emphasizing increased secular perfectibility and evolutionary development in the direction of human improvement. Such improvement, it is claimed, certainly involves knowledge—the cumulative development of science—as well as material goods—an expanding economy; less certain is whether it also entails progressively evolving morality.

In trying to understand the moral implications surrounding the idea of progress, much thought has been given to the contending forces of self-interest and altruism. Modernization in its capitalist form, as the engine of progress, postulates a particular kind of man (and the discussion tends to be sexist): a rationally maximizing man, possessed of complete information. Such an individual, pursuing his self-interest freely, automatically is led to better the general good as well.

Critics of this presumed happy outcome attack it both conceptually—rational economic man is a fabrication only partly related to reality—and morally—purely self-interested actions result in the "tragedy of the commons," not the providential good of all. Instead, they claim, one must put altruism at the center of one's actions, the visible hand of group interest before the invisible hand of self-interest. Sometimes, this opposition has taken the form of antimodernism, with the lamenters of modernization's pernicious effects attacking what they see as the antimoral and antihuman effects of modernism cum modernization.

Such critics, denying that the idea of progress is providentially and automatically connected to increased morality, also replace rational maximizing man with a being who is more fully human: one who has irrational impulses and altruistic needs. Such a human is also "local," that is, embedded in a specific historical and cultural setting, and not a "universal man" in an abstract time and space marked for single, linear

progress. Thus, the question on the very nature of humankind is intimately caught up in the conception of progress itself (as well as of global
history).

In any event, the idea of progress must be seen as a necessary complement to the modernization process, as well as a major element in modernism. Let us remember, however, as I have already noted, that modernism
itself is a contested arena, in which antimodernism (i.e., a challenge to
science and technology and the rationalism inspiring them) is already
present. As the sociologist David Frisby observed, "This transitory nature
of the new in notions of modernity was associated with crucial changes in
time consciousness—and especially a challenge to the notion of unilinear
progress."[18] In this light, then, one can see postmodernism as the triumph
of antimodernism not only over modernism but also over its accompanying idea of progress.[19]

VI

Having breathlessly sketched the features of modernism, postmodernism, and the idea of progress, I want to advance some views on their
relation to globalism and global history. First and foremost, I wish to
argue that global history, correctly conceptualized, allows us to incorporate some of the features of these other themes, as well as to transcend
them. Thomas Bender has suggested that postmodernism, with its deconstruction of "privileged" discourses, is a preparation for a post-Euro-
centric point of view—and thus for the perspective of global history.[20]

However, I am also arguing that globalization is a continuation of the
modernization project. It incorporates the expansionism and science/
technology-driven economic development of the modernization process.
But, and here is where global history has so important a role to play, it can
and must do so in a non-Eurocentric form. The present worldwide development no longer primarily follows the Western model; rather, it is a
concurrent development experienced, though in varying ways, by all
parts of the globe.[21]

All peoples are now subject to the global forces, some of whose features
I indicated in the introduction to this volume. We should no longer think
of some people as "primitives," i.e., backward in time, and others as
"civilized." Global time is now synchronic for all of us, subjecting us to
the same forces at the same time. For this reason, among many others,
global history is needed as a "modern" form of consciousness. It is also
why a short definition of *global history* might describe it as "a history with
which all peoples can identify, without being particular to any one of
them."

Global history also can be seen as a continuation of the idea of progress—Baudelaire, for example, spoke, though critically, of "Progress, the
great modern idea" (italics added).[22] What is more, global history can be
seen as a continuation of the project of modernism as well but a continuation that forcefully insists on taking seriously the concerns of antimodernism cum postmodernism about the purely beneficent effects of
"rationality," "development," and so on.

Thus, to give one illustration, the seemingly mindless though "rational" expansionism embodied in modernization on the Western model is
necessarily challenged by its threatening environmental effects. These
effects are now clearly perceived as global. And increasingly, some sort of
global response is dictated by the nature of the threat.

How will this be carried out? And what balance of reason and values
will be struck by widely differing social systems, faced with a global
challenge? How can we accommodate local concerns with global ones?
What accommodation between local and larger "rights" must be established? These are some of the questions that loom larger and larger as an
inquiry into the nature and significance of globalism and global history is
pursued.

VII

There is one more aspect I want to touch on before coming to an overall
conclusion concerning the relations of global history to modernism and
postmodernism. At the beginning of this chapter, I raised the question of
the relation of the city to modernism/postmodernism and to globalization. I now want to mention the way global life is substituting for
metropolitan life.

The initial "modern" attitude toward the metropolis can be traced back
to the very beginnings of the movement toward modernization and modernism. Francis Bacon, a main figure in promoting the idea of progress,
was one of the first, if not *the* first, to attach it to the rule of cities. Bacon
did even more; he realized that the coming of modernity, based as it was
in cities, reached out because of its universalizing science to the ends of
the globe: "The theatre of human endeavors," he declared, "is no longer
only the city but the whole world." As Paolo Rossi remarked concerning
Bacon's vision, "One can but acknowledge the 'modernism' of Bacon's
historical panorama."[23]

Indeed, it was Bacon who, focusing on the "Advancement of Learning," advocated a history that would go beyond the history of "a certain
kingdom or nation" and endeavor to describe "the memorable things,
which in their time happened over all the globe." For, as he continued,

"human affairs are not so far divided by empires and countries, but that in many cases they still preserve a connection: whence it is proper enough to view, as in one picture, the fates of an age."[24]

In this extraordinary anticipation, Bacon glimpsed the future of a global history. He did so, obviously, at the beginning of the "progress" toward modernization. His ship, allowing him to view the earth as a whole, was a sailing ship, not a spaceship. In a luminous phrase, worthy of his contemporary, William Shakespeare, he wrote "[that] little vessels, like the celestial bodies, should sail around the whole globe, is the happiness of our age."[25] The age he had in mind was the late fifteenth century, some 500 years before our own.

In acknowledging Bacon's pioneering role in envisioning some form of global history, I do not want to overlook the vast differences between his time and ours and hence between his conception and ours. Especially, though, I want to highlight his intuition about the way the global is connected to the metropolitan, seeing the latter as the indispensable base from which the ships set out and to which they would return.[26] New Atlantis, after all, is a city.

VIII

In speculating further, however, on what I am claiming to be a metropolitan basis for global history, I would ask whether, as a result of continued globalization, that basis is itself being radically transformed. Are we moving from rural to urban to global? As we know, the initial modernization and especially the first industrial revolution were coexistent with urbanization. In 1851, the census in Britain established that, for the first time, more of the population was living in urban areas than in rural ones. In that same year, the success of the dual movements to industrialization and urbanization was celebrated in England by the Crystal Palace Exhibition, with Prince Albert linking these movements to the "unity of mankind" in his opening speech.

From that time on, the pattern of industrialization and urbanization has repeated itself in all developing nations and become the model for those aspiring to be developed. Thus, in 1955, one-half the world's population was described as urban; in 1980, that figure climbed to two-thirds. It should also be noted that these modern or postmodern cities, often megacities, are, for the first time, not based primarily on agrarian resources. As Marshall Hodgson pointed out, this is not that people no longer have to eat but that the income of what he called the "crucial" classes no longer is derived from their relation to the land.[27]

The urban nature of modern life, while often deplored, has also frequently been celebrated. In the nineteenth century, for example, Baudelaire could characterize the city as the site of the "heroism of modern life" and exult at its exciting pace and variety, its ability to shock. He reveled in "the spectacle of fashionable life," on one side, and its "thousands of roaming existences—criminals and kept women—drifting about in the undergrounds of a great city," on the other side.[28] This attitude persisted, and one thinks of the sense of adventure awakened by the city in the characters of Gustave Flaubert or Theodore Dreiser or Thomas Wolfe. The city, for them, was where the action was.

Yet the seeds of its displacement were already being sown by the same agencies that had created the metropolis in its modern form. As early as 1884, as David Harvey reminded us, "the first moves were made towards international agreement on the meridian, time zones, and *the beginning of the global day*" (italics added).[29] This move toward global existence, the result of the conquest of space through the railroad, the telegraph, and then the telephone and radio, has intensified in our day. How far it may go is a subject of conjecture.

In the view of Jacques Attali, the French social theorist and adviser to François Mitterand, it will go quite far. According to a recent article, Attali

> predicts the emergence of a new class of nomads at the very top of the socioeconomic scale. As communications and computer technology grow in power, the notion of place will be fundamentally altered, he suggests. The wealthiest nomads will be freed to jet through the world, permanently attached only by their friendships and their work. After all, human beings have settled in villages and cities only during the last 10,000 years. Freed by new technologies that permit constant contact, he speculates, it will seem natural to roam the globe.[30]

In a rather different key, one may cite Salman Rushdie. In a recent interview, he gave the following self-description: "I think of myself as a metropolitan writer, and I think of myself as someone who has spent almost his entire life in gigantic cities—Bombay and London. . . . They define me. I know very well that London and Bombay have much more in common with each other than either have with the hinterlands behind them." So described, of course, these are global cities. But rather than being a glamorous jet nomad, Rushdie sees himself as a migrant, whom he described as "perhaps, the central or defining figure of the twentieth century."[31]

Rushdie may be said to be living *in* the global cities between which the new nomads are jetting, but spiritually, he, too, is inhabiting the spaces among them. In mentioning him and the jet nomads, I am simply trying to open up the question of whether global history, going beyond modernism

and postmodernism, may circle over a terrain that is no more metropolitan than it is nation-state.

Collapsing an argument that needs to be made at greater length, it can
be postulated that global life, not metropolitan life, is where the action is
now (thus possibly transcending modernism, which is based on the city).
The city as adventure may be a thing of the past in developed nations.
Bright young people may thrill not to Baudelaire's "shock" of the metropolis but to the "sonic boom" of the global world. They may live, exis-
tentially and sometimes literally, in Tokyo, New York, or London, for
example, either physically flying there in one day or, by communications
satellites, existing there mentally during the course of a global time of
twenty-four hours. (It should be noted, however, that modern communication may not only make jet nomads possible but may also abolish the
need for them by allowing instant networking from one's home.)[32]

A rather satiric view of this world is given by David Lodge in his novel
Small World.[33] It is a put-down of structuralism and postmodernism, and
its subject is the global conference circuit, with academics jetting hither
and yon. In many ways, it is a kind of Chaucerian tale about modern
pilgrims, who are not going to Canterbury but to innumerable cities in the
world. The double entendre is that the globe is a "small world," where the
academics keep meeting one another, never really leaving their narrow
selves. The book reminds us that there is a humorous or at least a sardonic
side to the global/local dichotomy and to the possible transcendence of
the urban frame.

IX

My central aim in this chapter has been to situate global history in a
postmodernist era. In touching on a range of subjects under this heading, I
have sought mainly to raise questions rather than to give final answers.
Even when I have made assertions, I have intended them to point to
problematics. It is in that same spirit that I make my final summary
statement.

Global history is an approach to historical analysis and interpretation
that asserts itself as a successor or at least an alternative to previous
analysis and interpretation centered around notions of modernism, postmodernism, and progress, as well as the idea of the nation-state. Recognizing that postmodernism, like modernism, is one of the cultural facets of
our emerging global epoch (though postmodernism itself may be an
ephemeral event), global history necessarily must consider it along with
the other evidences of globalization. In the process, the consciousness
embodied in our conceptualization of global history will, I hope, both

incorporate and transcend these constituent elements and make us better equipped to deal with the evolving global world.

Releasing these forces (industrialization, modernization, modernism, perhaps postmodernism, and so forth) from the geographical locus that gave them birth—cutting their umbilical cord to the West—is a kind of reordering of space. It coincides appropriately with the approaching third millennium—a sort of reorientation in time. (And as part of that reorientation, one must note that other calendars and other cultures do not always order *their* time as approaching 2000 A.D.; see the introduction) Today, in a "place" we finally recognize as global, it is only fitting that we raise our historical awareness to the level of the events actually surrounding us.

Notes

1. The advent of the "modern" is also often equated with the global. In an article on the Washington National Gallery show "Circa 1492", which displayed the famous photo from outer space called *Earthrise*, J. Carter Brown, the museum's director, was quoted as saying, "Well, 1492—that's where it started"; *The New Yorker*, September 3, 1990, 48. William Cronon emphasized the seventeenth century as the turning point: "By integrating New England ecosystems into an ultimately global capitalist economy, colonists and Indians together began a dynamic and unstable process of ecological change which had in no way ended by 1800. We live with their legacy today"; *Changes in the Land: Indians, Colonists, and the Ecology of New England* (New York: Hill and Wang, 1983), 170.

2. Marshall Berman, *All That Is Solid Melts into Air: The Experience of Modernity* (New York: Simon and Schuster, 1982), 102 and 133.

3. Charles Baudelaire, *The Painter of Modern Life and Other Essays*, trans. and ed. Jonathan Mayne (New York: A Da Capo Paperback, n.d.), 13. I prefer the translation in David Harvey, *The Condition of Postmodernity* (Oxford: Basil Blackwell, 1989), 10, which is essential reading on the subjects of modernism and postmodernism.

In his social theory, Georg Simmel captured the same tension. As David Frisby put it in his discussion of Simmel, "In the dimension of social theory, the presentation of the restless motion of everyday modern life—its snapshots, as it were—takes the form of highlighting their eternal forms *sub specie aeternitatis*"; *Fragments of Modernity*, (Cambridge, Mass.: MIT Press, 1986), 64.

4. Walter L. Adamson, "Modernism and Fascism: The Politics of Culture in Italy, 1903-1922", *The American Historical Review* 95, no. 2 (April 1990), 360.

5. Harvey, *The Condition of Postmodernity*, 31.

6. In North America, while modernization itself has proceeded apace, the concept of "modernity" has been given less attention than in Europe. See, for example, the issue of *The American Quarterly* 39, no. 1 (Spring 1987). In academia, however, postmodernism has been all the rage in the last decade or so.

7. Michael M.J. Fischer, "Is Islam the Odd-Civilization Out?", *New Perspectives*

Quarterly, (Spring 1992), 54 and 59.

8. Liah Greenfeld, *Nationalism: Five Roads To Modernity* (Cambridge, Mass.: Harvard University Press, 1993), 491.

9. See Piotr Sztompka, "The Bumpy Road from the Periphery to the Core of Global Society: Lessons from Eastern Europe", a chapter prepared for the second volume in our Global History series (Westview Press), on globalism and localism.

10. The indispensable book on the origins and meanings of modernism and postmodernism is Matei Calinescu, *Five Faces of Modernity* (Durham, N.C.: Duke University Press, 1987).

11. The Japanese scholar Nagayo Homma has commented that the Chinese characters for *modern* means "very American" and that the shift from "modern to chic" means from American to European.

12. Max Weber, *The Protestant Ethic and the Spirit of Capitalism*, trans. Talcott Parsons (New York: Charles Scribner's Sons, 1958).

13. For further discussion on the differences in meaning between such words as *modernization, modernity, industrialization*, and *Westernization*, see Bruce Mazlish, "The Breakdown of Connections and Modern Development," *World Development* 19, no. 1 (January 1991), pp. 31-44.

14. See, for example, Ian Weinberg, "The Problem of the Convergence of Industrial Societies: A Critical Look at the State of a Theory", *Comparative Studies in Society and History* 11, no. 1 (January 1969), 1-15.

15. What bedevils any treatment of modernism is the role that antimodernism plays in it. As I argue in my book *A New Science: The Breakdown of Connections and the Birth of Sociology* (New York: Oxford University Press, 1989; paperback ed., Penn State Press, 1993), the coming of industrialization and the values of the Enlightenment and the French Revolution were challenged *within* Europe and thus within modernism from the very beginning. Early nineteenth-century "Germany", for example, showed intense phobias as well as longings in regard to France, its more "advanced" neighbor. Jeffrey Herf, *Reactionary Modernism* (Cambridge: Cambridge University Press, 1984), effectively showed how this theme played itself out in the twentieth century.

16. In fact, a conference on exactly this subject, "The Idea of Progress Revisited," which I cochaired with my colleague Leo Marx, was held at MIT, December 6-7, 1991. A book based on the Conference papers is being prepared for publication.

17. See, for example, Charles Norris Cochrane, *Christianity and Classical Culture* (New York: Oxford University Press, 1957).

18. David Frisby, *Fragments of Modernity* (Cambridge, Mass.: MIT Press,1988), 13. Cf. Calinescu's statement: "Without entirely subsiding, the exhilarating belief in progress has been replaced during the last hundred years or so by the infinitely more ambiguous (more ambiguous because more self-critical) myths of modernity, the avant-garde and decadence"; *Five Faces*, 156.

19. Calinescu, went even further and said that "aesthetic modernity should be understood as a crisis concept involved in a threefold dialectical opposition to tradition, to the modernity of bourgeois civilization (with its ideals of rationality,

utility, progress), and, finally, to itself, insofar as it perceives itself as a new tradition or form of authority"; *Five Faces*, 10.

20. Personal comment to me, July, 1991.

21. See Tu Wei-ming, "A Confucian Perspective on the Rise of Industrial East Asia", *Bulletin of the American Academy of Arts and Sciences* 42, no. 1 (October 1988) for the argument on how modernization can take place on a Confucian, instead of a Protestant, basis.

22. The phrase from Baudelaire is quoted in Calinescu, *Five Faces*, 56.

23 The quote from Bacon is in Paolo Rossi, *Francis Bacon: From Magic to Science*, trans. Sacha Rabinovitch (London: Routledge & Kegan Paul, 1968), 35; this was originally published in Italian in 1957. Rossi"s own statement is on p. 69.

24. Francis Bacon, *The Advancement of Learning and Novum Organum* (New York: Colonial Press, 1900), 57.

25. Ibid., 59.

26. For similar emphases on the role of "world" cities, see the work of Fernand Braudel and Immanuel Wallerstein.

27. Marshall G. S. Hodgson, *The Venture of Islam. Conscience and History in a World Civilization*, vol. 1, *The Classical Age of Islam* (Chicago: University of Chicago Press, 1974), 108.

28. Quoted in Calinescu, *Five Faces*, 54. For the role of Baudelaire's ambulatory spectator, the flaneur, in "painting" the urban landscape and introducing modernity, as well as perhaps leading to postmodernity, see my "The Flaneur: From Spectator to Representation", in *The Flaneur*, ed. Keith Tester (London: Routledge, forthcoming 1994).

29. David Harvey, "Money, Time, Space, and the City", The Denman Lecture 1985 (Cambridge: Granta Editions, 1985), 10. See also my introduction in this volume.

30. *New York Times*, December 23, 1990.

31. Quoted in James Fenton's review of Rushdie's *Haroun and the Sea of Stories*, in *New York Review of Books*, March 28, 1991, 32. The last quote, however, is from a review of another of Rushdie's books, *Imaginary Homelands*, by Robert Towers, which appeared in the *New York Times*. In *Imaginary Homelands* (New York: Penguin Books, 1991), 17, Rushdie wrote that "the word 'translation' comes, etymologically, from the Latin for 'bearing across'. Having been borne across the world, we are translated men. It is normally supposed that something gets lost in translation; I cling, obstinately, to the notion that something can also be gained."

32. See the essays, of widely dissimilar importance, in the valuable collection *Cities in a Global Society*, vol. 35, *Urban Affairs Annual Reviews*, eds. Richard V. Knight and Gary Gappert (Newbury Park, Calif.: Sage, Publications, 1989). The volume's starting point is that "urbanized areas are entering a new era, one in which they will be shaped primarily by their responses to powerful global forces (11)"; thus, the collection tends to focus more on the impact of global forces on cities, rather than on the role of cities per se in global history.

33. David Lodge, *Small World: An Academic Romance* (New York: MacMillan, 1984), especially 339.

PART TWO

Applied Global History

6

Migration and Its Enemies

Wang Gungwu

This chapter approaches global history by looking at spatial relationships between people who live far apart, those who stay at home, and those who have moved away from their homes to foreign lands; more specifically, I look at the historical conditions under which people have migrated over great distances. Historians have always been concerned with the study of people over time, but the idea of global history requires that greater attention be paid to the linkages between the spaces people occupy. Thus, what is particularly relevant to our understanding of global history is migration in its external rather than internal form, notably in its concern with what people who move out of their countries do to the spaces they leave behind and to the spaces they come to occupy. The impact of individuals in shaping global history is increased (1) when more people are able to link the discrete and distant spaces they occupy and (2) when these spaces are more distant and different from one another.

Historians have often acknowledged the importance of geography in the study of migration, but usually in the context of the movements of people between chunks of territory. Traditional historians are, therefore, more concerned with those who controlled such territory—with tribes, kingdoms, empires, and their leaders and rulers—rather than with the linkages among the migrants themselves. People were identified by the territory, whether large or small, to which they belonged. Entities like communities, nation-states, confederations, and alliances were studied mainly in terms of the places occupied and fought over. Migration studies were generally placed in the context of local, national, and regional history or international and even an interdependent world history. Each of these approaches reflects a primary concern for the politics of physical space.

Globalization in the modern world, however, leads us to a more diffuse sense of extended space. It invites us to explore the more fragmented linkages between people in smaller groups, even as families and as individuals who live in different parts of the globe. In this way, global history is different from world history for it does not seek to cover everything that happened in the past. At the same time, it is different from international history because it is not primarily interested in developments affecting political entities. Perhaps it is most closely related to the idea of universal history, which might be seen as the abstract and ideological precursor of global history.

Both universal history and global history assume the linking of many people over time and space. But the former stresses ideals, common faiths, and values crossing national boundaries and even continents; it also points at features that show the oneness of humanity. Global history, on the other hand, arises when the regular linking of physical space becomes possible and significant because of the spread of people and technology. The more recent migrations of large numbers of people who had not been allowed to move freely in the past suggest that another way of looking at the use of physical space may now be more fruitful. Modern transportation and communications, together with modern education, have enabled and even encouraged more people to move from one place to another not just once but again and again, to settle or remigrate, and to do so quickly. Moreover, different kinds of people have begun to move, and the migration of educated people in small groups—as nuclear families and as individuals—has become legitimate and acceptable as a new norm. This, in turn, has contributed to a new emphasis on the autonomy of such groups and the individual rights of their members. Global migration seems to have brought forth a more abstract perception of physical space, changing the emphasis from territorial and historical space to finer distinctions and relationships between public and private space. The part played by migration in this change is an important one that deserves attention. Certainly, migration trends and patterns contribute to the definition of global history.[1]

This chapter focuses on developments that have been caused by the enemies of migration throughout history. A brief look at three major varieties of migration will establish what is meant by enemies. Large-group migrations of tribes, nations, or whole communities occurred from time to time in the past. They invariably led to conflict and then either to conquest of territory or defeat, slaughter, and possible enslavement of the losers. The new borders that were then erected would discourage, if not end, migrations for a long time. Later, there were enforced migrations of smaller groups because of famines, plagues, and other disasters. Some members of these groups became colonists or refugees or offered themselves if not as slaves then as bonded or contract labor of one kind or another. By this time, the obstacles to migration were more specific and less absolute, such as host communities that despised the newcomers and, in modern times, immigration officials and trade unions. Finally, a third variety of migration appeared—featuring "sojourners" who eventually became migrants.[2] These were individuals and families who had not intended to migrate but left their countries to trade, to seek skilled employment, to escape temporarily, or to look for adventure and fresh opportunities for betterment. These people were sometimes called economic refugees, and by and large, they eventually settled down. Their sojourning was actually a kind of experimental migration: Faced with uncertainty, suspicion, or the possibility of other options, sojourners extended their stays abroad indefinitely until a decision to settle was unavoidable. This type of migration has now reappeared in a new form and is increasingly the strategy of middle-class and educated people who wish to postpone as long as possible the final decision on whether to migrate and settle abroad. Many more people today, especially those with education and skills, have learned to appreciate this form of experimental migration.

Migration history is recognized as an important part of conventional history and has been well studied in terms of local, national, and world history. This is not the place to go over familiar ground. Rather, I would ask how migration history can contribute to our understanding of global history. Clearly, the enemies of migration, like the traditional bureaucratic empires and the modern nation-state, are also obstacles to any attempt to give shape to global history. Conversely, the notion of sojourning in relatively open trading societies was never threatening and therefore seemed to have been acceptable to most governments. Migration patterns based on sojourning were reinforced by safer and faster forms of transport and further encouraged and strengthened by the modern communications technology that is essential for international trade. And there is little doubt today that the great trading nations and their finance and marketing centers contribute much to our understanding of global development. They are the centers of wealth and growth that draw people toward them as sojourners or migrants.

It may be useful to reexamine migration history in the context of the globalization of commerce. Again, the large-scale movements of people in the formative periods of ancient kingdoms, empires, cultures, and civilizations are well known. Prior to the formation of strong centralized states, only natural borders existed, consisting mostly of mountains, deserts, swamps, and river valleys that, sooner or later, some powerful tribe or tribal confederation would cross in mass migrations. The stories of the Aryans who entered India, the Turks who spread to China, Europe and West Asia, the Arabs who fought their way across North Africa into the Iberian peninsula and traded south into sub-Saharan Africa, and the

Teutonic tribes who expanded at the expense of the Celts and the Slavs have all been central to conventional history; indeed, they have made such history exciting and comprehensible. But mass migrations of this kind normally led to settlement and the filling up of empty spaces and therefore to new state formations and defensive structures. These structures were set up against the challenges of further sizable migrations. Thus, migrants involved in large-scale settlement would very naturally have created their own instruments for self-protection and survival. This, in turn, led to the establishment of institutions that themselves became hostile to future migrations. The story of such migrations alone adds little to the idea of global history. The vast spaces they linked together were soon divided from one another: For such mass migrations, linked space was temporary and quickly succeeded by political and military barriers against future links.

The globalization of the modern world has changed that. In the initial stage, following the end of slavery, major migration of cheap contract labor was needed in various parts of the European empires to feed the industrial revolution in Europe. In the Americas, the demand was smaller because the freed slaves and their descendants could still work. And when American capitalists needed fresh industrial labor, they turned to the impoverished parts of Europe itself.[3] In Asia and the Caribbean, however, most of the coolie laborers were Chinese and East Indians. They were shipped overseas to plantations and mines to build roads and railways and clear jungles and bush. They were not skilled enough to be highly regarded or well rewarded, but they were useful and thereby fulfilled one of the principal conditions of migration. Because they were useful to the colonial territories, many stayed on after the end of their contracts and settled down as migrants.[4] Unfortunately for them, they encountered the phenomenon of white superiority that had emerged from the period of imperial power during the nineteenth century and was to last until the end of the Second World War. This had been tolerable in Asia, where the whites were few in number. But in the migrant states of America and Australasia, the Asian migrants could not assimilate as equal citizens, nor were they allowed to enlarge their communities through chain migrations. Many chose to go home instead, while those who stayed were allowed to remain on the periphery of white society as unwelcome sojourners. This was, to be sure, an ambiguous state to be in, but it was the only condition under which they could survive.[5]

The second stage, coming after the end of World War II, was an improvement for migration but only marginally so. On the one hand, concepts of racial superiority were on their way out, and greater compassion was found for the victims of war and deprivation, the millions of displaced people and political refugees (especially from Europe) for whom homes had to be found. On the other hand, the modern empires came to an end and were succeeded by scores of new nation-states. Although these new states subscribed to a UN Charter that endorsed great principles dedicated to supporting the poor and the oppressed, assisting migrant labor, and protecting persecuted refugees, the institutions available to implement these principles were still subject to the bureaucratic controls of national bodies. Migration was not a priority, and its enemies, especially those suspicious of what it might do to slow down nation-building efforts, stayed in control. What was remarkable, however, was the change in political conditions that created large numbers of upper- and middle-class refugees all over the world. This was followed by a change in values that permitted these people to become sojourner-migrants. Also unprecedented was the way the modern skilled and educated classes responded to the pull of the centers of power and wealth and the new transnational opportunities in trade and industry. These new types of migrants were articulate and politically sensitive, and they knew how to move in high native circles. They knew the law and their rights, and their successful adaptation to local conditions strengthened their capacity to transform the environment for all migrants. Most of all, as befitting their origins, they were masters in handling official and bureaucratic connections and in the art of informal linkages.[6] They quickly sought to lay the foundations for even greater changes.

The way that varieties of migration evolved and ebbed and flowed through time, I would suggest, is a major feature of global history. Modern sojourning, in particular, has contributed to a better understanding of what global history might mean. The rest of this chapter will examine the changes in two parts. The first will study sojourning in history as part of the traditions of two contrasting regions—East Asia and Southeast Asia—between which migration was discouraged, if not impossible. Eventually, sojourning became one of the strategies for dealing with the obstacles erected against migration. The second part will deal with the growth within modern nation-states of formal structures to control and assist migration. It will highlight the paradox of how restrictive institutions came to enhance the significance of the people movement they were created to control. It will look at new varieties of migration, as well as the advent of informal linkages across all boundaries in recent decades and how they redefine the global nature of migration.

There are excellent historical studies of migration world-wide. These include studies of the Jewish Diaspora and, more recently, the peopling of the Americas and Australasia and the large-scale importation of slave and then Asian labor.[7] These studies have enriched our understanding of how such people movements encountered resistance or created obstacles for themselves and for others. Furthermore, the studies have provided invaluable comparative material for any work of global history. Migration between countries in East and Southeast Asia has been less dramatic, but its importance in giving shape to the history of at least the latter region has been recognized. The contribution of migrations in Asia globalization trends are less obvious, but the two regions are key pieces of the jigsaw that must be put in place, if only to point out the differences between their migration histories and those elsewhere.

The historiography of the migrations of these regions is interesting. Indigenous writings have emphasized different features of migration: In East Asia, its involuntary nature is stressed, and in Southeast Asia, the focus is on the contrast between bonding the indigenous work force and tolerating outsiders. Modern historical writings have sharpened the picture further. For East Asia, especially for China, they have done so by placing migration in the context of a static agrarian society reinforced by Confucianized bureaucratic structures. In this way, migration has been seen as marginal to area history, and it seems to have had a minimal influence on the region's development. The enemies of migration—in this case, an orthodox philosophy and a highly centralized bureaucracy—prevailed.[8] For Southeast Asia, in contrast, scholarship since the nineteenth century has stressed the significance of people movements from the earliest times. Such movements included: the precursors of the Malays arriving from the Yunnan region in southwestern China; similar peoples spreading from Southeast China and Taiwan to various island groups in the Pacific and across the Indian Ocean to Madagascar; the Burmans and the Thais following later, also from southwestern China; the Vietnamese moving south at the expense of the Chams and the Khmers; and the coming of Indians, Arabs, Chinese, and Europeans in recent centuries. It appears that an unending process of peopling and successive dominance and retreat has enlivened the region's history. But that picture has been overdrawn. While the contrast with East Asia is clear, the impression of continuous mobility has also been greatly exaggerated.[9]

It is equally misleading to emphasize the relative immobility of the East Asian peoples. Filling empty spaces and displacing indigenous peoples from the borderlands have been major parts of Chinese history from the earliest times. Indeed, tribal migrations played an important role in the formation of petty states both in China and Korea, and ancient overseas migrations enriched and strengthened the early Japanese state. But with the smaller territories of Korea and Japan soon filled up, further migration both inward and outward was no longer encouraged. As in China, the increasingly Confucianized societies developed good reasons to persuade people to stay at home wherever they were, but China had many more reasons to allow the movement of people within the empire. For one thing, there was much more room and an evolving technology to make use of less fertile lands. For another, there were many periods of disorder, famine, barbarian invasions, and the breakdown of central administration, especially in northern China, when people were forced to leave home. Peopling the southern provinces remained a straightforward option until at least the Ming dynasty (1368-1644). And furthermore, moving people to the long land borders with various tribal confederations, whether Tibetan, Mongol, Turk, or Manchu, led to many official transfers of whole peasant populations to hostile frontier lands that were often unsuitable for intensive agriculture.[10]

Such internal migrations are part of conventional history and add little to global history. There were, of course, exceptional excursions far beyond Chinese borders. One could speculate whether Admiral Cheng Ho's famous naval expeditions between 1405 and 1435, which visited many countries in Southeast and South Asia and reached the East African coasts, might qualify as an early phase of global history, but they, in fact, led nowhere and were more of an aberration than a new trend. In any case, they had nothing directly to do with migration. Nevertheless, the abrupt withdrawal of the treasure ships did have consequences for Chinese trade with Southeast Asia. The expeditions had raised great expectations among the maritime peoples of Fujian and Guangdong provinces, who had been expanding their trade relations with the littoral states of the South China Sea since the tenth century. The lack of official support of any kind after 1435 drove the coastal traders to greater risk-taking and to a kind of extended sojourning or long periods of "temporary" absences from China that verged on migration.[11]

Why the extended periods of sojourning by the Chinese did not lead to colonization or full-scale migration is relevant to migration history. The *qiao* ("sojourner") or *qiaoju* ("sojourning") phenomenon was a product of Confucian rhetoric, of the exhortations to be filial and loyal to heads of family and the clan-based village so prevalent in southern China. This was a powerful value system that enjoined everyone never to move away from *his* ancestral home (women were carefully excluded from any form of sojourning to ensure that the men returned). Migration was simply not an option; only sojourning on official duty or as a trader was permissible. Any other kind of departure amounted to rejection of the family, and life as an exile from home was punishment indeed in China because no other place would normally receive such people except in bondage. Leaving home was feared, and seeking settlement elsewhere was an unwelcome prospect.

Chinese traders sojourned in Japan, Korea, and Southeast Asia. Most of them returned after a few years overseas, but many stayed on to marry locally and establish second homes abroad. Some had, for all intents and purposes, settled down with their local families. But with advances in transportation during the preceding two centuries, links with their ances-tral homes became easier, and regular visits home were possible. Then came the massive migrations of largely unskilled labor during the nine-teenth century, not only to Southeast Asia but also to the Americas and Australasia. As the Chinese saw it, this was not migration but mere sojourning. But calling the phenomenon sojourning did not prevent mi-gration and settlement. By the twentieth century, Chinese women could also leave their homes to join their husbands abroad, and the conditions for settlement were complete.[12]

Yet the concept of sojourning persisted, even though its meaning had been modified. Now, sojourning was not necessarily temporary but could be for life and could stretch over generations. It also meant that a highly particularistic loyalty toward family and the clan-based village could be the basis of linked space over great distances. This created the conditions for the kind of small-group autonomy (independent of states and govern-ments) that would be strengthened and supported by later advances in communications technology. This kind of linkage has been compared to the kind of autonomous space that enabled Jewish communities in differ-ent parts of the world to survive for centuries. But the Chinese idea of sojourning was not expressed in terms of nationality or a single unified and structured religion. Sojourning for the Chinese was predicated on trading relations and physical ties with their ancestral homes. The Chi-nese sojourners never experienced the intensity of emotional and spiritual power that characterized the relations between Israel and the Jewish Diaspora.[13]

The bulk of the Chinese sojourners went to Southeast Asia, and mil-lions of their descendants are still there. What has changed for them, however, is that new nation-states emerged after the period of Western colonialism. In the context of local nationalism and the powerful pres-sures of nation-building, those Chinese who have decided to settle have adopted the nationalities of their adopted homes. But Southeast Asian national governments continue to wonder if many of their local Chinese are still unrepentant sojourners. Meanwhile, other local Chinese who have become loyal nationals find the tradition of linked spatial relation-ships with ancestral homes still invaluable for long-distance trade with China and with other descendants of Chinese elsewhere in the world.[14] One might add that the hundreds of thousands of Chinese who traveled even greater distances—to other parts of Asia and other continents like the Americas, Australasia, Europe, and Africa—had extended their so-journing pattern of spatial relationships everywhere. Also, it is interesting that other East Asians with comparable Confucian familial backgrounds, the Koreans and the Japanese, practiced a diluted form of sojourning but nevertheless achieved, in their own way, the same kind of linked spatial relationships over great distances. Despite the differences among the three major groups of East Asians, it is noteworthy that their behavior patterns and cultural manifestations are often perceived by other ethnic groups as the same, and there is a tendency to group them all together. What is striking, however, is that they are all attuned to the modern communications technology that makes the linking of spatial relationships relatively easy and makes their autonomy as small groups seem unusually well protected, if not invulnerable.

The Chinese concept of sojourning largely evolved in Southeast Asia. The centuries of experience there taught the Chinese what was possible in long-distance spatial relationships. But even more important was the nature of the Southeast Asian societies where the efficacy of these sojourning links was proven. I will return to the somewhat overdrawn picture referred to earlier, which seemed to suggest that most peoples migrated into the region from somewhere else from the earliest times. In its extreme form, this image seems to suggest that the cultures of the region also originated from somewhere else—from India (Hinduism and Buddhism) or further west (Islam and Christianity) or from China (Confucianism and a sinicized Buddhism in Vietnam). In addition, during the Western colonial domination from the eighteenth century to the first half of the twentieth century, modern political and economic institutions, as well as most of the Chinese sojourning communities in the port cities of the region, were established.[15]

The picture of extensive migrations of peoples and cultures that made Southeast Asia what it is today is overdrawn and misleading because it neglects indigenous attitudes toward migration. Migration in Southeast Asia was either peripheral to mainstream society (as in the mainland states around the great valleys of the Irrawaddy, Salween, Menam, Mekong, and Red rivers) or integral and vital (as in the coastal and trading ports and kingdoms of the Malay archipelago). In the mainland states, migration communities were rarely significant. But in the archipelago polities for all the centuries before European dominance, overseas trade was an overriding concern. For them, migrant traders in their port cities brought wealth and power. They were therefore welcome for their role in linking these ports with the great ports of other regions, be they Chinese, Indian, Arab, or Persian. The spatial links were essential to the trading relationships. The autonomy of the small groups was a necessary part of those links, and although many of these migrant groups settled down as loyal subjects to the local rulers, they did not have to lose the autonomy that made them the wealth-creating communities they had become. In this context, migration was not associated with absorption or assimilation or integration but with the migrants' usefulness as economic actors across great distances overseas, especially as skilled labor or as commercial agents and advisers. Certainly, superior transport technology (in this case, shipping) had an impact in ways that were impossible for overland trade until the advent of modern railways and highways. Hence, before the nineteenth century, migrants or sojourners who were masters of shipping technology were invaluable, and even those who accompanied them as merchants and skilled hands were welcomed.[16]

The contrast between East and Southeast Asia is clear. People movement was difficult in East Asia: In that region, the enemies of migration were dominant, there were strong local identities in closed societies, there was a centralized bureaucratic state, and foreign trade was not important. This was also true in the mainland Southeast Asian states, which resembled their northern neighbor, China, in many ways. But in the archipelago states of Southeast Asia, there were few enemies of migration before modern times, that is, before the creation of the nation-states that replaced the colonial administrations after the end of the Second World War. Today, the nation-state as an obstacle to the easy movement of peoples (in other words, as an enemy of migration) seems to have come to stay in Southeast Asia. Yet there are extenuating factors that are worth noting in the archipelago states that, together with Thailand, have formed the Association of Southeast Asian States (ASEAN). While they are all building central bureaucracies and emphasizing strong local identities, they have affirmed the great importance of foreign or international trade and investment and kept their societies relatively open to outside influences. Their history of valuing the long-distance links that were vital to their trading economies and their tolerance of autonomous migrant groups in their midst over the centuries have made them more open to external opportunities. In that way, they have made their contribution to the globalization of history.[17]

The suggestion that the modern nation-state is an enemy of migration needs modification. This institution was created in the modern West, but it had evolved from powerful kingly states, some of them (like the British Isles, Scandinavia, the Netherlands, and Portugal) not unlike the trading port cities and kingdoms of Southeast Asia. Because these nation-states have evolved over time, they are relatively open. There had been no need for painful and melodramatic efforts at nation-building (with the exception of Nazi Germany). Thus, it is not the nation-state itself that is necessarily hostile to migration. Rather, it is the artificial boundaries of some of the Southeast Asian states and the haste with which they were created that made people in these states feel politically insecure and, as a consequence, actively opposed to migration. Yet useful migrant groups in the ASEAN states remain free to participate fully in commercial and industrial enterprises and even play a global role in international finance and trade.

In the nation-states, despite many kinds of newly erected barriers, migrations by individuals, families, and small groups continued as long as they were nonthreatening to those who were already settled. Furthermore, it was expected that the migrants would eventually be absorbed into the native populations. And until modern times, this was inevitable if only because the means of transport allowing the migrants to return to their original homes were limited and difficult. Perhaps the only exception to the norm of assimilation involved some groups of Jews, whose struggle to survive as a distinct people was a truly exceptional story that would later play a part in global history.

Before I turn to that topic, it would be useful to focus on the paradoxes of migration history in the two major North Atlantic regions: Europe and North America. Like many other aspects of modernization and globalization, the key ideas and institutions underlying the paradoxes originated in these regions.

Europe, fragmented throughout its history, may be compared to Southeast Asia, but it has been culturally homogeneous in ways that Southeast Asia has never been. Except for brief interludes when Muslim forces led by the Arabs and the Turks dominated the Mediterranean and southeastern Europe, respectively (and an even briefer period when Mongol armies rode in from the east), the European heritage has been Christian. With a common religion, small group migrations before modern times from one part of Europe to another were never a problem, and they were rarely mentioned in the history books. Much of conventional history has been concerned with dynastic, civil, and sectarian religious wars, defenses against the power of Islam, and the political and constitutional evolution from monarchies to democracies; with qualitative changes in the feudal and capitalist economies of the region; with overseas expansion since the sixteenth century; and with the scientific and technological revolution that is still with us. The dynamics of such historical developments, including the increasingly major migrations across the Atlantic from the 1500s onward, led to worldwide modernization and obviously are part of global history. But insofar as those developments also produced the conditions leading to a plethora of nation-states around the world—one manifestation of the enemies of migration—they have also produced paradoxes that need to be explained.

The roots of the paradoxes may be found in the unique separation of church and state that evolved gradually in most of the western and central regions of the Christian world. That eventual separation produced parallel legal concepts, if not systems, that protected subjects from their rulers, individual citizens from the authorities, minorities from majorities, and even migrants from the natives. These radical changes were indeed slow to come about whether under monarchic rule or in republican nation-states. For a long time, even when the legal provisions were agreed upon, they were often poorly administered or not followed. And when they were too slow in coming about, the subjects or citizenry who felt disadvantaged, dispossessed, and oppressed and those who knew they were discriminated against voted with their feet and migrated to new lands, especially those opened up for settlement in North America.[18]

Of course, not all migration from Europe to the Americas was of this kind. More common were poor and landless migrants in search of land and new opportunities. Others were recruited for jobs not available at home. There were also better-off people, sojourners of a type, who could afford to try to seek their fortunes in the New World. For example, many of the soldiers and officials who set up the administrative and legal structures, the adventurers who probed the frontiers and opened up the wilderness, and the traders who linked the newly settled places with the centers of civilization in the Old World had not intended to migrate but eventually either did so themselves or made it possible for their families or descendants to do so. But unlike the usual migrants in search of land and work, there were also those who wanted to be free and equal—more specifically, free to worship in their own faith and be equal before God and the law. Theirs were far-reaching goals that proved difficult to achieve. But the ideals that were transplanted to the migrant-established new nation-state known as the United States of America found the soil congenial. And the leaders there established new and higher standards of rights and duties in order to protect those who came after them. These standards, in turn, greatly influenced several other migrant states that also drew their populations from Europe.

Thus, in the course of the past two centuries, the Old World states and societies of Europe spawned a number of migrant states in the Americas and Australasia. Thankfully, these new states have sustained the peoples' desire to start afresh in the New World and have not reproduced all the narrow-minded traditions and practices of the Old World. On the contrary, they have translated most of the Old World's arbitrary migration controls into channels of regular and continuous migration.[19] Such a transformation was by no means straightforward: Indeed, the convoluted story of the different migration stages—freedom-seeking colonization, convict transportation, markets for slave labor, refuge for the poor and the persecuted, down to the selective "brain-draining" immigration of recent years—makes fascinating reading. By the beginning of the twentieth century, these developments had become part of the larger picture of globalization.

More specifically, four factors have assisted the transformations in the migrant states that have challenged the enemies of migration. These factors have, in turn, influenced migration policies of the old nation-states of Europe and, to a lesser extent, even of some of the new nation-states elsewhere. The four are the Holocaust experience in Central Europe and its ramifications; the new categories of political refugees; the communications revolution; and the evolving concept of universal human rights. I will briefly outline the reasons for their powerful influence on patterns of migration.

The story of the Jewish Diaspora, an unfinished migration history, stands alone. As a chain of anti-Semitic pogroms and a symbol of unrelenting religious persecution, it also surpasses the experience of all other migrant groups. How that extraordinary heritage of an unassimilated migrant minority led to the Holocaust perpetrated by Nazi Germany belongs to the history of the explosive power of nationalism and the new nation-state. Had the Germans succeeded in establishing the Third Reich in Europe, their racial policies would have led to the end of migration as we know it in that part of the world. The only exceptions would have been the returning migrants of the same nation and culture, for example, the Sudeten and Volga Germans and the German settlers in the Americas. Beyond that, Hitler's solution was to expand Germany to encompass all people of the same "race." Ultimately, however, the horror of the Holocaust challenged some earlier claims to European civilization. The Second World War led to the creation of the state of Israel, which embodied the idea of a historic homeland that migrating Jews could return to or identify with. That is still a mixed blessing, encompassing, on the one hand, the ideals of the rights of minorities and, on the other, also representing the narrow interests of a nation-state. But the overall effect of the tragic events of the Holocaust is still a positive one.

The gains in standards of tolerance and in policies toward minorities and immigrants are clear, even though far from secure in most countries. The migrant states, as well as some of the wealthier nation-states, have set good examples on how governments and communities should behave toward all their people. The persecution of small groups of minorities has become unacceptable to more people. Although the idea of ethnic and even subethnic rights, including the right for immigrants to remain different and unassimilated, is still evolving, the legal and philosophical justification for the ideals of multiculturalism and cross-cultural understanding is now much more sophisticated. There is still considerable resistance, even in the migrant states, but the ideals and the arguments in support of them are now unlikely to go away. And the chances of these ideals being increasingly embodied in law and turned into practice through a common basic education are now better than anyone could have expected earlier this century.[20]

The second new factor concerns a subtype of migratory peoples, the refugees who had never sought to migrate but were forced to leave their homes because of religious and political persecution or because of their racial or ethnic origins. The flood of refugees driven from one territory to another is not a new phenomenon. The idea of the exodus or the exile (of the Jews from Egypt or from Babylon) has come down to us from ancient history, and there have been many other equally dramatic examples of enforced migration through the centuries, most of them related to religious or racial persecution. But it was not until the late nineteenth century that national borders became barriers to refugees. And following the large-scale displacement of people in Europe during and after the First World War, Western governments were forced to take the problem seriously and acknowledge the need for joint international efforts to deal with it. Organizations within the League of Nations and then, after the Second World War, the United Nations were created to take care of the millions of refugees created by wars both large and small.

The problem became global when more and more refugees had to be shipped thousands of miles in every direction. The idea of refugeeism itself, especially in terms of political refugees persecuted for holding dissident views, had to be further refined and related to the wider question of migration. In particular, refugees had to be clearly distinguished from different kinds of involuntary migrants in a world ever more divided between very rich and very poor countries. As more people feel compelled to leave their homes in search of a livelihood and to escape not only from war and chaos but also from dire poverty, death by disease, and starvation, the claims to refugee status—seeking freedom from want—have grown rapidly and globally. And as with the early migrations of pilgrims and religious minorities to North America, the new categories of migrants now include those seeking freedom and protection from political persecution.[21] This recent development, which blurs distinctions, adds a political dimension to the concept of linked global space. It enables migrants of like political faiths and goals to globalize their ideals and have their values physically linked through networks independent of the nation-states and their narrowly defined migration targets. It has given new meaning to small groups, families, and individuals scattered about the world. And it has joined them together, through their political beliefs, within the realm of global history.

The third factor, the communications revolution that made fine technical networks of spatial relationships possible, also sprang from Europe and North America. But today, these networks now reach every corner of the globe. All they need are people to use and service them, and migrants, especially better-educated ones, are well positioned to take full advantage of the power and range of these networks. The rapid rate of scientific discovery in the field of transport and communications and the speed at which these discoveries have been translated into practical applications have been sources of wonderment for decades. This is even more true of the ability of every country, city, and territory in the world to respond quickly and acquire the skills to use these applications effectively.

The technological links now established between distant places have strengthened the spatial relationships created by past and present migrations. If the links are also open and accessible, they further reinforce the idea of ethnic minority rights, as well as the multicultural conditions that several migrant states have consciously supported. And not least of all, such links and conditions may ultimately encourage the globalization of the special form of migration found in East and Southeast Asia, known by the Chinese as sojourning—being temporarily away from home for generations. The new communications links would enable many migrants or migrant communities to live, behave, think, and feel as if they had never really left home. The influence such developments would have on cultural renewal, exchange, and intercrossing is considerable. But more immediately, the challenge they pose to older ideas like settlement and assimilation would have to be met, not by violence and force, it is hoped, but with patience and imagination. Certainly, if the phenomenon has come to stay, much rethinking in the context of global history will be needed. [22]

The fourth factor is connected to the three already outlined. The concept of universal human rights has become less abstract because of the shock of the Holocaust, the plight of political refugees, and the widespread access to speedy communications. Although human rights appear superficially comparable with other, more traditional ideas about fellowship, compassionate humanity, and equality before God and are therefore generally appealing to the common man or woman, the concept is different in nature and goes much further than the earlier ideas. Human rights must be traced to the same tradition of church-state separation that was there at the beginning of modernization in western Europe. Hence, there is a strong connection with the law that protects one's rights and with individuals who wish to guard the right to be true to their own consciences. The concept of human rights has already found application in the right to migrate, whether as free labor or as refugees, and no doubt it will be further refined to defend the rights of migrants to preserve their cultural values and their private relationships with their ancestral homes. There is still a large gap in understanding between peoples and also in the institutional structures needed to implement such rights. Moreover, there are political barriers, both national and international, that may inhibit the rapid promotion of the idea of human rights for decades to come. But the first step has been taken in the attempt to globalize the right of individuals to his or her own private spatial relationship with whomever he or she likes in the world. That migrants might choose to use this right to intensify their relations with their original homes would be understandable. It also seems clear that this could minimize the difference between these migrants and sojourners. The decision, then, for migrants to redefine themselves as sojourner-migrants would not be a difficult one to make.[23] It is not too early to recognize this step as a part of global history,

Many remarkable developments have followed the globalization of issues and problems in modern history. There is the fact that the enemies of migration are being challenged, if not undermined. And there is the paradox that the attempts to control migration have actually led to greater protection of migrant and refugee rights. In turn, closer study of migration issues should throw much light on global history.

This outline of the way migrations illuminate the emergence of global history threatens to lead to a new Whig or positivist interpretation of history. Let me hasten to check myself from offering such a view. Global history is no substitute for the conventional local and national histories that more accurately reflect the immediate, actual concerns of governments and societies, including their glories and successes and their mistakes and disasters. Nor is this chapter, which outlines changes in the status and position of some more fortunate migrant groups (even communities), meant as an attack on the nation-state as an institution. Although it appears here as an enemy of migration—an entity that has controlled and organized migration systematically—the nation-states is still evolving and is here to stay. And it can be developed as a benign and progressive force for social and economic betterment for all its citizens. Together with those citizens, sojourners and new migrants could be expected to contribute to the development of their temporary or adopted homes and to help make their countries advanced and prosperous political entities. These individuals must be both useful and nonthreatening if they are to enjoy the privileges of residing in a globalized environment.

Placed in the larger perspective, migration is but one feature of the general trend toward globalization. It must be set beside other major developments and examined with different approaches to the study of the globalization phenomenon. One such approach highlights the universality of science and technology; the common appreciation of popular art, music, and literature as well as some aspects of high culture and their effects on local native cultures is another; and the integration of multinational networks of trade and finance is yet another. In comparison, the growing range of linked spatial relationships that people are now beginning to cultivate may be no less significant.[24]

The way sojourner-migrants have responded to the informal linkages now open to them is of particular interest. Whether these linkages will last and whether new enemies of migration may appear and find new ways to erect barriers or restore the obstacles of the past is as yet uncertain. What is unmistakable is that, for now, many more migrants can choose to become long-term sojourners more easily than ever in the past. Furthermore, there is a growing awareness that the difference between sojourner and migrant may have been, to some extent, due more to differences in function and class (marked in many cases by wealth, education, and political and cultural superiority) than to differences in motivation and intent. Insofar as migration suggests leaving home permanently in a major and normally single move to settle elsewhere, there have always been elements of regret, necessity, and force of circumstance, accompanied by the expectation that the new place will be better and linkages with those left at home unnecessary, if not undesirable. In comparison, the rich, the powerful, and the venturesome were never migrants. They traveled, sojourned, moved on, returned home, or stayed on to settle if they wished, almost at will. They have now been joined by the educated, professional middle classes who have always admired their life-styles and who themselves have begun to redefine the meaning of migration as applied to their own movements from place to place. The access to informal linkages seems to be the key to that redefinition.

The contrast between migration today and earlier migrations is obvious. In ancient times, whole tribes migrated, often joining related tribes in larger armed confederations. If they succeeded, they took over the spaces they marched into and either put the defeated to the sword or enslaved them. Such powerful migrant groups were collectives; loyalty was not only expected but often also absolute. The idea that smaller groups, families, or individuals should be free to migrate or remigrate out of the new territory or return home without the agreement of the tribal leaders or the kings was unthinkable. No such group or individual would be so foolish as to cross over the borders controlled by their own kin. Only in times of great disorder would it ever be necessary for any of them to move away on their own, and such a move would be generally involuntary. The results were often tragic. Unless there were new empty spaces to move into or spaces occupied by groups who were even smaller and weaker, the small groups, families, or individuals from an alien tribe would meet hostility wherever they went. The question of maintaining linkages, however informal, with their own tribes was highly suspect and often unthinkable.

The only safe scenario for small-group migrations was when the group possessed some special skill or skills that their hosts needed and did not have. Historical records show that the arts of the smith, the potter, and the apothecary were often welcome, and artists, performers, and cooks could hope to survive. Religious men and nimble fortune-tellers sometimes did well, and with salesmanship, entrepreneurship, courage, and a bit of luck, the sojourning merchants would prosper. Of course, there was always room for the polyglot, the ubiquitous interpreter. Most of them traveled in small groups, some alone, and a few with their families, depending on the skills they had to offer. But until modern times, they could not remain in touch with their homes without incurring great expense or inconvenience. Even the Chinese merchant sojourners were forced to stay away for long periods, and many established second or third families who would normally identify with the maternal homeland and grow up as natives rather than migrants. Thus, successful migrants had three choices: settling down and bringing up native families; returning home with their fortunes after decades, even generations, of sojourning; or, if there was enough time, arranging chain migrations for kinfolk to join them and organize new migrant communities abroad. For the most part, it was easiest to settle down and be assimilated into the host culture, provided the hosts allowed them to do so.[25] But changes around the world have brought forth new possibilities especially in modern times.

The most dramatic transformation came about in the migrant states of North America and Australasia. These states were strongly affected by the four factors outlined earlier: the Holocaust, the politicization of refugees, the communications revolution, and the issue of human rights. Within a couple of decades after the Second World War, as a result of political challenges within and international pressures without, a radical revision of assimilationist ("melting pot") migration policies took place. In their stead were: calls for racial equality, however bitterly fought; programs to promote multiculturalism, however defined and misunderstood; and selective but nondiscriminatory migration, however reluctantly agreed upon.[26] Much sooner than anyone expected, many migrant communities found themselves formally legitimized. They discovered that they were free to have their contacts with ancestral homes restored (in some cases, with official encouragement) and that the rights of migrant individuals and nuclear families were, for the first time, carefully protected.

These developments are recent and still evolving, especially within the new nation-states, where they are yet to have any marked influence. It is difficult to evaluate them before they have worked themselves out and even more difficult to predict if they will have any lasting impact on the emigration or immigration policies of indigenous or nativistic polities in the Old World. What is clear is that they reflect the globalization of major issues and problems that touch on the lives of individuals, families, and small minority groups. Where migrants and their communities are concerned, surprising progress has been made in enhancing informal linkages over great distances, which are now more or less affordable: the right to communicate freely beyond national boundaries and the means of staying in close personal touch. For the more successful, the professional, and the middle classes, there is the further possibility of using international investment and financial connections to bind distant kin together.

It is too early to say if these tolerant and often beneficial conditions have been entrenched in the migrant states. Nor do we know now if they could ever be fully accepted into the older and somewhat defensive nation-states like Japan and China or the newer ones that have emerged in Asia and Africa since the 1940s and recently re-created after the breakup of the Soviet bloc in Eastern and Central Europe. But global migration and the extension of the concept of sojourning to those who, in the past, could only have been migrants or descendants of migrants is a significant new development that has contributed toward the unfolding of global history. In response to the changes accompanying the globalization of trade, information technology, and the movements of educated people, governments everywhere may do well to consider how they can benefit from the advantages arising from these developments.

Notes

1. There is as yet no accepted distinction between terms like *world, international, universal* and *global history*. This chapter on migration drawing on the processes of globalization in modern times (especially the technological changes enabling close linkages over great distances) points to the way in which global history might be delineated in future.

2. The literature on migration is vast. I have found the most useful to be William H. McNeill and Ruth S. Adams, eds., *Human Migration: Patterns and Policies*, (Bloomington: Indiana University Press, 1978) and Sydney Goldstein and Alice Goldstein, *Surveys of Migration in Developing Countries: A Methodological Review* (Honolulu: East-West Population Institute, 1981). On sojourners, see Wang Gungwu, *Community and Nation: Essays on Southeast Asia and the Chinese,* selected by Anthony Reid, (Singapore and Sydney: Heinemann Asia and George Allen and Unwin Australia, 1981), pp. 118-127.

3. S. Lebergott, *Manpower in Economic Growth: The American Record Since 1800* (New York: McGraw-Hill, 1964); Charlotte Erickson, *Emigration from Europe, 1815-1914: Select Documents* (London: A. and C. Black, 1976).

4. Morton Klass, *East Indians in Trinidad: A Study of Cultural Persistence (New York:* Columbia University Press, 1961); Gunther Barth, *Bitter Strength: A History of the Chinese in the United States, 1850-1870* (Cambridge, Mass.: Harvard University Press, 1964).

5. Mary R. Coolidge, *Chinese Immigration* (New York: Holt, 1909) (Taipei reprint, Ch'eng-wen, 1968); Stuart C. Miller, *The Unwelcome Immigrant: The American image of the Chinese, 1785-1882* (Berkeley: University of California Press, 1969); Sucheng Chan, *This Bittersweet Soil: The Chinese in California Agriculture, 1860-1910* (Berkeley: University of California Press, 1986).

6. Wang Gungwu, "Sojourning: The Chinese Experience in Southeast Asia," in

Anthony Reid, ed., *Strangers, Sojourners and Settlers: Southeast Asia and the Chinese* (forthcoming).

7. From the rich literature on migration, two books by Bernard Bailyn have greatly influenced my thinking: *The Peopling of British North America: An Introduction* and *Voyagers to the West* (New York: Alfred A. Knopf, 1986 and 1987). Another important book is Charles A. Price, *The Great White Walls Are Built: Restrictive immigration to North America and Australasia, 1836-1888* (Canberra: Australian National University Press, 1974).

8. Yen Ching-hwang, *Coolies and Mandarins: China's Protection of Overseas Chinese During the Late Ch'ing Period, 1851-1911* (Singapore: Singapore University Press, 1985).

9. For early history, see Peter S. Bellwood, *Man's Conquest of the Pacific: The Prehistory of Southeast Asia and Oceania* (Auckland: Collins, 1978) and George Coedes, *The Indianized States of Southeast Asia* edited by Walter F. Vella and translated by Susan Cowing (Honolulu: East-West Center Press, 1968); for all periods, with an attempt to modify the somewhat overdrawn picture, see D.G.E. Hall, *A History of South-East Asia* (London: MacMillan, 1964).

10. This happened many times in Chinese history; a sustained policy of this sort was followed by the founder of the Ming dynasty. An excellent recent study is Arthur Waldron, *The Great Wall of China: From History to Myth* (Cambridge: Cambridge University Press, 1990).

11. Wang Gungwu, "Merchants Without Empire: The Hokkien Sojourning Communities," in James D. Tracy, ed., *The Rise of Merchant Empires: Long-Distance Trade in the Early Modern World, 1350-1750*, (Cambridge: Cambridge University Press, 1990), pp. 400-421.

12. Lee Lai To, ed., *Early Chinese Immigrant Societies: Case Studies from North America and British Southeast Asia* (Singapore: Heinemann Asia, 1988).

13. Maurice Freedman, "Jews, Chinese, and Some Others," *British Journal of Sociology* 10, pp. 61-70; W. F. Wertheim, *East-West Parallels: Sociological Approaches to Modern Asia* (Chicago: Quadrangle Books, 1965).

14. J.A.C. Mackie, "Overseas Chinese Entrepreneurship," *Asian-Pacific Economic Literature* 6, no. 1 (May 1992), pp. 41-64; Jennifer W. Cushman and Wang Gungwu, eds., *Changing Identities of the Southeast Asian Chinese Since World War II* (Hong Kong: Hong Kong University Press, 1988).

15. David J. Steinberg et al., *In Search of Southeast Asia: A Modern History*, (New York: Praeger, 1971).

16. Anthony Reid, ed., *Slavery, Bondage and Dependency in South-East Asia* (St. Lucia: University of Queensland Press, 1983).

17. The success of ASEAN as a regional group has surprised many of its neighbors; this is systematically recorded and examined in several books and journals published by the Institute of Southeast Asian Studies in Singapore during the past twenty years. Also, see Linda G. Martin ed., *The ASEAN Success Story: Social, Economic, and Political Dimensions*, (Honolulu: East-West Center and University of Hawaii Press, 1987).

18. Marcus L. Hansen, *The Atlantic Migration, 1607-1860* (Cambridge, Mass.: Harvard University Press, 1940) is still the most useful introduction to the subject.

19. Price, *The Great White Walls;* Robert A. Divine, *American Immigration Policy, 1924-1952* (New Haven, Conn.: Yale University Press, 1957); Richard Plender, *International Migration Law* (Leiden: A. W, Sythoff, 1972).

20. James Jupp, *The Australian People: An Encyclopedia of the Nation, Its People and Their Origins,* (Sydney: Angus and Robertson, 1988), pp. 1-4, 853-967.

21. Louise W. Holborn's article on refugees in *International Encyclopedia of the Social Sciences,* (vol. 13) (New York: MacMillan, 1968), pp. 361-371.

22. Detailed monographic studies have yet to be made but, given that the phenomenon of "cultural persistence" among some groups of Jews, East Indians, and East Asians is now well recognized, research on this subject is likely to show that the communications revolution has greatly strengthened the predispositions of these migrant communities. If this means that future migrants would find it much easier to behave as sojourners, there may be negative reactions in either nation-states or within certain urban complexes, and new kinds of enemies of migration will evolve.

23. J. R. Pole, *The Pursuit of Equality in American History* (Berkeley: University of California Press, 1978); Nathan Glazer and Daniel P. Moynihan, *Beyond the Melting Pot: The Negroes, Puerto Ricans, Jews, Italians, and the Irish of New York City* (Cambridge, Mass.: MIT Press, 1963); Richard P. Claude, *Comparative Human Rights* (Baltimore, Md.: Johns Hopkins University Press, 1976); Tom Campbell et al., eds., *Human Rights: From Rhetoric to Reality* (Oxford: Basil Blackwell, 1986).

24. Specifically, these are relationships brought about and sustained by cheap air travel, the telephone, computers, and facsimile machines, as well as by video-cassettes, satellite transmission, and the global entertainment industry, to mention a few examples.

25. Miller, *The Unwelcome Immigrant;* Milton R. Konvitz, *The Alien and the Asiatic in American Law* (Ithaca, N.Y.: Cornell University Press, 1946); H. I. London, *Non-White Immigration and the "White Australia" Policy* (New York: New York University Press, 1970).

26. Donald J. Phillips and Jim Houston, eds., *Australian Multicultural Society: Identity, Communication, Decision-making* (Melbourne: Drummond, 1984); Jerzy Zubrzycki, *Multiculturalism for All Australians: Our Developing Nationhood* (Canberra: Australian Government Printing Service, 1982).

7

A Globalizing Economy:
Some Implications
and Consequences

Richard J. Barnet and John Cavanagh

As human interconnectedness over great distances keeps growing at an ever-increasing rate, *globalization* has become the buzzword of the moment. The constantly expanding network of commercial, cultural, and financial ties across the planet is defining a new reality. The disappearance of the familiar landscape of the Cold War, the failures and disappointments of twentieth-century political ideologies, and the questioning of Enlightenment orthodoxies—ideas of progress, faith in reason itself—all feed our collective craving for a new paradigm and a new language. *Globalization* has become a popular term in both the academy and the press because it seems to capture the essential changes in the human condition that are taking place in our time.

Just as bards and court musicians celebrated the rise of the nation-state, today's corporate managers, environmental prophets, business philosophers, rock stars, and writers of advertising copy offer themselves as poets-laureate of the global village. It is only in the past twenty years that global technologies have extended the reach of factory assembly lines and financial institutions across the entire planet. It is less than a quarter century since the unforgettable pictures taken from space of the fragile blue planet swathed in its thin membrane of life-sustaining gases were broadcast around the world. In Spaceship Earth, humanity had, for the first time, a unifying metaphor to awaken the planetary consciousness of which poets, prophets, and philosophers had long dreamed. But thinking globally takes many forms. This chapter is a beginning effort at clarifying the concept of globalization, especially in its economic manifestations, and to assess some of what we believe to be its most significant consequences. Behind the poetry is a complex and contradictory reality with implications for humanity that are both promising and disturbing.

There are hundreds of millions of actors at work weaving the web of global interconnectedness, but a few hundred space-age business enterprises provide most of the drive and the dynamism behind the process. The transnational megacorporation is the first human institution with both the ideology and the technology to operate on a global scale. A handful of large corporations are able to develop truly global products and earth-spanning factories, to supply the financing, and to acquire the channels of communication. In the process, they have become the revolutionary force of our time.

Just as the world of nation-states that has evolved since the seventeenth century has been the handiwork of kings, generals, and individual entrepreneurs, the emerging global order is principally the creation of large industrial and commercial institutions and their transnational networks of suppliers and customers. By operating across borders, they are integrating a new world economy that bypasses all sorts of established political arrangements and conventions—tax laws, traditional ways to control capital flows and interest rates, full employment policies, and older approaches to resource development and environmental protection. Laws and methods of governance intended for another age are becoming obsolete. National governments are losing control over the space they are supposed to govern because they are being confronted with seemingly impossible choices. More and more, they must adapt to a world not of their making.

About 200 corporations and 100 global banks are spearheading this process by developing the capacity to burst old limits—of time, space, national boundaries, and ideology. As the hopes and pretensions of governments shrink virtually everywhere, institutions we traditionally think of as economic rather than political, private rather than public, are occupying public space and exerting a powerful influence over the lives of ever-larger numbers of people. The architects and managers of these space-age economic institutions have the hardware and know-how to operate globally, the vision to conduct their business as if national borders no longer exist, and the growing confidence that governments everywhere have little choice but to give up the illusion of controlling them. By developing the arts of planning, producing, and marketing on a planetary scale, the global corporation is rushing into the vacuum left by the crisis of national governments.

Assuredly, globalization encompasses far more than the plans and products of these large business operations. But the global dreams of large corporations, made real by technologies that annihilate time and distance, supply the driving force behind economic, political, and cultural interconnectedness. By virtue of their size, their power, the relative clarity and single-mindedness of their objectives, and the inability of governments to comprehend (much less control) them, they are changing the character of civil society across the globe. What nation-states can do—even their very nature—is not what it was as recently as ten years ago. The shifting relationships between the managers of global corporations and political authorities across the planet are creating a new politics.

II

In the ordinary course of doing business, global corporations are becoming the midwives of a political economy characterized by the emergence of four dynamic global networks. All have roots that can be traced to past centuries, but each has developed so rapidly and so pervasively in the last fifteen years that, taken together, they are shaping a new world economy. One way to describe this new world is to focus on these four emerging institutions that increasingly define our age and determine how we live today.

We will start by mentioning the first, which we call the global financial network. For reasons of space, we will have little to say about its far-reaching implications in this chapter beyond defining it and noting its most novel feature. The network is a constantly changing maze of Mastercards, "Euroyen," "swaps," "ruffs," and an ever-more innovative array of speculative devices for repackaging and reselling money. This network is more reminiscent of Las Vegas than the dull gray banks of yesteryear. Twenty-four hours a day, every day, more than $500 billion flows through the world's major foreign exchange markets, trillions of bits of data traveling millions of times faster than the snap of a finger.[1] No more than 10 percent of this staggering sum has anything to do with trade. International trade has become an end in itself, a highly profitable game. John Maynard Keynes, who had only intimations of how technology might one day be harnessed in the service of nonrecreational gambling, predicted the rise of this "casino economy."

The second global network that is transforming world civilization is what we call the global cultural bazaar. This is a worldwide communications network and permanent world's fair featuring cultural products designed for an international audience. The technology for spreading commercial culture around the world is new, and the global culture industry is the most dynamic agent of change in the new world economy. Films, television, radio, music, magazines, T-shirts, games, toys, packaged food, and theme parks are the media for broadcasting global images and spreading fantasy.

Global commercial culture is largely American in inspiration and conception. Unlike automobiles, television sets, and machine tools made by U.S. corporations, American cultural products—movies, TV programs, videos, records, cassettes, and CDs—are sweeping the globe. Reruns of "Dallas" and "The Cosby Show" fill TV screens on every continent. The 1990 fairy tale hit *Pretty Woman* became the all-time best-selling film in Sweden and Israel within weeks of its release. Disneyland is now a global empire; its Japanese incarnation outside Tokyo draws 300,000 visitors a week, and despite a disappointing start, the Euro Disney Resort, a theme park on the outskirts of Paris occupying space one-fifth the size of the city itself, still claims that it will draw more tourists than the Eiffel Tower, the Sistine Chapel, the British Museum, and the Swiss Alps combined.

In 1989, packaged cultural products netted a U.S. trade surplus of some $8 billion, which made entertainment the second largest surplus item that year, right after aerospace products. Include such mythic amenities of American life and leisure as McDonald burgers (Teriyaki Mcburgers in Japan), Coke, Levis, Marlboros, and a variety of licensed spin-offs from films, TV, and sports—Teenage Mutant Ninja Turtle bubble bath was a planetary hit a few years back—and the conclusion is inescapable: The American dream is the nation's number one export. But foreign corporations have bought major Hollywood film studios, and only one of the six worldwide producers of popular music is still owned by a U.S. corporation. One does not have to be American to sell American culture.

The third global commercial network we call the global shopping mall. It is a planetary supermarket with a dazzling spread of things to eat, drink, wear, and enjoy. The customers are the rich and the expanding middle class in some of the poorer countries and virtually everybody in the richer countries. Of the six billion people on the planet, almost four billion are primarily window-shoppers. As recently as World War II, most people consumed products that were grown or made close by, often in the plot or the shed behind the house. Today, this state of affairs hardly exists in developed industrial countries. For the most part, people neither grow their own food nor make their own clothes. Imports are within reach of almost everybody, and more and more products are hybrids combining capital, labor, and materials from all around the world.

Many of the materials and much of the labor originate in the former colonial appendages of Africa, Asia, and Latin America. Here, flowers for export are grown, televisions sets for the world market are assembled, and data are cheaply processed and transmitted across the world at the speed of light. Hair from Pakistan and India is sold in the beauty parlors of Brooklyn—at a little over a $100 a pound. Sand from the coral beaches of the Philippines is marketed in Japan. At the same time, global goods are making their way into once-remote regions of developing countries. Chopsticks from Minnesota are sold across Asia. Even the furthest reaches of the globe are Marlboro Country; 344 billion Marlboro cigarettes were sold around the world in 1990.

The fourth worldwide network has the most immediate and far-reaching impact on the economic prospects of people across the world: The global factory is a network of plants, contracts, offices, and communications links for the production of goods, the processing of information, and the performance of services of every description. Everything from cigarettes to cars contains materials from dozens of countries, pieced together in a globally integrated assembly line driven largely by the logic of the bottom line. Data processors, law offices, advertising agencies, and insurance companies have become global assembly lines of a different sort. There is an international labor market for brawn, and creative merchandising ideas, computer knowledge, patient fingers, managerial know-how, and every other marketable skill coexists with a global labor pool in which more and more of us, from the chief executive officer to the wastebasket emptier, are swimming. Hundreds of millions more of the world's uprooted and dispossessed are desperate to jump in.

Mammoth assembly plants of the sort that thrilled Henry Ford and Joseph Stalin are still in evidence, many of them now in out-of-the way places, a few bigger than ever. But less and less of the world's work now takes place within such monuments to mass production. In part, this is because the production of goods is increasingly dispersed to smaller facilities around the world, to subcontractors, suppliers, and casual workers who cut and sew at home. But the main reason is that more and more of the world's work is not in manufacturing.

In 1950, a factory was a place that produced steel, cars, machine tools, and all sorts of other products big and small. While the factories of the 1990s still produce goods of these sorts in greater numbers than ever, a growing percentage of the world's work force is engaged in producing, marketing, and distributing paper of symbolic value of one sort or another or in providing all sorts of other services to feed, cure, comfort, and entertain people or to pick up after them in their houses, hotels, and other public places. According to the Random House Dictionary, the second meaning of *factory* is "any place producing a uniform product, without concern for individuality," and the example given is the "degree factory." We live in a world of factories that turn out services instead of goods— data factories, design factories, law factories.

Of the 100 most valuable, i.e., wealthiest, corporations in the world as of May 29, 1992, as judged by Morgan Stanley, almost half manufacture nothing in the old-fashioned sense of the word. They are banks, telecommunications firms, insurance companies, holding companies, public utilities, and retailers, and their products are deals, value-added paper, communication, and marketing expertise. If you subtract all these, the character of large manufacturing enterprise in the late twentieth century begins to emerge. Twelve of these surviving industrial giants manufacture drugs and medical supplies. Nine are petroleum giants. Eight produce packaged food and drink. Five make cars and trucks, and one makes airplanes. Four are chemical companies. Two produce cigarettes, and there is one steel company on the list. All operate on a global scale.[2]

By 1989, the sales of the world's top 200 "industrial corporations"—all hybrids turning out goods and services but not including purely financial institutions—had jumped sevenfold from their 1970 levels and stood at $3.4 trillion. This amounted to almost 20 percent of the gross world product of what was then known as the non-Communist world. Even the smallest of these giant firms had revenues exceeding the gross national product of the vast majority of the world's sovereign nations.

It should be noted that between 1970 and 1989, the number of U.S. firms in the top 200 had slipped from 123 to 69, and the number of Japanese firms jumped from 13 to 43. Changes in the hierarchy of global banks have also been striking. The combined assets of the world's top 100 banks jumped from $4.4 trillion in 1981 to over $11.4 trillion in 1989. Japanese banks increased their share of this huge accumulation of capital from 25 to 46 percent, while the share of U.S. banks dropped from 15 to 6 percent. Three years later, Japanese banks hit hard times, but they still dwarfed their U.S.-based competitors.

In 1945, almost half the world's goods were made on American soil by American companies. Ten years later, a number of U.S. firms already felt such strong competition from Europe and Japan that they began to move their manufacturing facilities overseas, primarily in search of cheaper labor and proximity to promising markets; within the next few years, this happened at a swiftly accelerating pace. To be sure, American manufacturers had been locating production facilities abroad since the turn of the century. Singer Sewing Machine and other U.S. firms were already playing a highly visible role in the British economy by 1902, the year a London publisher brought out a book on American corporate penetration entitled *The American Invaders*. By the outbreak of World War I, Henry Ford had become the premier automaker in Britain. (In 1915, his highly publicized efforts to keep American boys out of the trenches aroused such anger that he had to take in British minority shareholders to cool nationalist feelings.) By 1926, Fords or Ford parts were coming off the line in nineteen foreign countries.[3] The company had assembly operations in Argentina, Brazil, India, South Africa, Mexico, Malaya, Australia, and Japan. Its Yokohama plant, established in 1925, soon took the largest share of the Japanese market; nationalists called for Ford's expulsion, but the plant was still managing to produce 12,400 cars a year in Japan when it was shut down three years before the outbreak of World War II.[4]

In the second half of the twentieth century, the global spread of manufacturing facilities took off. Consider what happened to the television
industry. In 1948, at the dawn of the TV era, 100 percent of all televisions
were produced on American soil. By the 1960s, as the competition between GE, RCA, and twenty-five other American TV producers intensified, manufacturers were looking for ways to cut costs and expand their
markets. Locating production facilities in Europe appeared to be a way to
do both. By 1976, there were only twelve U.S. firms assembling television
sets in the United States. The American makers moved much of their
production of black-and-white television receivers to the Mexican border
and to Taiwan. The same process was repeated with the introduction of
color television. By 1976, 90 percent of the value of an "American" television consisted of subassemblies and parts produced abroad. "Made in the
USA" now meant little more than the addition of the U.S.-made cabinet
and knobs.[5] As wages rose in Europe, American manufacturers moved
their production to Taiwan, Hong Kong, and Singapore. The deindus-
trialization of the United States resulted in the loss of millions of high-
paid jobs in the nation's industrial centers.

These same trends spread to the other great manufacturing centers in
the industrial world. In the United Kingdom, there was a net decline of
more than a million manufacturing jobs between 1966 and 1976. Employment in the motor vehicles, shipbuilding, metal manufacturing, mechanical engineering, and electrical engineering industries fell from 10 to 20
percent in that decade alone. In the West Midlands, a leading industrial
region, 151,117 more manufacturing jobs were lost than were created in
just three bad years—1978-1981. In Lancashire, the textile industry lost a
half million jobs. In the industrial areas of northeast France and western
Belgium, the unemployment rates shot up from 1 or 2 percent in 1973 to a
range of 8 to 12 percent by the mid-1980s. Traditional industrial regions in
Northern England, Northern Ireland, Wales, Hamburg, Nordrhein-West-
falen, Saarland, Auvergne and the Paris basin became pockets of severe
and chronic unemployment.[6]

What was still being produced in the advanced industrial countries,
what neighborhoods, cities, and regions were attracting the production,
and what the work force was coming to look like were all caught up in a
vortex of change. The closing of factories that had been located in or near
the heart of America's industrial cities caused an exodus from what came
to be known as the *inner city*, a term dating from the early 1960s. A
generation before, many of these same blocks and census tracts were the
heart of the city; now, people spoke of them almost as if they were
festering sores.

The result—a local result of globalization—was that virtually all the
older cities developed "inner city problems"—50 percent unemployment

rates for undereducated youths, crime, declining educational facilities, inadequate health facilities—and as cities became increasingly expensive, unpleasant, and dangerous places to work and live, the flight to suburbia of large corporations, their executives, and blue-collar workers took off. As the great corporations merged, automated, exported jobs, and relied increasingly on subcontractors and temporary employees, the global factory took on a new look. And so did cities across the world. In Washington, D.C., for example, large tracts within a mile or so of the White House were abandoned to a black and Hispanic underclass. In others, most prominently Paris perhaps, the city prospered by exporting its slums to the surrounding sprawl. Old jobs were lost by the millions, but new jobs in manufacturing and related areas were created in substantially lower numbers in high-technology industry; in the production of aircraft, industrial robots, new synthetics, chemicals, and ceramics; in the technology of sophisticated assembly; and in the fashion industry—clothes, furniture, and specialized fittings of all sorts for the upscale market. More "service" jobs, mostly on the low end of the wage scale, were created. As labor critics had predicted twenty years earlier, the United States was becoming "a nation of hamburger stands." All this changed the way cities looked. Right next to row on row of dilapidated buildings, where former factory workers waited for government checks and young men without hope of a job supported themselves by running drugs or by violent crime, there rose gleaming "miracle miles" of shopping malls, hotels, and globally connected offices. For some workers, regions and city blocks around the world, this shift in production brought unparalleled prosperity, and for others crushing poverty. Everywhere, the gap between city blocks with a future and those with memories of a once-prosperous past widened.

III

These four networks play the key role in the integration of the world economy, but they are far from global in a literal sense because most people on the planet do not participate in their activities either as workers or regular customers. But the changes wrought in civil society by the processes of globalization are felt almost everywhere. These worldwide webs of economic activity, having already reached a scale never before achieved by any world empire or nation-state, touch virtually everybody in the industrial world and, indirectly, billions more in nonindustrialized countries. The driving force behind each of them can be traced, in large measure, to the same few hundred giant corporations and banks, most of which are headquartered in the United States, Japan, Germany, France, and the United Kingdom.

Yet as global cultural and economic integration accelerates, a process of political and social disintegration is also under way. Everywhere, the nation-state faces a crisis of identity. Trading blocs, politically organized regions, and transnational markets developed by global corporations have become more politically and economically relevant units than nation-states. As Peter Drucker put it, the nation-state is no longer "the predominant unit of economic life."[7] As a consequence, certain economic and political laws that national leaders take for granted have been quietly repealed. It used to be that the agricultural economy, the raw materials economy, and the industrial economy were more or less in sync with one another. Within some countries, these disparate sectors of the economy continue to be reasonably well integrated, but for the world economy as a whole, the food, raw materials, and industrial economy are all going their own way. The agricultural and minerals economies continue to decline even when industrial economies boom. The world money economy has less and less to do with commerce.

As the twentieth century draws to a close, the most striking characteristic of world politics is the collapse of so much of the "official truth" of the Cold War years. The repudiation of socialism is, of course, the most spectacular ideological turnabout of the 1990s, but the inevitable intrusions of a world economy over which national governments exercise diminishing control have drained other established political orthodoxies of meaning and power. Like Leninism, Keynesianism also was premised on the idea that national economies were real. Within the borders of a nation-state or at least within militarily powerful, advanced industrial nations, the state could provide economic stability, development, and social progress.

The Leninists believed that they could accomplish these worthy objectives through state planning and a command economy. The Keynesians thought it could be done more humanely by more modest government intervention in the marketplace, essentially by adjusting the incentives of producers, buyers, and sellers through the "fine tuning" of interest and tax rates. For more than twenty years, it has been obvious that economies do not react well to either medicine, and what it takes to manage a successful national economy to achieve stability and growth without wrecking the environment has become increasingly unclear. Political programs can stimulate short-term booms, but all across the political spectrum, long-term economic management has become a mystery since nothing quite works as theory prescribes. Juggling interest rates and exchange rates and raising and lowering taxes all produce unwelcome surprises. Free market, free world, national security, national unity, and economic stability have become secular credos, but they neither describe reality nor prompt sound policy. By and large, the goals cannot be realized by the political authorities who promise to achieve them.

In large measure, this crisis is the result of growing tension between global corporations—which are able to exploit their mobility and to distance themselves from the problems of any piece of real estate anywhere—and local business, workers, and citizens, who are rooted in a particular place. The faster the processes of globalization accelerate, the more traditional connections are being cut be they family ties, bonds of village life, or cultural traditions linking people with their local history or a tribal past. As the Cold War ends and the great powers, pressed by corporations and banks, struggle to create great global markets, a local backlash is taking place. The fever of nationalism is sweeping across the former Soviet Union and Eastern Europe. Canada, India, and many other countries are wracked by secessionist movements of one sort or another. In the age of globalization, everyone from the Ukrainians to the Sikhs wants a nation-state to call their own. Every tribe, it seems, wants its own flag.

Why has this paradoxical burst of nationalist fervor occurred at a moment when the nation-state increasingly looks like a relic of a bygone age? To a great extent, the separatist wars of the post-Cold War era are throwbacks. In some cases, the conflicts go back centuries, suspended for the last seventy-five years by the intervention of cataclysmic events, two world wars, and the eight-decade-long fight over communism. These ethnic conflicts are frozen in time, sparked by old grudges about race, religion, language, and wars fought long ago. These feelings were long squelched by the intervention of the great powers, which could control them as long as the central government could deliver on its economic promises or keep hope alive that prosperity was around the corner. The urge to secede is a consequence of the breakdown of larger political communities, which is traceable to the failures of the nation-state itself. In an interdependent world, national leaders are no longer in sufficient control of their own economies to be able to deliver on their electoral promises. And as more and more people around the world face unemployment, grim economic prospects, and a decline in services and benefits, the national capital becomes the symbol for all that is wrong in their lives. The reflex reaction is to opt out of failing political structures.

IV

The relationship between nations and the corporations that, legally speaking, are their creations is being transformed, and in the process, the nation-state itself has been changed. The differences in the ways governments deal with their own corporations have become heated issues of international diplomacy. The Japanese government is committed to advancing the interests of Japanese companies around the world, to opening up new markets, to preserving a business culture in Japan that is hostile to hostile takeovers, and to making sure that a highly skilled work force will always be on tap. In the United States, various national policies are also designed to favor corporations flying the nation's flag—"Buy American" legislation, tariffs and nontariff trade barriers, and hundreds of billions of dollars in subsidies to arms manufacturers, electronics firms, and agribusiness—but American ideology is laissez-faire.

Government intervention in behalf of corporations is different in Japan and in the United States, not only for cultural but also for specific historical reasons. In Japan at the end of World War II, the government mobilized industry to reconstruct the war-ravaged nation. Its focus was domestic, and its goal was to rationalize manufacturing and finance by organizing corporations and banks into a powerful industrial machine to rebuild and sustain the nation. The United States, on the other hand, was producing more than 40 percent of the world's goods on its territory, and it occurred to neither corporate executives nor government bureaucrats that a coherent, sustained industrial policy was needed. There was nothing General Motors could do to expand its business that was not also good for the United States. Government policy favored corporations deemed vital to national defense and U.S. energy needs, and various financing efforts (such as the Export-Import Bank) were designed to promote American exports and investment overseas. But today, while the United States government actually spends a greater share of the gross national product than does the Japanese government, the intervention of the state into the economy in behalf of American corporations is much more random and much less planned, coherent, and consistent than in Japan.

Japanese companies cooperate with one another in a variety of ways, subtle and not so subtle, but they see their fate as bound up in the economic health of the Japanese islands. U.S.-based companies are more apt to view one another as predators to keep at bay rather than long-term allies. American law and custom frown on the cozy relationships at the heart of Japan's corporate culture even though, for the most part, antitrust laws have gone the way of cowboys and spittoons. Under the American system, the primary commitment of U.S. corporations is to their shareholders—mostly insurance companies, pension funds, other large institutions, and, increasingly, non-Americans. None of these are likely to have a long-term commitment to the future of the firm—much less to the economy, to the territory, or to the people of the United States. U.S. companies, thanks to the individualistic American culture and its laissez-faire ideology, see themselves as free spirits in search of profits, preferably quick profits, wherever they are to be found. They will do whatever it takes to produce an impressive bottom line. On any given day, Japanese corporations are more likely than their U.S. competitors to put customer satisfaction and employee security ahead of concerns about the price of their stock.

The deregulation of industry and the sharp decline in the bargaining power of organized labor are both consequences of globalization. Governments have made a virtue of necessity by shaping national policy to suit the global interests of the largest economic units operating on their territory; the theory is that these are the engines of growth on which the prosperity of the nation depends. Corporations can, in important ways, escape the regulators and tax collectors by locating their assets, their production facilities, and their profits beyond the jurisdiction of their home governments. As yet, there is little in the way of international regulation. The ability to move factories abroad has rendered the strike, which was the chief weapon of organized labor and the major source of its political power, largely obsolete. The power of government to influence corporate behavior in ways that protect the environment, workers, and long-term economic growth has been weakened. As a result, the older American ideology voiced in 1953 by Charles E. Wilson, president of General Motors, that "what was good for our country was good for General Motors, and vice versa" is much less true than it ever was.

In a climate of intense global competition, the managers of U.S. corporations do not believe that they can afford to put America first when it costs money. As a high executive of Colgate-Palmolive put it in 1989, "The United States does not have an automatic call on our resources. There is no mindset that puts this country first."[8] As it has become harder for U.S. companies to make things in the United States and realize a profit, they have moved away or gone into new businesses. All this activity is a result of individual firm decisions in response to opportunities overseas encouraged by incentives—unplanned and often unintended—that originate in U.S. tax, labor, and environmental laws. But more important than any of these is the American ideological credo: A corporation is private property, and as long as no laws are violated, it can do what it likes and go where it pleases.

V

In his *Competitive Advantage of Nations*, Michael E. Porter, after studying competitive strategies in ten different countries, concluded that although companies in the age of globalization seem to have "transcended countries," the "role of the home nation seems to be as strong as or stronger than ever." He pointed out that "the home nation takes on growing significance because it is the source of the skills and technology that underpin competitive advantage."[9] The different strategies for achieving corporate growth in the United States and Japan are rooted in the fundamental differences in history, culture, and social system we have been discussing. Of course, there are many differences in strategy among Japanese corporations and even more among American-based companies. But in important respects, the strategies to which U.S.-based companies have resorted are a reaction to U.S. government policies. In turn, these corporate strategies weaken the regulatory power of the national government and the social coherence of the nation.

The divergent behavior of U.S.-based and Japanese-based global corporations and the different degree and character of government support in the two countries is becoming central to the debate about U.S.-Japanese relations. Japan has moved to accommodate American fear and anger in a number of ways. Its market is becoming more open. Government policy now favors more mass consumption and more imports. In some industries, it is becoming easier for American companies to do business in Japan, including manufacturing. Tariffs, quotas, and other legal barriers to foreign goods have come down. Japanese firms have become too big to be significantly influenced by government subsidy, and so the role of the Ministry of International Trade and Investment, the object of great American concern, is much less important than it was.

In their effort to solve the trade crisis, both American and Japanese politicians are demanding that their commercial adversary change its social culture and economic system in significant ways. In obedience to foreign pressures, Japan has made some effort to promote domestic consumption and to build up the market for foreign goods. At the same time, Japanese politicians, executives, and publicists feel no compunction about attacking American society for its weakening work ethic, its profligate spending habits, and its lack of investment in the future because of its obsession with quick profits. In the Structural Impediment Initiative talks between the two nations, the United States concluded the negotiation by admitting that its budget deficit and the failures in its educational system were contributing to the trade deficit. This was the first time in living memory that the U.S. government assumed obligations of this magnitude to a foreign power to reshape its domestic policy.

The growing differences in national business cultures and government-corporate relations are becoming a major strain on international relations. Ever since the Peace of Westphalia of 1648, the international system has rested on the notion that the beliefs of sovereign nations were their own business; wars to force changes of religion in foreign countries were declared to be over. To be sure, the internal affairs of nations were never kept out of international politics to the extent the Westphalia system seemed to prescribe. But it has been 400 years since the belief systems and cultural traditions of sovereign nations became so central to the major international conflicts of the day. Although the Cold War was presented

as an "ideological struggle" (and in some ways it was), the conflict between the United States and the Soviet Union was largely about behavior
in foreign affairs and armaments. The mounting tension between the
United States and Japan, between the United States and a united Europe,
and between Europe and Japan are rooted not just in what nations do but
also in what they are.

The demands laid on one nation by another to change its business
culture are prompted by the pressures of globalization. How Japan or-
ganizes its economy to compete is a matter of concern to the United States,
and it matters to Japan if the government of the United States is driven to
retaliation because its corporations are unable to compete without aban-
doning the home country. U.S. trade negotiators have pressed the French
government to stop subsidizing their farmers so generously, in effect
demanding changes in the rules of French politics. But as the demands for
intranational change become more shrill, nationalist, protectionist, and
isolationist sentiments are rising almost everywhere.

VI

The twentieth-century nation-state, that extraordinary creation of Lin-
coln, Bismarck, Wilson, Keynes, Roosevelt, Stalin, Mao, Nehru, and the
millions all over the world who have died for it, looks more and more like
a remnant of the past. In much of Asia, Africa, and Latin America, the
state is collapsing under the weight of debt, bloated bureaucracy, and
corruption, and local people's movements and more sophisticated "informal" economies are growing up to fill the vacuum. The United States,
although still the largest national economy and by far the world's greatest
military power, is increasingly subject to the vicissitudes of a world
economy over which it exercises less and less control. In the process, the
economic health of the United States is, to a greater degree, at the mercy of
the decisions of foreign banks and governments. The years of increasing
dependence on the world economy have, for the most part, been boom
years, but the economic prospects of large numbers of Americans have
declined, and the quality of life—as measured by job security, sense of
personal safety, educational opportunity, decent and affordable health
care, habitable and convenient housing, confidence in the banking and
insurance systems, and breathable air and drinkable water—has dropped
precipitously. In the years of globalization, the fortunes of corporations
chartered by political authorities in the United States and the fate of many
U.S. citizens have diverged.

Nevertheless, paradoxically, the nation-state is far from disappearing.
Indeed, in Ronald Reagan's America and Margaret Thatcher's Britain, the
size and budget of the state expanded even as leaders campaigned for

office by denouncing government and preaching "privatization." But although the state grew, it did not become more effective. Nor did it command greater legitimacy, much less affection. National governments, either acting unilaterally or in concert, still set the rules under which the world economy functions, and, as mentioned earlier, national policies for economic development continue to exert a profound influence on the competitive position of particular corporations. Thus, for all the talk of professors and corporate leaders (and our own earlier statement) about the twilight of the nation-state, it is altogether obvious that what governments do or fail to do is still important. Politicians and generals determine when and where the dogs of war are unleashed—not tycoons or commodity traders.

This is the dilemma facing the nation-state in the era of global integration. As an institution, it is largely a product of wars. Its *raison d'etre* has been national security, defined primarily as a strategy of preparing for and fighting wars. In the mercantilist era, the object of economic activity was to accumulate gold and silver so that kings could finance their wars and maintain large standing armies.[10] In the twentieth century, the most powerful industrial countries, notably the United States in World War II and Japan in the Korean War, have had their economies resuscitated by wars at critical moments. But as the experience in the 1991 Gulf War showed, the limits to war as an instrument of politics increasingly frustrate national leaders who, for many reasons, are becoming loathe to pay the price of imposing unconditional surrender on a defeated enemy. (The main reason is that the alternatives are either to turn their backs on the mass suffering caused by their punishing attacks and leave a ruined country as a gaping hole in the world economy or to spend a few billion dollars to teach the defeated Hitlerite states and terrorist nations "to elect good men," as Woodrow Wilson once put it, and tens of billions more to "jump-start" their ruined economies, as the United States did in Germany and Japan at the end of World War II.) Even the largest and most powerful nations can no longer preserve their economies from the unwelcome consequences of prolonged war preparation or from the boomerang effects of victory. Because of increasingly unpleasant side effects, war is no longer an effective instrument for advanced industrial societies to stimulate their national economies, to mobilize their populations, or to achieve control over valuable real estate. All these objectives can still be achieved for a time, but the benefits have shrunk as the costs have become prohibitive.

VII

For all the inspirational talk about humanity's common fate on a small planet, the global village remains deeply divided along economic, cultural, and political lines. An extraordinary global machine has been developed to make, sell, and service commodities, but no political ideology or economic theory has yet evolved on which to base a stable, legitimate world order. All over the world, politicians are counting on this machine, which destroys ecological capital even as it creates wealth to usher in a world of freedom and abundance. The ideology that provides the inspiration and legitimacy for this emerging global order is different from the notions on which political communities throughout history—from the Greek city-state to the modern nation-state—were founded. Even when they espoused a universal spirit, these ideologies were celebrations of particular slices of territory. But contemporary strategies that shape corporate and governmental behavior in the age of globalization place much less importance on attachments to particular pieces of geography. People and places have become more fungible. For practical purposes, vast regions of the world are deemed by some to be expendable, and this can be expressed in a number of ways. Underdeveloped countries can serve as dumping grounds for garbage. Their best workers can be put to work stitching or sewing twelve or fourteen hours a day for less than a living wage as their compatriots sink into deeper poverty. Or hot, poor countries that offer little in the way of resources or markets can be simply ignored even as millions face starvation—Somalia may be the exception—since there are so many better sources of labor, raw materials, and customers.

Because of the revolution in communications and transportation, distance is less and less significant—that is, for those who are in a position to take advantage of these globalizing technologies. For the increasingly mobile owners and managers of capital and the peripatetic lawyers, economists, accountants, and advertising executives who serve them, economic dependence and emotional attachments to hometowns and native lands are weakening everywhere. As they lubricate the wheels of commerce, these jet-age nomads scan the globe and see a giant menu of personal and professional choices. They have the education, training, and psychological outlook to find a niche in the global economy anywhere in the world. Yet for most people, place and rootedness are as important as ever. For billions of people, their very identities are tied to places either because they cannot conceive of living anywhere else (which is true of most people on the planet) or because they are dependent on a piece of ground or a factory job for their livelihood. For these individuals, the forces of globalization threaten to bring life-transforming changes far beyond their control. Hundreds of millions of people have left farming in the last generation, and as people migrate to the great cities of the world, old ways of life, family traditions, childrearing practices, and local authority structures are swept away. Unlike the jet-age nomads, most of these people have choices of a very different sort; the prospects for most are marginal employment in the capital city, if they are lucky, or migration to new lives of insecurity in faraway lands. The processes of economic integration that are transforming the planet are creating a crisis not only of politics but also of culture. The effects of globalization are increasingly felt where people live and work.

The potential market for global goods designed for middle-class living is not growing rapidly in the United States or in other affluent countries with little or no population growth. Marketers look to constant, speedy technological innovation to maintain the flow of new products and product wrinkles that will keep mature economies growing. They also look to the most promising developing countries as the places to repeat the success they have had over the last fifty years in the industrial world. However, ever since the boom years from 1950 to 1970, the middle class has been growing slowly in the Mexicos and Brazils of the world. The places that have had a big expansion in their middle-class populations—the South Koreas and Taiwans—tend to have highly protected markets that limit the horizons for the global shopping mall. In Latin America, Africa, and Asia, thirty-five million people enter the labor market each year. The majority of the people have neither steady jobs nor secure incomes, and most are much too poor to buy global products. The explosion of urban populations, particularly in what used to be called the Third World, will bring growing numbers of people into contact with shopping centers and malls, and they will be subjected to more and more advertising messages. But the very processes of urban growth—mainly, the huge migrations into the cities of former subsistence farmers who enter the money economy without prospects of steady work—lead to further impoverishment. The world's urban population is projected to grow by 29 percent during the 1990s—only 10 percent in rural areas—but most of those pouring into Mexico City, São Paolo, and Calcutta have little more than the clothes on their backs.[11]

Working for global corporations is an option for more people in poor countries, but these men and women barely make a dent in the growing unemployment problem. Because of the competitive pressures on global companies to keep wages down, to automate, and to cut back their work forces, only a small proportion of workers in the global factory can afford to shop at the global shopping mall. Marlboros sold by the "stick," in the lingo of the trade, and bottles of Coke are bought by very poor people all over the world, but women who earn fifteen cents an hour sewing basketball shoes in Indonesia are not good prospects even for these.

Three-quarters of the people on earth live in 130 poorer countries. Donald Halper and H. Chang Moon, professors of international business, pointed out that countries such as India, Indonesia, and Brazil are so populous that even a small percentage growth can deliver a highly profitable market to the suppliers of global goods. "India has a low per capita income of $350, but it also has an expanding middle class, currently estimated at 100 million citizens—the upper 8 percent of the population. Sales of consumer goods are rising at 10 percent to 20 percent annually."[12] However, over the past decade as the Third World debt crisis has deepened, most people have watched their real incomes shrink. In the Philippines, as in most countries of Asia, Latin America, and Africa, well over half the national income is earned by the top 20 percent of households. (In the United States, less than 40 percent of all income comes from the richest 20 percent of households). In Brazil, Panama, and Peru, the top 20 percent of households take home over 60 percent of the income, and in Argentina, Chile, Costa Rica, Mexico, and Venezuela, the figure hovers around 50 percent.[13]

In the Philippines in the mid-1980s, the average Filipino family was spending over half its income on food and beverages. The rest went for housing, utilities, transportation, and education, almost all of which are locally provided.[14] Unless the Philippines becomes another newly industrialized country like South Korea (and the prospects for this in the next decade are minuscule), this densely populated archipelago has little prospect of becoming a major market for global companies. In the global village, 80 percent of people in the industrialized world and less than 20 percent in underdeveloped countries make up the worldwide pool of consumers of global products. Under presently foreseeable conditions, it appears there will not be enough buying power to absorb the ever-expanding output of the global factory.

Because the gulf between the winners and losers in the race toward globalization is widening, global economic integration is almost always accompanied by processes of social and political disintegration. For some farmers, workers, regions, and city blocks all around the world, the process brings unparalleled prosperity. For others just across town or across the highway, the consequence may be crushing poverty. The inhabitants of a city block on the upper east side of Manhattan are drawn by taste, style, and class into a closer relationship with similarly situated citizens of Brussels, Rio, or Tokyo; they move further and further away from poorer, less mobile residents who may live a block or two away.

These fissures within territorially based societies are not only making governance difficult but are also provoking a local cultural backlash almost everywhere. Social issues—questions of religion, tradition, family, language, and morals—are often more powerful determinants of political direction in many parts of the world, including the United States, than the traditional who-gets-what questions that theorists have held to be the substance of modern politics. The desire for global commodities appears to be a powerful force all over the world. But for many people throughout the planet, globalization comes with its own nightmares: the disruption of family life, the overwhelming of cultural heritage, the despoiling of the environment—in short, the loss of the sense of place and the sense of self that gives life meaning. The fundamental political conflict in the opening decades of the new millennium, we believe, will not be between nations or even between trading blocs but between the forces of globalization and the territorial-based forces of local resistance seeking to preserve and to redefine community.

Notes

1. James Robinson, chief executive officer of American Express, in his address to Executives Club, Chicago, September, 1989.

2. "The Business Week Global 1000," *Business Week*, July 13, 1992, pp. 53-104. Fifty-four produced goods in the traditional sense, forty-four did not, and two produced both goods and services.

3. James P. Womack et al., *The Machine That Changed the World* (Rawson Associates, 1990), p. 35.

4. Ward's *Auto World*, November 1985, pp.81-83.

5. Joseph Grunwald and Kenneth Flamm, *The Global Factory: Foreign Assembly and International Trade* (Brookings, 1985), p. 19n.

6. Paul Knox and John Agnew, *The Geography of the World Economy* (Edward Arnold, 1989), pp.182-184.

7. "The Post-Business Society," *New Perspectives Quarterly* (Fall 1989), p. 24.

8. Robert Reich, *The Work of Nations* (Alfred Knopf, 1991), pp. 140-141.

9. Michael E. Porter, *The Competitive Advantage of Nations* (Free Press, 1990), p. 19.

10. Reich, *The Work of Nations*, p. 14.

11. United Nations, *World Economic Survey, 1990* (New York, 1990), p. 205.

12. Donald Halper and H. Chang Moon, "Striving for First-Rate Markets in Third World Nations," *Management Review*, May 1990.

13. *Statistical Abstract of Latin America*, p. 299.

14. "Metro Manila: The Urban Challenge," *Consumer Markets Abroad*, (June 1987), pp. 7-8. The per capita GNP figure is for 1988; see World Bank, *World Development Report, 1990*, p. 178.

8

Human Rights
as Global Imperative

Louis Menand III

The perfection of human society, consists in that just degree of union among individuals, which to each reserves freedom and independency, as far as is consistent with peace and good order.

—Thomas Jefferson, 1787

To those who have accepted Enlightenment teaching, it may seem incredible that any rational person would not readily accept as self-evident truths individual freedom and equality regardless of sex, race, or religious belief. To others, it may seem incredible that any person would willingly inject some notion of individualism into a belief system and thereby disrupt the sense of community essential to that system. It is this tension between an essentially secular worldview and more proscribed belief systems that sets the stage for the extension of human rights doctrines. Add to this the autocratic bullies in some nations who will let nothing stand in the way of their bullydom, and the tension becomes more acute. Whither, then, human rights?

In the last years of the twentieth century, there has been an explosion of interest in and a declaration of faith in international standards of human rights. In 1992, the twelve-member European Community agreed to grant diplomatic recognition to each of the emerging states resulting from the breakup of Yugoslavia, provided that these new units each agreed to institute democracy and guarantee respect for human rights. A similar position was taken in late 1991 by the EC, the United States, and other democracies vis-à-vis the republics created by the dissolution of the Soviet Union. The king of Saudi Arabia proclaimed a change in his autocratic form of governance in early 1992 by making provision for citizen consultative councils, and he suggested that some measures for human rights be instituted. The U.S. Congress attempted to establish a human rights standard in that nation's trade relations with China (although the president ultimately vetoed the measure). And in early 1992, the minority white population of South Africa voted overwhelmingly to move toward a new constitutional system granting full electoral and other participation to the black majority, thereby moving closer to an end to apartheid. In addition, there was a growth in the number of plebiscites calling for ethnic autonomy in Russian Armenia and a continuing search for independence for Quebec. In short, plebiscites, elections, and human rights standards were all a significant part of world politics in the early 1990s. Writing in 1991, political scientist Samuel Huntington noted that "between 1974 and 1990 more than 30 countries in Southern and Central Latin America, East Asia, and Eastern Europe shifted from authoritarian to democratic systems of government."[1]

All of this comes as the human rights emphasis in world politics by the United Nations continued. Since 1948, eight conventions on human rights have been adopted by decisive votes in the General Assembly. And yet a series of contrary moves in several areas occurred at the same time. In Algeria, a military junta annulled a national election because voters showed overpowering support for Islamic fundamentalists. In Mynamar, a military junta not only annulled a national election but also put under house arrest the newly elected leader, Daw Aung San Suu Kye, who was subsequently awarded the Nobel Peace Prize for her efforts toward establishing a democratic regime for her country. Meanwhile, the troubled peoples of Africa were still seeking stability between autocracy and democracy in lands populated for centuries by proud tribal groups for whom clan relations are paramount. And much of the Middle East remained governed by autocracies with no regard for human rights—Syria, Saudi Arabia, Kuwait, Iraq, Iran. In short, establishing a human rights standard for the world's population remained a tenuous proposition.

In this period, private international agencies such as Amnesty International continued to document, nation by nation, severe human rights infractions: torture, terrorism, brutal treatment of prisoners, and less violent but equally firm suppression of individual rights. Index on Censorship publicized infractions of speech, press, and assembly rights around the world. Individual rights organizations like Human Rights Watch continued to note human rights abuses in South and Central America, Africa, and elsewhere. And the United States Department of State, under congressional mandate, again published its annual review of human rights issues, by nation, as part of the effort to determine whether the United States should grant aid to specific nations. Terrorism has been stopped in Argentina and Chile but not in Haiti, and only in 1992 did a semblance of domestic peace return to El Salvador. In 1992, Peru abrogated its democratic institutions. Repression and street-fighting erupted in Thailand once again, and universities on the West Bank in Israel/ Jordan had been closed for over four years as of 1992.

In the midst of these events, the United Nations Committee on Human Rights and the Center for Human Rights in Geneva are increasingly active in monitoring such rights around the globe and considering cases of individual abuses brought to their attention by citizens in countries that are party to the International Political Rights of the Economic and Social Council Convention of 1966. The UN Human Rights Commission is now in its fifth decade, and it has been repeatedly noted that the issue of human rights has been embraced as an important concept by almost all the nations of the world and that, at least on paper, a standard is acknowledged. Writing in 1983, John Ruggie, professor of international relations at Columbia University, said:

> Virtually every state in the world accepts the concept of human rights, and most grant that human rights are an appropriate area of international concern. A substantial number of states have accepted the United Nations Conventions on Economic, Social and Political Rights, all members of the Council of Europe have ratified the European Convention for the Protection of Human Rights and Fundamental Freedoms, and seventeen states in the Western Hemisphere adhere to the American Convention on Human Rights. In addition, numerous other international human rights instruments are in place. What do all of these developments signify?[2]

It is precisely that question that I will address in the pages that follow.

I

How did all of this concern for human rights emerge, and what does it mean, if anything? Is the concept of human rights an operative one, or is it more frequently cited as a pious talisman by people and governments? Is the concept of human rights essentially a secular notion of individualism, and if so, how does it relate to religious and ideological fundamentalism? If historically the parties at law in international affairs have been states recognizing the nation-state system, how can an individual have standing in the international community? Are these so-called rights individualistic or communal, and if the latter, how can the individual assert a right against the community? Is there a history to all this that will assist in creating a global future in which these questions can be discussed and answered?

The proximate cause for the development of human rights concerns can be traced to World War II and the conditions that gave rise to it and followed in its wake. The growth of military power in the Axis nations was accomplished domestically by a suppression of parliamentary pluralism in Italy and Germany; by the elimination of freedoms of speech, press, and religion; and, in Germany, by a declaration of war on German and, subsequently, all European Jews.

When the war started, the Western democracies' response to fascism was couched in the language of civil liberties so important to their pluralist societies. The "four freedoms" of Franklin Roosevelt (freedom of speech, freedom of worship, freedom from want, and freedom from fear) became an important standard for the Allied governments in prosecuting the war (including the Soviet Union, itself a totalitarian state). In January 1942, the Allied nations organized themselves as the United Nations and called for "complete victory" and, among other things, the preservation of human rights. This group's concerns included the nature and shape of the world organization formed to help keep the peace and the commitment it would make to guarantee certain human rights as international standards to forestall the recurrence of totalitarian governments in the aggressor nations and elsewhere in the world.

Finally in 1945, the fifty-five-member group calling itself the United Nations completed a charter for a permanent UN, with each nation pledging, in Articles 55 and 56 of the new charter, to promote human rights. The document provided for an economic and social council, which would include human rights in its purview (Chapter X, Article 62.2). Thus, for the first time in international organizational life, the concept of human rights was advanced. Despite the growth of democracy in Western Europe and the Asian subcontinent, it is remarkable that the concept of an international standard of human rights had not emerged until then. But it was not the gulag in the Soviet Union, the dictatorships in South America, or the arbitrary rule of French, Dutch, or British imperial commands that caused the emergence of human rights. Rather, it was Fascist totalitarianism and the tragedy of World War II that illuminated the need for standards of individual rights. And oddly enough it was the world imperial powers—France, the Netherlands, and the United Kingdom—that joined the United States, Canada, Australia, and the Scandinavian countries to secure the adoption of the UN charter and launch the subsequent drive for human rights. It is pointless to speculate on whether human rights concerns on an international scale would have emerged had there been no war, but it is true that, unlike the development of the hapless League of Nations, the creation of the United Nations after the war was the single most important factor in setting the world agenda for human rights.

In the affairs of humans, great good occasionally comes from great evil. As historian Gordon Craig said about Hitler and Stalin:

It is fair to say that between them they were the makers of the world in which we have lived for the past forty-five years, and from which we are now [1992] only beginning to emerge. Without them, none of the slaughter that attended the Second World War, with the irreparable loss of forty million military and civilian lives, would have taken place; without them there would have been no divided Europe, no headlong dissolution of the European colonial empires, no cold war, no Korea and Vietnam, without them no debauching of the economies of the great nations to support the burden of the arms race. It is easy enough to find, in the years that followed the First World War, general causes for the ills of European civilization, but its near destruction was the result of individual decisions and the most baleful of these were made by Hitler and Stalin. One may gag at the attribution to them of historical greatness, but, whatever one calls them, it is necessary to study their careers.[3]

I would add simply that they made our world.

No sooner had the United Nations begun its organizational life than the Economic and Social Council created the Commission on Human Rights. Its central task was to devise from political history a statement of human rights that would be applicable globally. And as the world knows, the General Assembly adopted the Declaration on Human Rights in 1948, not as a prospective treaty but as a statement made by the forty-eight nations that voted for it. (No one voted against the declaration, and eight nations abstained.[4]) The declaration has two undivided parts. The first twenty-one clauses concern what are called political and civil rights; the later clauses address so-called social rights. The early clauses begin with a statement that all human beings are free and equal in dignity and rights (Article 1). Articles 2 through 21 enumerate rights regarding speech, press, due process, religious beliefs, migration, marriage, property, assembly, and periodic franchise. It is this set of political/legal rights that I refer to when using the term *human rights* in this chapter. Articles 22 through 29 of the declaration address social and economic rights, such as the right to a job, to social security, to a decent standard of living, and so forth. While the declaration should be understood to view the rights of individuals as indivisible or, more particularly, as the qualities necessary for a dignified life, my references will be confined to the first list.

Generally recognized as the spirit behind the UN declaration, Eleanor Roosevelt guided the document with great care through its many iterations to the final result. But though it was a major new charter for international policy, important as that is, the declaration was not designed to create and codify new international law. And thereby hangs a tale.

II

It is frequently stated—and believed—that the worldwide interest in human rights is a direct result of the Enlightenment's Age of Reason and its three most famous political/legal documents: the U.S. Declaration of Independence (1776), the French Declaration of the Rights of Man and the Citizen (1789), and the U.S. Bill of Rights (1791). The Bill of Rights was adopted as part of a written constitution; the Declaration of the Rights of Man enunciated a revolutionary policy. It is the difference between a declaration of policy and a constitution that must concern us. Clearly, however, the French Revolution of 1789-1794 captured the world's attention for its quick, sudden, and violent break with ancient and entrenched autocracy and the real emergence of a republican ethos in France. The events have captured revolutionary imaginations ever since.

The rebellion of England's North American colonies, starting in 1775, was something else again. It produced warfare but not much internal, local violence, and the revolutionary document that came out of it was a statement claiming the same rights as those held by citizens in England who lived under the same monarch. The Declaration of Independence of 1776 was a quite different document from the 1789 French declaration, and it sprang from different sources. An understanding of this difference may assist us in thinking about the fate of global human rights in the century that lies ahead.

Of the four important revolutions of the last 300 years in Europe and North America—that of the English in 1688, the American colonies in 1775-1783, the French in 1789, and the Russians in 1917—two (the French and Russian) were abrupt and violent rebellions against all authority, religious and secular, against social hierarchies and old social values, and against the dominant legal systems. The other two (the English and American) were, by contrast, wholly prosaic. In neither the English Glorious Revolution of 1688 nor the American Revolution of 1776 was the social structure uprooted or abandoned, and in neither were parliamentary government and law discarded.[5] Indeed, in England, the Parliament benefitted from the distribution of kingly and representational power set forth in the famous English Bill of Rights of 1688. The centuries-old traditions of English law continued unchanged, and the 1688 document set the stage for one of the most important developments for any legal system, namely, the independence of the judiciary, established by Parliament in 1707. In his *Second Treatise on Civil Government*, John Locke, writing in 1690, stipulated: "Whoever has the legislative or supreme power of any commonwealth is bound to govern by established standing laws, promulgated and known to the people, and not by ex temporary decrees; by indifferent and upright judges who are to decide controversies by those laws; and to employ the force of the community at home only in the execution of such laws."[6]

This dictum has become standard constitutional language in the development of democracies and the rule of law across the globe. And Locke is universally recognized as the early Enlightenment philosopher who provided the theoretical justification for the social contract and for government limited by law, reflecting the English tradition in which he was writing. The combination of Locke's writing, the English Bill of Rights, and the establishment of an independent judiciary were crucial to in the growth of a right-based tradition—now exportable globally.[7]

Other methods for strengthening the rule of law followed in the eighteenth century, including freedom of the press, the right of citizens to send representatives of their own choosing to Parliament, and, at the end of the century, the guarantee of access to habeas corpus proceedings. Each of these developments seem, in retrospect, to be logical movements preceded by an even earlier recognition of citizen rights. It is important to realize that what is called the rule of law in the legal rights jurisprudence of the late twentieth century actually saw its first manifestations in written form in 1215. In the famous Chapter 39 of the Magna Charta, the English barons induced King John to proceed against citizens only according to "the law of the land," a concept that came to be known as the rule of law. It is crucial to acknowledge this concept when tracing the evolution of rights for it occurred against monarchical power, a power almost absolute in its centralization and totality and with all the authority of the Roman Catholic church behind it. At the end of the thirteenth century, it was King John's grandson Edward I who agreed not to attempt to tax without the approval of Parliament—establishing yet another "right," namely, a freedom from arbitrary taxation. And in the twelfth century, it was King John's father, Henry II, who instituted a legal procedure we now call a jury system to evaluate evidence and determine guilt or innocence—a right, that is, to be judged by one's peers and not arbitrarily by the king's handpicked judges. Each of these rights—jury trial, procedure according to the rule of law, and freedom from arbitrary taxation—evolved slowly over the succeeding centuries. By the early 1600s, a legal system in the fullest sense was in place, a system of jurisprudence that formed the basis of the English rights that the American colonists claimed in the middle of the eighteenth century.

When Thomas Jefferson wrote the Declaration of Independence in 1776, he coined a phrase that was, in itself, not revolutionary in England or the colonies but that became a rallying point for human rights activists globally in the following 200 years. That well-known phrase, "inalienable rights, among which are life, liberty, and the pursuit of happiness" encapsulates what the evolution of English law had created.

American colonists also drew on classical writings about law and power, on the English experiences, and on the jurisprudence of lawyers such as Sir Edward Coke and Willam Blackstone—and, of course, John Locke. The classical scholar and political leader most frequently mentioned was Cicero, who gave voice to the growth of natural law (*jus natura*) and the laws of the citizens in Rome (*jus gentium*). A law-based polity is part of the heritage of both republican and imperial Rome, and present-day Europe is a legatee of this significant Roman contribution, eventually codified by Justinian in the sixth century CE.[8] This entire evolution is best seen in the oldest written constitution in the world still in force, that of the Commonwealth of Massachusetts, adopted in 1780. The first articles in that constitution form a slate of rights that served as one of the models for the U.S. Bill of Rights. Article 30 also contains the phrase universally regarded as crucial for democracy and human rights—"a government of laws and not of men."

In sum, then, the growth of rights under law in Anglo-American history occurred over six centuries, from 1215 to the American Revolution, and continues near the end of the twentieth century.

In contrast, the French Declaration of the Rights of Man was promulgated as doctrine, but no legal system capable of securing the declaration's principles was nurtured simultaneously. Indeed, in the subsequent violence of the revolution itself and in the dictatorship of the Napoleonic era, there was no opportunity for the growth of rights-sustaining law, accepted by government and people alike. The mere assertion of rights was undoubtedly satisfying, but the pious statement had no other utilitarian purpose. As a useful prescription for limitations on power, the declaration was ineffective.

Similarly, the development of international law in the nineteenth and twentieth centuries was predicated on the assumption that parties at law are national states or abstract entities such as corporations or ships. The individual had little or no standing in international law, except as noted in bilateral treaty arrangements concerning extradition and the like.[9] While the French declaration is a strong statement about the universality of human rights, it has no enforcement mechanism. Even the United Nations Protocol on Civil and Political Rights of 1966 has not matured into a meaningful form or court for the adjudication of rights.

Curiously, however, an important development from 1945-1947 was a mirror image of an international law centered in the individual. Holding the Nazi, Fascist, and Japanese war leaders individually accountable for crimes against humanity was a major development in international law. The Nuremburg trials were the world's first attempt at an international level to establish individual responsibility for aggressive acts of war and for violation of treaties designed to protect conquered peoples, such as the

Hague Convention of 1899, the Geneva Convention of 1907, the Kellogg-Briand Peace Pact of 1927, and other international agreements. Beyond law, a presumptive world human rights standard was set forth, which the Fascist leaders had transgressed; for that, they were deemed liable. Hence, a precedent was established to hold individuals responsible for war crimes, in contrast to the 1919 Versailles Treaty's stance that Germany *as a nation* was guilty of aggressive acts of war.[10]

As I have noted, there has been significant growth of democracy and the rule of law since 1945. The three Axis powers—Germany, Italy, and Japan—were forced to forswear totalitarianism, and each adopted a strong democratic system of government patterned after the Anglo-American, Scandinavian, and Western European models. Now, over forty-five years later, the notions of democratic pluralism, human rights, and the rule of law form the basic fabric of these countries. And it is because of this extraordinary development—over a period of forty years, not six centuries—that democracy and law are now proclaimed in much of the world as the accepted standards for political systems.

A significant development in human rights law can be seen in the European Convention of Human Rights and Fundamental Freedoms and the European Court of Human Rights created by that convention. The signatories now comprise twenty-one nations, which have agreed to accept the jurisdiction of the court's human rights judgments in their domestic law. The convention, adopted in 1952 and entered into force in 1961, made a significant change in the concept of standing in international law by endowing the individual citizens of a member nation the "right" to have a legal judgment made by the European Court in a dispute with his or her own government. The individual must exhaust national remedies before approaching the court in Strasbourg. But if the court, applying the list of rights contained in the 1952 convention, finds for the individual, then each member nation has agreed to accept that judgment. This is a magnum jump in the evolution of international law, and by 1992, after some 400 or 500 cases, it was clear that the system works.[11] A similar court, sitting in Luxembourg, was established under the twelve-nation European Community. It considers economic, labor, finance, and market issues that concern the EC, headquartered in Brussels.

Without being too chauvinistic, it is possible to say that Western European democracies and the rule of law under which they are now functioning are the outgrowth of the early Anglo-American experience. The task of political science has always been to attempt to understand power and the institutions that try to control the exercise of power: Terms of office, periodic franchise, pluralist politics, and due process under law are among the most important of these. In every society, throughout history, political and religious powers have almost always been sought by those who gravitate toward forms of control for whatever reasons. And the individuals in any society are affected by the ways in which those powers are exercised, all too often without having any voice in controlling power themselves. Mystery, magic, and authority formed the basis of community in Sumeria, Egypt, India, China, and Babylonia. Not even in the brief experience of the Greeks in the fourth and third centuries BCE and, somewhat later, of the Romans under the law of *jus gentium* has there been "freedom" in the sense in which it is used in the late twentieth century, and certainly, no agreed upon mechanism has existed for controlling political and other forms of power.[12] It is the late twentieth-century experience of the English-speaking nations and of Western Europe that motivates the current insistence on democracy and human rights for the emerging nations of Eastern Europe. It also stimulates the continuing activities of the Human Rights Center of the United Nations and the Inter-American Treaty statements about human rights, and it plays a central role in congressional concerns about the foreign policy of the United States. In short, it is only now at the end of the twentieth century, that democracy, human rights, and the rule of law seem to dominate public discourse.

III

Or does it only seem so? If human rights are at the top of the international agenda for much of the world, why are they in jeopardy? Amnesty International, which won the Nobel Peace Prize in 1977, continues to document worldwide cases of torture and repression and to work for the relief of individuals caught in lawless situations. The roster of persons engaged in Amnesty activities is impressive. London-based Index on Censorship documents, country by country, egregious examples of press and speech censorship. Human Rights Watch and its regional watch committees (America's Watch, Asia Watch, Middle East Watch, Helsinki Watch, and Africa Watch) continue a daily monitoring of human rights abuses and actions of governments that violate rights, and Article 19 in London is concerned with censorship worldwide. Many countries now have human rights groups struggling to create an environment in which rights might come alive and flourish. There is a growing interest in sharing information about the protection of privacy, particularly in an electronic era that promises to revolutionize the handling and manipulation of information.[13] All these groups and movements and many more like them monitor and publicize derogations of rights not only in those countries that are only partial democracies or those with no pluralist tradition at all but also in the so-called Western democracies that usually stand at the forefront of human rights concerns. Because of the changes in the former USSR and Eastern Europe, there is (at least, as of 1992) no longer a need for clandestine rights groups intent on realizing the human rights provisions these governments agreed to via treaties or their own constitutions. A classic case involved the so-called Basket Three rights incorporated in the Helsinki Accords signed by thirty-five nations in 1975. Frequently, citizen pursuing these rights were abused and jailed and, as individuals, became symbolic figures in their own countries and around the world for the protection of rights. Notable among them were Adam Michnik, Vaclav Havel, members of the Czechoslovakian group known as Charter 77, and Andrei Sakharov of the Soviet Union. Sakharov, for many years the most famous scientist working for human rights, was sent into exile for his efforts, despite having received the Nobel Peace Prize. But in his case, as in that of so many others, the political wheel turned, and he became a national and world hero. Obviously, a signature on parchment (the Helsinki Accords in 1975), a vote for a human rights agenda (the UN protocol in 1966), and an acceptance in theory of human rights as a universal principle (the UN declaration of 1948) do not guarantee the operational reality of human rights.

Does this mean, therefore, that without constitutional, pluralist democracy and the rule of law, there can be no effective protection for human rights? The response to this question is complex. And if there is to be a future for global human rights, the nature of the political complexity involved must be clearly understood.

So far, my history and examples have concerned the essentially Western European and former British colonial nations in which English legal history and the doctrines of the Enlightenment have been central to political growth. After all, that is where the concern for human rights originated. But what of the larger world of Asia and Africa that has been barely, if at all, touched by Western influences, and, more importantly, that has religious and political traditions older and more time tested than English law, (with merely 800 years of history) or the traditions of the 250 years of the Enlightenment? China and, until 1945, Japan have had high cultures that have not depended on a calculated doctrine of individualism. Forms of law have been consistent with the prevailing systems of government and quite unlike the Anglo-American law or the European civil law set forth by Justinian in the sixth century CE. The notion of political rights like free speech, a doctrine of privacy, the sanctity of the home, or speedy trial—those so common in any twentieth-century listing of human rights—had no analog in China and Japan.[14]

In the Asian subcontinent of Malay, India, and Indonesia, the political and social structures were also historically different. But all that changed in these areas and in Western Asia, first with the emergence of Islam and then with the coming of British colonialism.

Islam is, by far, the stronger of the two "systems," with over, 1,350 years of history. It is a highly developed religious/political doctrine emanating from the Koran, the Hadith Reports, and the teachings of Mohammed. The body of doctrine and subsequent legal writings by Islamic scholars compose Shari'a Law, the basic religious and political/legal foundation for all of Islam.

In Islam, the individual is not the center of the universe; rather, he or she is to be governed by the word of Allah as presented in the Koran and Shari'a Law. Hence, the notion of individualistic human rights does not exist in Islamic political theory. From the end of the seventh century CE to the end of World War I, much of Western Asia and North Africa was under the dominion of various Muslim caliphates and, after 1453, under the Ottoman Empire, which continued to administer Shari'a Law in those vast domains. In India's many states and under its occasional empires, a Hindu/Muslim society existed in which each group could seek its own reality under local monarchs of one persuasion or the other, although Muslim states predominated in the Indian subcontinent.[15]

The other significant legal development came in the eighteenth and, nineteenth centuries, late in the histories of Asia and Africa: English settlers' use of rudiments of their common law and practice in considerable areas of both continents. In India and Sri Lanka, in part of the Malay, in Kenya, Zimbabwe, and South Africa, this slow growth of English legal institutions helped set the stage for some evolution of rights and common-law procedural juristic practices. The well-known story of Mohandas Gandhi—who was educated in the law in England, lived and practiced law in South Africa, but personally held in second-class status because he was Indian—illustrates the difficulties (at least in the early twentieth century) of attempting to live and work by one legal standard in a social and political setting that had scant regard for the rights of another.

The English practices evolved in many and varied circumstances. By and large, this process was an overlay of English concepts on Hindu, Muslim, and clan traditions, most of which were stronger than the common law and its derivatives. These traditions remain strong today. The imposition of English practices were, in part, upheld by the pressure of the English overlords, in company with the army and navy and the ever-stronger commercial grip of the East India Company and, later, the abundance of English owners and traders. Islam, by contrast, relied on myth, mystery, and authority, historical methods of control over populations. Of course, Islam gained its dominance by warfare during the century after Mohammed's death, but once the territories and people were subject to Muslim rule, the religious authority of the occupying caliphs became the law. While Britain allowed proselytizing, it did not use religious myth as a method of control but relied on trade and the army instead. And unlike the Spanish in South America, the British did not attempt to impose Christianity on the Indian population. This is not to say that the British experience did not have an impact—indeed, it did. In fact, the entire subcontinent of India and Sri Lanka today has parliamentary and pluralist democracies freely adopted when the British voluntarily left in the middle of the twentieth century. While uneasy tension continues in Pakistan between the secular and Islamic fundamentalist forces, India is frequently cited as the world's largest democracy, with its population approaching one billion people.

South America has had a wholly different political history. The millennia-old populations of Aztec, Maya, and Inca populations lived under autocratic regimes and religious symbols and powers not unlike those of ancient Egypt, Sumeria, and Babylonia. Again, mystery, myth, and authority were the controlling factors, but all of this would be altered dramatically in the sixteenth and seventeenth centuries by Spanish conquest from Mexico to Tierra del Fuego. This meant the imposition of both Catholic Christianity on this vast subject population and Spanish legal doctrines, primarily about religion but also covering property and individual "rights."[16] The resulting mixture of ancient and Christian religions and symbols of power made for an uneasy truce in South America for over 250 years, until the nineteenth-century revolutions against Spanish imperialism and the emergence of the present national entities.[17] The political and legal systems that evolved in these nations were not based on any concept of individualism or of pluralist democracy, but these ideas did develop in the twentieth century, particularly after World War II and the growing world emphasis on law-based democracy. But even that is a sometime thing.[18]

The present (1992) nations of Eastern Europe offer a quite different history. When the Roman Empire was at its zenith in northern and eastern Europe, it butted up against tribal populations about which little was known. Over the centuries, the movements of northern and eastern European people and the shifting of political authorities resulted in the evolution of generally stable societies that, by the end of the eighteenth century, had long since converted to Christianity—in either its Roman or Byzantine form—and had adopted parts of the civil law. Subsequently, Sweden, Poland, and Russia were nation-states ruled by monarchs who, though they professed Christian beliefs, did not promote any political/legal systems of a democratic character. Some civil law traditions took hold in these states, as they did in the central European Austro-Hungarian Empire and in what was called the Holy Roman Empire. But all of these people were governed by autocratic, landowning, and domineering autocracies adhering to the Christian faiths as declared by the recognized powers of the Roman-dominated clergy. In parts of eastern Europe, the

Eastern Orthodox religion was the ruling belief system, and in most of
Europe before the French Revolution, it and Roman Catholicism worked
hand-in-hand with political leadership to retain the faith and obedience of
the people vis-à-vis the religious doctrine and the dominant autocracy,
however changing that may have been from generation to generation.
(This was yet another example of myth, mystery, and authority.) In none
of this was there any ground in which what we now call Western notions
of rights might take root.

A similar evolution took place in Asiatic and European Russia. Dominated by the Orthodox church and the ancient political units, the various
ethnic groups came under the control of Russia and the Romanov dynasty. Over the seventeenth and eighteenth centuries, imperial Russia expanded eastward to the Northern Pacific, overrunning ancient tribes and
national entities that had their own belief systems or that had adopted
Islam. The resulting Greater Russia was therefore a vast land mass encompassing a diverse group of people all in some measure governed spiritually by Islam or the Orthodox church and politically by the imperial
army and, in the nineteenth century, the Romanov secret police, the
Okhrana. After the 1917 revolution, Russia continued under new management and with a wholly new belief system that brooked no deviation
from its rigid tenets and practices. Even within that system, both Islam
and Christianity continued underground although they were not, of
course, sanctioned. Free religious practice as well as free expression in
other matters did not exist. It is commonplace and true to say that Russian
communism accommodated no recognition of Western ideas of pluralism
or rights. Even the old czarist secret police evolved into the Cheka under
the Bolshevik government (with many of the same officials), then the
NKVD, and, since the 1940s, the KGB, merely updating the same techniques of social and political control exercised under the czars. This
development illustrates an important political lesson: Once a secret police
and investigative system is in place in any nation, it is virtually impossible
to get rid of it. Power seekers, democratic or otherwise, seem fatally
attracted to secrecy (section VI). For seventy years and forty years, respectively, Russia and Eastern Europe had no rights tradition, even though the
Soviet Union and some of the Eastern European nations participated in
UN-sponsored human rights initiatives and all become signatories of the
Helsinki Final Act in 1975, with its well-known Basket Three of some
human rights.

However, the Helsinki meeting created the Commission on Security
and Cooperation in Europe, which, after the breakup of the totalitarian
system in Eastern Europe and Russia in 1989, continued to meet. In 1990
in Paris, the contents of Basket Three were confirmed. The new (1990)
charter was signed by the original thirty-five nations, and its provisions

commit the member nations to accept, among other things, several rights-related ethics:

We affirm that, without discrimination, every individual has the right to:

Freedom of thought, conscience, and religion or belief
Freedom of Expression
Freedom of Association and Peaceable Assembly
Freedom of Movement.

No one will be:

Subject to arbitrary arrest or detention,
Subject to torture or other cruel, inhuman, or degrading treatment,

Everyone also has the right:

To act upon his rights,
To participate in free and fair elections,
To fair and public trial if charged with an offense.

The charter also lists additional economic and social rights to which the participating nations have agreed. These rights, agreed to in Paris, are now held to be essential for developing a pluralist democratic tradition and, with all the other protocols, are now dominant in world political activities.

In coming to accept democracy as the governing politics of their nations, each of the Eastern European and former Soviet republics explicitly recognize that for the new system to work, there must be a commitment by citizens to the rites and rituals of democracy. This includes making distinctions within society between what is good and what is not, what government should do and what it should be prohibited from doing, and how an individual should be free to live his or her life. That means, therefore, a commitment to free assembly, free expression, and freedom from arbitrary power. When those conditions are met, diverse centers of politics evolve that compete for citizens' support. Such a plurality of actors, each able to exercise singly or in groups their freedom of expression and movement, amounts to pluralist democracy. Representation in a legislature is one of the consequences of a democratic and noncoerced franchise. When these principles are incorporated into a system of enforceable law, then a law-based pluralist democracy exists. But it takes all of these elements for such a system to evolve and work. And it takes both restraint by those who lead *and* practice on the part of citizens. Pluralist democracy is erratic, at best, even in societies with a long tradition of

freedom; in new democracies, a tendency toward impatience is understandable but must be resisted. The habits of democracy must be
learned—perhaps the most important quality in a nation's evolving drive
for human rights.[19]

IV

Much of the world's population in 1950 lived in political systems that
did not recognize the basic Western doctrine of rights inhering by natural
law in individuals. This is what Jefferson inscribed for the world to see in
the U.S. Declaration of Independence—namely, the inalienability of rights
to life, liberty, and the pursuit of happiness. If one accepts that individuals
have rights that antedate political society and exist even against political
society, rights that inhere and are not entitlements or privileges, then one
has to agree that a legal/political structure must exist to guarantee those
inalienable rights. But individuals live within communities, and the tension between the citizen and the community establishes a dialectic that is
not easily resolved. In a freewheeling society like the United States, un-
constrained by any history of domineering religious institutions or any
rigid political or economic ideology, a sense of community revolves
around adherence to the Constitution, which embodies the Bill of Rights.
In a nation endowed with vast natural resources and a thriving agriculture, the constraints on the citizens are far fewer than in less well-
endowed societies in geographic regions with much scarcer resources;
such are the societies that comprise the overwhelming masses of mankind. Nonetheless, even in the United States, there is some concern that
certain communitarian values need to be articulated and supported and
that this may call for the restraint of certain freedoms. Some think speech
that harms groups of citizens (such as women and racial minorities)
should be muted. Clearly, a more harmonious republic would result from
such constraint. But if a communitarian ethic of this type is to be established, who would implement the necessary restraint on speech and
against what standards? Can such a standard evolve without governmental or other coercion?

In the United States, the choices are different from those in societies less
well situated or with traditions that seem antithetical to the full range of
freedoms. In the United Kingdom, there is complete freedom of religion
despite the fact that religious instruction is required in all schools—and
this in a society in which the head of state is also the head of the established church. This seems to be an anomaly.

At the other extreme, to what extent can freedoms of speech and
religion be made compatible with official systems of ideology or religion
that do not recognize individualism, such as those in China and societies
with fundamentalist Islamic governments? Between Islamic republics and

the United States, there are many states whose sense of community creates some dialectical tension and other states with an ever-changing authoritarian bent, at times benign and at other times brutally authoritarian (as in parts of Latin America, Asia, and Africa). Stanley Hoffman directly addressed this issue by warning against sliding into vulgar relativism. He agreed with Herbert Kelman that to excuse infractions of internationally accepted human rights would "erode the moral force of transnational efforts to promote human dignity."[20] Perhaps it is the search for dignity that can be an accepted standard, but any *coerced* action to support the search for dignity would be antithetical to the main principles of evolving human rights. Freedom of belief and expression are not inherently opposed to communitarian values—it is how the two are reconciled that will always be at issue. One of the tasks is to assure a measure of civility or community compatible with individualism. It is my belief that the development of standards of decency and civility requires the efforts of many elements within a community, not just the legal system. The law can be used to enhance individual rights: It cannot coerce sense of dignity or taste.

So-called democratic constitutions must, in some fashion, provide the procedural and juridical mechanism to make rights real. A constitution like that of the United States is quite explicit about rights, and, by virtue of an independent judiciary, it provides neutral tribunals to consider differences between an individual or groups and the state. The United Kingdom, which has no written constitution, has seen a legally sanctioned independent judiciary evolve since the early eighteenth century, as well as a strong tradition of rights similar to those in the U.S. Constitution and the European Covenant on Human Rights and Fundamental Freedoms, which Britain has joined. Other Western nations have moved to adapt their systems to the prevailing paradigm, as has Japan. The big question is whether the rest of the world, probably comprising three-fifths of the global population, will do the same. It may be an overstatement to assert in the 1990s that the nations of the world are moving inexorably toward a law-based set of rights for their people. To restate the question asked earlier, does the Western message mean that without a law-based rights system accompanied by a pluralist system, there can be no expansion of human rights as understood in the West and as internationally proclaimed in the UN declaration or in the 1966 UN protocol? The answer is probably yes.

V

Throughout this chapter, I have used two terms, most frequently together: *law* (or *law-based rights*) and *pluralist democracy*. To this point, I have stressed the importance of law as a determinant of the reality of human rights. But in any political system, a legal establishment of lawyers, jurisprudence, and a judiciary does not exist in isolation, nor did it emerge suddenly. Rights were not granted by a munificent priest or king—in fact, the granting of rights is an oxymoron if one accepts the Jeffersonian formulations. *The fact is that citizens fought to ensure that their rights would be recognized.* The evolution of rights in the English system took centuries. Perhaps this began with jury trial and subsequently encompassed the right to choose one's representatives in a parliament or even to arrive at some understanding of the felicitous phrase the barons had wrung from King John—the *law of the land*, known in later generations as the rule of law or, in the jurisprudence of the United States, as the due process of law. What *did* happen over time was a continuing *political* struggle on each issue leading to a rights-based law. Certainly, the barons confronting King John were early political actors seeking satisfaction of their demands. Even though it was wrung by the threat of force, the Great Charter survived and is now counted as one of the world's great and noble documents. But that had to be followed by other action. England was fortunate in that after the Norman Conquest in 1066, much attention was paid to the law, and both royal courts and the common law deeply concerned both jurists and legal commentators who had great influence on subsequent generations—men like Ranulf de Glanville, Henry Bracton, and Fleta, the unknown author of a treatise by that name, written around 1290. After the Protestant Revolution under Henry VIII came a slow and tortuous growth of the law, and by the early seventeenth century, such a magisterial figure as Sir Edward Coke could galvanize Parliament to stand against royal pretensions to authority by voting for the Petition of Right in 1628. In the 1640s, men like John Lilburne, (who was in and out of jail), insisted on the right not to be required to incriminate themselves.[21] In the same period, John Milton wrote eloquently about freedom of the press, and by 1688, all of Parliament insisted on legally binding limits on royal power.

Among all these great events, untold numbers of people attempted to assert rights—some successfully, some notably and mortally unsuccessfully. But to the extent that Parliament allowed, a more open political/ legal system did evolve, however slowly and hesitantly. It featured a recognizable party system of government, a plurality of groups seeking voice in English life, and a dissenting religious tradition. By the time John Wilkes, an independent publisher jailed for allegedly libeling King George III (in 1763), finished his litigious career, he and his thousands of supporters had laid the basis for a free press and for the right of the people to send to Parliament persons of their own choosing.

Politics in the broadest sense was making it possible for citizens to argue and "lobby" for recognition of rights. The American colonists became the eighteenth century's prototypes of a citizenry using the free press and the protections of the common law to agitate for rights and eventually to proclaim independence as free and equal states under law. Agitation, speaking, petitioning, lobbying, and writing—the tools of democracy—came alive in the eighteenth century. Their analogs today are radio and television (although there is a major qualitative difference, I believe). The French Revolution had its own political and philosophical background and was equally political, yet, for other reasons, the Declaration of the Rights of Man had a different career, in considerable measure because the mechanisms of democracy did not exist in France as they had in England. It took two Napoleonic empires before France could organize itself in 1871 to give some meaning to its declaration.

In the century and a half after 1789, democracy had a checkered career: partial free press in central and eastern Europe; parliamentary elections in some European nations (which were annulled on occasion); fitful acknowledgment of democratic forces in Latin America); colonial empires emerging in sub-Saharan Africa; and Japan and China isolated from much of the world, especially Japan, with extraterritorial jurisdictions forced on China by the western European powers. The development of democracy took a major turn after 1945, and, as I noted, at the time of the adoption of the Declaration of Human Rights in 1948, the West assumed that the world could and would become progressively more democratic and law-centered, a harbinger for a vigorous human rights movement globally.

However, if there is no rights law, how then do citizens assert their political rights, and how can they be helped to do so? Can a nation or group of nations interfere in the internal affairs of a country whose system, tradition, ideology, or authoritarian structures do not support human rights? In one sense, these questions have been answered. The 1948 declaration set a human rights standard, subsequent protocols further that standard, and in the last two decades of the twentieth century, diplomatic recognition and trade in many democratic governments are, in part, contingent on some form of adherence to democracy and human rights. The twenty-five year-long condemnation of South Africa is probably the most well-known and widely subscribed to diplomatic initiative. But governments and international organizations are not the only actors. Nongovernmental organizations devoted to human rights become the necessary instruments to work for progress in that sphere.

In 1966, the United Nations sponsored two important protocols, one on political and civil rights and a second on social rights. On the non-governmental level in the 1970s, international watch groups were being formed; the 1975 Helsinki Accord provided the backdrop for political agitation for rights in Central and Eastern Europe and in the Soviet Union; and the United States created the first subcabinet-level post in its State

Department explicitly concerned with civil rights. Index on Censorship and Amnesty International began systematic documentation of human rights abuses, country by country, and organizations in many nations, such as the Tunisian League for Human Rights, the Egyptian Human Rights League, and, in the United States, the U.S. Physicians for Human Rights, work assiduously to document and help to ameliorate human rights abuses. Through some osmotic process, a human rights standard became, in the final two decades of this century, a central ingredient in the world's foreign policies. And the Nobel Peace Prize has frequently been awarded to individuals and groups who are prominent international spokespeople for human rights. Among these are Amnesty International, Andrei Sakharov, Lech Walesa, Daw Aung San Suu Kye, and Martin Luther King, Jr.

By 1990, the Islamic world was torn between a fundamentalist and rigid move to adhere strictly to Koranic law and reject Western belief systems and a modern push for Islamic nations to become engaged with the West and the United Nations. Middle East historian Bernard Lewis described the matter as follows:

> By a sad paradox the adulation in the nineteenth and twentieth centuries of democratic constitutions guaranteeing equal rights for all citizens, in the Ottoman Empire, in Iran, Egypt, and elsewhere, on the whole weakened rather than strengthened the position of minorities. On the one hand it deprived them of the limited but substantial and well-grounded rights and privileges which they enjoyed under Islamic dispensation. On the other, it failed to make good the new rights and freedoms offered to them by the newly enacted constitutions which, in this as in many other respects, proved a dead letter.

Lewis went on to note:

> From the beginning, that is to say from the first impact of these ideas (Renaissance, Reformation, Enlightenment, French Revolution) at the end of the eighteenth century, there were few who saw that they could threaten not only Christianity, which did not concern them, but also Islam, and who, seeing this, gave warning. For a long time they had little influence. The small minority who were at all aware of European ideas were, for the most part, profoundly attracted to them. Among the vast majority, the challenge of Western secular ideas was not so much opposed as ignored. It is only in comparatively recent times that Muslim religious thinkers of stature have looked at secularism, understood its threat to what they regard as the highest values of religion, and responded with a decisive rejection.[22]

And it is fundamentalist Iran that issued to the Islamic world a death sentence on Salman Rushdie for his novel *Satanic Verses*, which Muslim leaders found offensive and blasphemous. A reward has been announced for Rushdie's death—a reward potentially sought by hundreds of millions of people against a single man exercising his rights to free press and speech—and ironically issued by a nation whose 1948 government voted for the UN Declaration of Human Rights.

It is difficult to deny that a growing interest in a human rights standard will increase. But such a standard must be accompanied by more than conventions and protocols. The acceptance of the position that rights inhere in the individual and should be protected by law and are not privileges must be accompanied by a communal sense of dignity.

To the extent that there is an expert on these matters, Vaclav Havel is the most experienced and vocal. Not only was he jailed several times for attempting to exercise his freedom in Czechoslovakia but, when his nation underwent its Velvet Revolution for freedom (largely at his urging), he became the Czech president, hoping to heal the wounds of forty years of tyranny and to press a sense of humanity and civility on his fellow countrymen, who were prone to be vindictive against those who had betrayed their rights in the past. Unable to hold his country together, Havel lost the support of his parliament and was forced to relinquish his post as president of a federal republic. Speaking at the World Economic Forum in Davos, Switzerland, in early 1992, Havel said:

> We must try harder to understand than to explain. The way forward is not in the mere construction of universal systemic solutions, to be applied to reality from outside, it is also in seeking to get to the heart of reality through personal experience. Such an approach promotes an atmosphere of tolerant solidarity and unity in diversity based on mutual respect, genuine pluralism and parallelism. In a word, human uniqueness, human action, and the human spirit must be rehabilitated.

> Sooner or later politics will be faced with the task of finding a new, postmodern face. A politician must become a person again, someone who trusts not only a scientific representation and analysis of the world, but also the world itself. He must believe not only in sociological statistics, but also in real people. He must trust not only his own soul; not only an ideology, but also his own thoughts; not only the summary reports he receives each morning, but also his own feeling.[23]

Law-based democracy requires just the qualities Havel has worked for as political agitator, playwright, and national leader. The spirit of rights is crucial to implementation of the law. A people must want to create an environment within which human dignity and capacity for free expression and free movement are guaranteed.

In one sense, the technologically based information systems now available globally do, in fact, make the world a global village, to the extent of transmitting images and facts. But the transmittal of human values is something else again. Satellite TV transmissions, computers, fax machines, and radio combine to make the people of the world capable of knowing what is happening and able to respond. Pluralist politics is being played with many actors, fulfilling one of the aspirations of democratically inclined nations and peoples. The more that is known, so this political theory holds, the healthier will be people's responses to events—in their own nation and elsewhere. This sort of politics is successful where governments allow it to be practiced and to the extent that governments are weary of being badgered on their human rights records. After all, it took 500 to 600 years for the political system in England to develop the prerequisites for law-based government. Why should it take less time for nations to evolve a law-based politics that would have the same beneficent human rights results?

VI

A major variable to the full exercise of human rights is a nation's sense of security, most frequently meaning what is called national security but also trade security and, increasingly, resource security. In defense of interests and borders, governments implement policies designed to limit or prohibit migrations of individuals and groups of citizens. For example, while there was free movement across national boundaries in Europe prior to 1914, the introduction of passport on a large scale put a stop to such movement. But that was a small matter when compared to the prohibition of migration for hundreds of thousands of Jews wishing to flee the Soviet Union after World War II. And legislation in the United States—keeper of the flame with its Bill of Rights—prohibited the immigration, even for short visits, of people who had an affiliation with Communist groups; in essence, this was a limitation on political speech for those denied visas and for those in the United States who wanted to talk to such people.

The existence of a so-called national security issue is recognized even in treaties written to expand human rights. The European Convention on Human Rights noted in Article 10, paragraph 2, that the charter's freedoms "may be subject to such formalities, conditions, restrictions, or penalties as are prescribed by law and are necessary in a democratic society, in the interests of *national security.*" In the 1966 International Covenant on Civil and Political Rights, adopted by the General Assembly and ratified in 1992 by ninety-two nations, Article 12 stipulated that "the above-mentioned rights shall not be subject to any restrictions except those which are provided by law, and necessary to protect *national security.*" (In both quotations, the emphases are mine.)

The national security standard is, of course, nation-specific, whereas human rights are thought to be global-specific. The instances when and where a nation invokes national security are many and varied. What these provisions imply is that the undersigned nation subscribes to an international human rights standard—except for reasons sufficient to itself. In the name of national security, it may decline to follow that standard. It should not be a surprise, although it is undoubtedly regrettable, that this should be so in a world of nation-states. For those who search for a more serene global standard, the national security rationale does not ring true.

In addition to these caveats in international treaties, there are the ever-present national intelligence agencies whose concerns run from high-technology spying to gathering information about people exercising some aspect of supposedly protected freedoms. In sixteenth-century England, for example, Queen Elizabeth's officials had a most remarkable espionage network targeting Catholics in a Protestant society. This was only one of the many "intelligence" functions carried out in secret and reporting to the highest authorities. Looking for heretics from officially sanctioned ideology is very old hat, indeed. One hesitates to mention the Holy Catholic church inquisitions in Europe in the Middle Ages for fear of sounding trite. More recent organizations include the Okhrana in Czarist Russia, the Mossad and Shin Bet in Israel, the Savak in Iran, the KMT in Taiwan, and the FBI and CIA in the United States. The existence of such intelligence agencies has historically chilled, if not prohibited, free speech and the free exercise of religion, and in modern democratic societies, they have often created a chilling environment in which citizens have been loath to fully exercise their guaranteed rights. In fundamentalist societies, as in China or in much of Islam, the same sorts of institutions exist to guarantee loyalty to the power structure. Thus, the intelligence agency is the instrument most frequently created and turned to in efforts to protect "national security." In a democracy, the control of such agencies in the interest of freedom becomes one of the most important of tasks. In non-democratic nations where there is no a spirit of openness, the opportunity to control the "thought police" is that much more difficult to realize.

The search for "national security" through such instruments creates a system of secrecy in government that is distinctly antithetical to democratic government and to citizen's effort to acquire the knowledge needed for forming a political view. Without information, the citizens' right to free expression becomes devalued. In the United States, James Madison, the father of the U.S. Constitution and the principal author of the Bill of Rights, aptly remarked that "a popular government without popular information, or the means of acquiring it, is but a Prologue to a Farce or a

Tragedy; or perhaps both. Knowledge will forever govern ignorance: And a people who mean to be their own governors, must arm themselves with the power which knowledge gives."[24]

The triad of national security, secrecy, and intelligence, when invoked by any government, can nullify expressive freedoms. It is this triad that can and does stand in the way of the full exercise of human rights. Indeed, I believe that the first obstacle to a healthy rights tradition is the obsession of those in power for *control*. This obsession is independent of governmental systems. It is defeated, however, when the practice of democratic politics and adherence to law prove too strong for the strongman, for the "democrat" who wants to rule by plebiscite, or for the bully who would destroy democracy and the law for personal satisfaction and for power and control.

At the same time, in many nations a university or university system has evolved that, by the very nature of education, embodies many attributes so essential for democracy—high literacy; a search for truths in the natural and social sciences; an acknowledgment of complexity; a willingness to investigate, to weigh evidence, and to test hypotheses; and a strong sense of history. When these universities have had a semblance of freedom, they have frequently provided the student shock troops to work for and to fight (often literally) for democracy and rights. Beijing University was the source of the democracy movement so brutally crushed in 1989. University students in Thailand have frequently had to take to the streets, as have students in Korea and as students in the United States and many other countries certainly did over the conflict in Vietnam. Why but for fear of what the university might project did Israel close the colleges in the occupied West Bank? The free university is a blessing in any nation, particularly as a countervailing center of power against injustice, the arbitrary exercise of power, and the denial of democratic rights. The purpose of the university is education and not the accumulation of power or political agency, but the essential attributes of the university are the very reasons its students and faculty act as a conscience for the society.

VII

Three centers—the Western democratic states (mainly those in Western Europe), the English-speaking community, and Japan—have now assumed responsibility for furthering democracy and human rights in the world. They have made clear their determination to stand by their national and community policies and insist on measures of democratic representation and law-based rights for themselves and in their dealings with other nations. Individual national policies vary, however, sometimes insisting on national rights in favor of dealings with other nations and sometimes muting the insistence on human rights in favor of some other objective—as exemplified by the U.S. trade policy toward China and the West's pusillanimous dealings with much of the Arab world for, among other things, oil. Ultimately, individual national policies may come and go, and the natural supply of oil will vanish, but world citizens and their pursuit of rights will continue, just as the individual existed for many millennia before world trade, rigid ideologies, oil, or other modern factors came into being. Nonetheless, it is to the examples and policies of the Western democracies that nascent human rights groups turn for guidance and assistance.

A second source of support is the multitude of nongovernmental rights groups around the world, aided and abetted by the private rights groups in the United States and Western Europe. Human Rights Watch in New York City is one of the most significant, with its regional watch groups. Such groups have many tools at their disposal, including fact-finding, publicity, litigation when the legal system permits, and direct involvement with government policymakers. To the extent that their research and formulations of rights positions are credible, such organizations have access to government and business leaders. They write, they speak, they organize arts and film festivals to benefit rights causes, and they make themselves visible. They cannot sail into a nuclear test zone as Greenpeace can, but their fleet, though not waterborne, is powerful and composed of policies, facts, and peaceful agitation.

A strong network of rights groups has emerged around the globe, attracting academics, lawyers, physicians, business people, and citizens of all kinds. Many of these individuals are active in their domestic parliaments or universities, and they serve as nongovernmental observers to the varied regional and UN activities centered on human rights. The 1993 United Nations Conference on Human Rights will demonstrate the numbers and resources of these groups.

The third and definitely not the least of the centers for human rights advocacy is the United Nations itself. From the outset in 1946, the UN has been considered the world's spokesgroup for human rights, particularly since the General Assembly adopted the Universal Declaration in 1948. The Human Rights Commission has, over the past forty-six years, continued monitoring human rights and, in recent years, has grown evermore active. At the forty-seventh session of the commission in early 1991, 43 member nations attended as did more than 130 nongovernmental "consulting" associations, ranging from Planetary Citizens, International Federation of Newspaper Publishers, Friends of the Earth International, Disabled Peoples International, World Muslim Congress, Amnesty International, and many world religious groups.

The agendas for meetings like that are long and varied, covering the general furtherance of human rights as well as specific topics; "the right to development," the "human rights and dignity of migrant workers," and "rights of the child" were among the twenty-seven issues considered at the 1991 UN sessions. This range of issues and the many groups attending the session further attest to the role the United Nations plays as the world's forum. Among the decisions made at that meeting were recommendations for a study on human rights and the environment and a decision to send the commission's special rapporteur as an observer to the preparatory meetings for the 1992 Brazil United Nations Conference on Environment and Development.

The commission and the individual organizations that serve as consultants to it have long since begun to take a global view by urging that rights and human dignity, as envisaged in the universal declaration, are now very much tied to the world's environment. Their insistence on the need to protect individuals, their communities, and the fragile ecology suggest the obvious—that humanity is part of a natural community and thrives or suffers along with it. In 1948, the year the universal declaration was promulgated, Fairfield Osborn published *Our Plundered Planet*, and read together, these two works depict a central portion of the globe's agenda at the end of the century.[25]

The Third Committee of the General Assembly has assumed responsibility for the United Nations Human Rights Committee, which concerns itself with the record of activities in light of the 1966 International Covenant on Civil and Political Rights. As of 1991, ninety-two nations had ratified the covenant, making it possible for their citizens to request a hearing on instances of alleged human rights abuse before the Human Rights Committee. (Of all the Western democracies, only the United States had failed to ratify the covenant by 1991; finally, in late spring 1992, it did so, some fifteen years after President Jimmy Carter had submitted the covenant to the U.S. Senate.) In its 1991 report, the Human Rights Committee noted,

> Referring to certain positive developments of the previous year and to the fact that the importance of human rights was receiving greater international recognition, the Under-Secretary-General stressed that, nevertheless, the underlying reality of the era continued to be marked by massive and widespread violations of human rights. The challenge to the international community to promote and ensure respect for human rights was in fact greater than ever. The Center for Human Rights was seeking, within the means at its disposal, to respond to that continuing challenge as energetically as possible. The General Assembly's decision in 1988 to launch World Public Information Campaign on Human Rights had greatly enhanced the practical possibilities in the month and years ahead for collaborating with various United Nations bodies, Member States, and non-governmental or-

ganizations in an effort to reach out to the hundreds of millions of human beings who needed information about fundamental human rights.[26]

At that meeting, recommendations to the Preparatory Committee for the 1993 World Conference on Human Rights were adopted. Among the recommendations for strengthening UN and world concern for human rights was a suggestion that the group create a high commissioner for human rights, an international court of human rights, and a human rights institute. Any or all of these would be significant steps forward, particularly a court if it is fashioned after the European Court of Human Rights, which has, in essence, compulsory jurisdiction in cases brought before it.

Complementing the commission and the Committee on Human Rights is the United Nations Development Programme (UNDP). The 1992 Human Development Report, issued in March of 1992, was both a sobering and a hopeful document. The UNDP has developed two indices to bring some measure of comparative analysis to human development. The Human Development Index in 1992 examined "the links between human development and the environment—between human development and global markets."[27] In its first Human Development Report in 1990, the UNDP defined human development as "a process of enlarging people's choices." The report placed the responsibility for enlarging choices squarely on the individual state, describing this as the "the real challenge at the national level. Each country, developing or under trial, must set its own goals and design its own strategy."[28]

To complement the Human Development Index, the UNDP has now created the Political Freedom and Human Development Index. The 1992 report noted that "democracy and Freedom rely . . . on much more than the ballot box." In urging world consideration of developmental growth and political freedom, the UNDP has developed a checklist of indicators of political freedom: "personal security, Rule of Law, freedom of expression, political participation, and equality of opportunity." (It should come as no surprise that these six points are a 1990s counterpoint to Franklin Roosevelt's four freedoms proclaimed just fifty years earlier.) The report insisted that "the personal freedom index is a reflection of people's lives. The sum-total is human freedom. People know when they are tortured, when they are without a political voice, when they are unable to express views and preferences, when they are discriminated against and when they fear that, if detained, they may be without defense. They know what and how much they have lost." The report also noted that "there are no development institutions managing the new integrated global economy— much less doing so democratically in the interests of the world's people. Democracy may be sweeping through individual nation-states, but it has yet to assume a global economic dimension." The report stated that "visionary blueprints must at least be prepared."[29]

All three of the 1991-1992 reports (Human Rights Commission, Committee on Human Rights, and the Human Development Report) strongly reflect a growing consensus that development, environment, the world economy, and the planet's ecology are intertwined and indivisible. They remain divisible as long as individual governments over time fail to recognize the limitations of the earth's carrying capacity, as well as the limits of sovereign power. The Rio Conference of 1992 clearly demonstrated an awareness of the interconnectedness of these issues. It underscored democracy and freedom of political expression and itself demonstrated ways by which citizens around the globe can participate fully in helping address each and all of the interlocked issues.

The globe's peoples, living in a natural environment shared by all, have created a system of livelihood and governance that is still fractured but that is so clearly an indivisible unit. One is now reminded of the title of Barry Commoner's path-breaking ecological study of 1971, *The Closing Circle.*[30] Everything correlates.

VIII

There are, in my judgment, four issues that will impede movement toward a broader pluralist democracy and respect for human rights globally: unchecked population growth; ethnic, religious, and nationalist xenophobia; the world's fragile ecology; and the baleful results of unrestrained trade in armaments and the heedless industrialism that makes such trade possible. Each of these issues separately and together can present us with terrible choices about our cultures and life-styles. International competition for resources alone can have a severe adverse impact on food availability and on attempts at population control. And should there be a significant shift in the ecological balance of the earth and its atmosphere, there may be a further mad scramble by nations to secure and protect scarce resources. There is mounting evidence that this is already happening in concerns about the ozone layer, the depletion of fish stocks and rain forests, and solid waste management. The list of horrible scenarios is endless, but the reality of these scenarios is real: Just see the agenda of the Earth Summit for Brazil in June 1992. (For an extended discussion of ecological issues, see Chapter 1.)

The "luxury" of having a human rights standard is to be expected in advanced industrial democracies of the world because of current economic stability, flourishing agriculture, and reasonably stable populations. But in the nonindustrialized world, the situation is more often reversed. Poverty in India, hunger in the Saheel, population pressures in China, and war, terrorism, and vast hunger in Somalia all speak of continuing difficulties. The so-called North-South dichotomy is a real one— part economic, part ideological, part ecological. The 1992 Human Development Report noted that "developing countries enter the market as unequal partners and leave with unequal rewards." Furthermore, "In 1960, the richest 20% of the world's population had incomes 30 times greater than the poorest 20%. By 1990, the richest 20% were getting 60 times more. And this comparison is based on the distribution between rich and poor countries, the richest 20% of the world's *people* get at least 150 times more than the poorest 20%."[31] It is crucial to acknowledge these issues while at the same time attempting to move the global system toward a greater human rights standard.

Do human rights have a future globally? The evidence presented here suggests that with sufficient political pressure and an outcry about every known situation—torture, terror, suppression of religious expression, restriction on migration, genocide, and other violations of the several extant human rights protocols—individual nations can be muscled into some agreement. But this will take enormous and continuing political activity and steadfastness on the part of the present world's democracies. The funding of private international rights organizations is a major task, and those concerned nations will have to stand by the NGOs and help expand the existing machinery for human rights concerns. Moreover, each nation will have to fully fund its stipulated contributions to UN activities— supporting the Center for Human Rights, ratifying and implementing treaties, adhering to human rights standard for a nation's diplomacy and trade policies, and issuing a clear, positive statement of adherence to human rights. In any case, it will be a long leap from a *politics* of human rights to a *law* of human rights. The European Convention is, thus far, unique in this process. A similar inter-American effort has never taken hold, and there is no similar effort in Asia or Africa. In the long run, a functioning law of human rights must be governed by a law-based polity. In the short run, over many decades, a vigorous international rights movement must be funded to continue to alleviate human rights abuses and to help more nations move toward recognition of the need for a human rights law. After all, this is what democratic politics is all about.

In his closing address at the Nuremberg trials of the Nazi leaders in 1946, Chief Counsel Robert H. Jackson said, "If you were to say of these men that they are not guilty, it would be as true to say that there has been no war, there are no slain, there has been no crime." Similarly, to say that humankind cannot move toward respect for the freedom and dignity of each person is to say that democracy cannot be realized—that those global citizens not enjoying protection of their inalienable rights face arbitrary autocracy forever, and that, for them, that is the way the world will end—with a whimper.

Notes

1. Samuel P. Huntington, "How Countries Democratize," *Political Science Quarterly*, Winter 1991-1992, p. 579.

2. John G. Ruggie, "Human Rights and the Entire International Community?" *Daedalus* 112, no.4 (Fall 1983).

3. Gordon Craig, "Above the Abyss" (review of Alan Bullock's *Hitler and Stalin: Parallel Lives*), *New York Review of Books* 39, no. 7 (April 9, 1992), 3.

4. The eight abstaining nations were Byelorussia, Czechoslovakia, Poland, Saudi Arabia, South Africa, the Ukraine, the USSR, and Yugoslavia.

5. Catherine S. Menand, "The Revolutionary Moment and the Supreme Judicial Court," *Massachusetts Law Review*, 77 no. 1 (March 1992). Menand showed that even after independence was declared and warfare broke out in Massachusetts, the business of the Supreme Judicial Court went on, and despite revolution, the forms and traditions continued unchanged from British colonial rule into independent statehood for Massachusetts—not the typical revolution discarding the past.

6. John Locke, *Second Treatise on Civil Government*.

7. Peter Gay noted that the "patron saints and pioneers [of the Enlightenment] were British: Bacon, Newton, and Locke" (p. 11); he also referred to "the great preceptors of the Enlightenment—Bacon, Newton, Locke" (p. 135). Peter Gay, *The Enlightenment: An Interpretation—The Age of Paganism*, (New York: Alfred Knopf, 1967).

8. The American historian Bernard Bailyn counted classical influences among the four major sources of political and legal ideas for the American colonists, the others being the common law, religious sermons, and political pamphlets reasserting eighteenth-century ideas. The pamphlets were an important development in the politics of human rights that I will refer to later in this chapter. Bernard Bailyn, *Ideological Origins of the American Revolution*, (Cambridge, Mass.: Harvard Press, 1967).

9. Louis B. Sohn and Thomas Buergenthal, "The Position of the Individual Under International Law," in *Regional Conventions on Protection of Human Rights*, (New York: Bobbs Merrill, 1973).

10. Robert H. Jackson, *The Nuremberg Case as Presented by Robert H. Jackson, Chief Counsel for the United States* (New York: Alfred A. Knopf, 1947).

11. Andre Dzremczewski, "The Domestic Application of ECHO as European Security Law," *International and Comparative Law Review* 30 (January 1981). See J. G. Merrills, *The Development of International Law by the European Court of Human Rights* (Manchester: Manchester University Press, 1990).

12. Herbert J. Muller, *Freedom in The Ancient World* (New York: Harper, 1961).

13. A growing worldwide concern with privacy issues, prompted by the growth of electronic information systems (largely since the 1960s), has spawned

several important journals. In the United States, the most significant is the monthly *Privacy Journal*, edited by Robert Ellis Smith, Providence, R.I.

14. For a comparative comment on the United States and China vis-à-vis community and individual rights, see John K. Fairbank, *The United States and China*, 4th ed. (Cambridge, Mass.: Harvard University Press, 1983).

15. N. J. Earlson, *A History of Islamic Law* (Edinburgh: Edinburgh University Press, 1964). See also Marshall G.S. Hodgson, *The Venture of Islam* (Chicago: University of Chicago Press, 1974).

16. The Dominican friar Bartolome Da Las Casas viewed the Christian slaughter of Indians in person in the middle of the sixteenth century and wrote vigorously against the brutalities he witnessed. His work is powerful because it remains contemporary and was written by the first priest to be ordained in the New World. He wrote *A History of the Indies*, but his most dramatic book is *The Devastation of the Indies*, first published in 1542 and now reissued by Johns Hopkins University Press, Baltimore, Md., 1992.

17. F.S.C. Northrup, *The Meeting of East and West* (New York: MacMillan, 1947), especially Chapters 1 and 2.

18. An amazing analysis of South American rights concepts and experiences is contained in the work of Tom J. Farer. See his "Human Rights and Human Welfare in Latin America", *Daedalus* 112, no. 4. (Fall 1983).

19. The human tragedy of authoritarian behavior in a system committed on paper to rights has often been repeated. A 1992 comment by Mark I. Kogan, a Russian lawyer who survived twelve years in Stalin's gulag, is revealing. "You know, Stalin's constitution was wonderful, on the surface. You could find any sort of rights in it." *New York Times*, May 11, 1992, p. 8. In this interview, Kogan went on to say, "While our old bosses are still running the system, either openly or hidden, and *until people's mentality changes*, there can be no real talk of a law-based state" (emphasis added).

20. Stanley Hoffman, *Duties Beyond Borders* (Syracuse, N.Y.: Syracuse University Press, 1981).

21. Leonard Levy, *The Origins of the Fifth Amendment* (New York: Oxford University Press, 1968). This work won the 1968 Pulitzer Prize.

22. Bernard Lewis, "Muslims, Christians, Jews: The Dream of Coexistence," *New York Review of Books* 29 (March 26, 1992).

23. Vaclav Havel, "The End of the Modern Era," *The New York Times*, March 1, 1992.

24. Gaillard Hunt, ed., *Writings of James Madison* (New York: Putnam's, 1900-1910), 9:103 (letter to W. T. Barry, August 4, 1822). Quoted in Franklyn S. Haiman, *Speech and Law in a Free Society*, (Chicago: University of Chicago Press, 1981), p. 368.

25. Fairfield Osborn, *Our Plundered Planet* (Boston: Little, Brown, 1948).

26. *Report of the Human Rights Committee*, Official Records: Forty-Sixth Session, New York, 1991.

27. *Human Development Report, 1992*, United Nations Development Programme (New York: Oxford University Press, 1992).

28. Ibid.

29. Ibid.

30. Barry S. Commoner, *The Closing Circle* (New York: Alfred A. Knopf, 1971). See also his *Making Peace with the Planet* (New York: Pantheon Books, 1990).

31. *Human Development Report, 1992*, p. 1.

9

The Globalization of Music: Expanding Spheres of Influence

John Joyce

If global history is an incipient field in search of a viable subject matter, surely there can be no more exploitable topic than the unique state of music in the modern world. I refer here, in particular, to a phenomenon of the past hundred years that the ethnomusicologist Bruno Nettl has called "the intensive imposition of Western music and musical thought upon the rest of the world."[1]

The introduction of Western music to other parts of the globe is, in itself, hardly recent: In most post-Columbian colonized regions, it goes back several hundred years—as early as the first half of the sixteenth century with the incursion of the Spanish conquistadors and their attendant missionaries into Mesoamerica and the Andes. What is unique to the past hundred years is the vastly more intensive imposition of Western music abroad. This is a genuinely contemporary phenomenon, beginning about a century ago but accelerating and expanding dramatically after World War II. How has this phenomenon taken shape?

To begin with the present, a record review, entitled "Global Rachmaninoff," crossed my desk. It is a glowing report of S. V. Rachmaninoff's Second Symphony, performed with a Japanese conductor leading a Welsh orchestra. The conductor in question was trained at a Tokyo conservatory and did master classes in Sweden with an Estonian conductor and, later, with another Japanese conductor in Boston. According to the reviewer, the BBC Welsh Symphony Orchestra, a little-known provincial group, has been welded by Mr. Otaka into an absolutely first-rate ensemble. The term *global* has been used increasingly of late to characterize just this kind of phenomenon in the field of European concert music. A century ago, such a juxtaposition of geographically disparate music and musicians would have been unimaginable, and even as recently as the 1950s, it was more than a little unusual.

Until the past generation, the world of European art music was almost entirely Western, that is, bifurcated between Europe and the Americas, especially the United States. By the turn of the present century, the United States possessed a half dozen symphony orchestras as good as the best of Europe. A majority of the personnel of these orchestras were Europeans, as were all of the conductors, without exception. The same was true of the major American opera companies in this period, and following this tradition, it was de rigeur for American composers to hone their craft by finishing their studies in Europe.

By midcentury, with the maturing of American conservatories, the balance shifted. Well over half of the instrumentalists in U.S. symphony and opera orchestras were American born and trained, a new generation of American conductors were taking the helm of the top U.S. orchestras, and American opera singers were increasingly being imported by major European opera houses. The status of American composers, too, had risen, to the point that by the 1960s, their compositions were becoming part of the fixed repertory of European orchestras.

The entry into this close-knit and highly specialized field of music by non-Western musicians was entirely unexpected by most Western concert and opera audiences. Beginning in the 1960s and rapidly accelerating since then, instrumentalists and singers from a remarkable range of non-Western nations joined European and American orchestras and opera companies; many of them were thoroughly trained at Western music schools in their own countries, and others came to the West to perfect their craft. A new generation of non-Western piano and violin virtuosos, opera stars, and conductors have moved into the forefront of what is now a globally international concert scene, jetting not only between European and American cities but to the growing number of non-Western capitals boasting Western orchestras and concert halls. A casual survey of classical recordings of the past ten years offers eloquent testimony to this global development: Japanese conductors leading orchestras in Boston, Berlin, and Melbourne; Israeli conductors in Frankfurt and Arnhem; Hindi conductors in Tel Aviv, Vienna, Los Angeles, and New York; an Egyptian conductor in Toronto; an African-American conductor in Helsinki; a Korean conductor in Gothenburg and Paris; a Mexican Amerindian conductor, in Dallas; Korean and Japanese violinists recording major violin concertos with orchestras in London, Berlin, Leningrad, New York, and Montreal; and a Japanese pianist, trained in Tokyo and Vienna, recording the complete sonatas and concertos of Mozart. To this I can add recent "live" performances: of Palestrina masses by a Polynesian choir in Samoa; a Japanese baritone performing Schubert's song-cycle, "Die Winterreise," on five successive nights to packed theaters in Tokyo; one of Tokyo's six major symphony orchestras playing Strauss waltzes with sobbing Viennese "glides" and luftpausen after upbeats, another doing the cycle of nine Beethoven symphonies, and a third devoting a concert to the works of the American composers Aaron Copland, George Gershwin, and Charles Ives. Perhaps most remarkably, given the radically dissimilar singing methods of the two source cultures, there is the quite recent entry of singers of Asian-Pacific provenance into the bel-canto style of European opera. There are video recordings of a young Japanese coloratura soprano executing, with great virtuosity, the role of the Queen of the Night in *The Magic Flute*; a Chinese lyric soprano singing the role of Mimi in *La Boheme*; a Maori dramatic soprano performing, with an appropriately opulent vocal tone, the role of the Marschallin in *Der Rosenkavalier*. Nor has there been a dearth of non-Western composers working in contemporary Western idioms. Japanese and Korean as well as Greek and Turkish composers have mastered, with effortless facility, such abstract, nationally "neutral" styles as atonality, serialism, and various forms of electronic music.

In this closing decade of the twentieth century, the remarkable embracing of Western classical music by culturally alien societies proceeds apace and would, indeed, appear to be a primary example of the process of globalization in the field of music. And yet, while this striking development is certainly an important aspect of cultural interaction in music, it must be regarded in the first instance as a further expansion of the history of Western music—a unilateral and, therefore, a more superficial manifestation of musical globalization.

To be sure, Nettl's phrase, "imposition of Western music," implies a one-way flow of influence, in which the recipient culture simply adopts, through strict emulation and training, a particular form of Western music. This process was the example in most earlier encounters between European and non-European peoples. In sixteenth-century Mexico and Peru, for example, the Amerindian hosts were soon taught to sing, reportedly with great expertise, the sophisticated Gregorian chants and polyphonic masses and motets of the Spanish Catholic missionaries. An adoption of much the same repertory took place among the Japanese in the late sixteenth century, under the tutelage of Portuguese missionaries.

By the mid-nineteenth century, as Western imperialism approached its greatest range and influence, adoption continued to be the "official" form of musical exchange. By this time, the process had become more intensive, with colonial subjects everywhere being systematically taught to sing, from the written music, harmonized Protestant church hymns and to play European band instruments for the purpose of forming "homegrown" military bands to perform at diplomatic and other ceremonial events.

By the end of the nineteenth century, a watershed had been reached in Western musical influence. A wide repertory of church hymns and Western band music had been absorbed by these far-flung colonial choirs and wind ensembles. The universal adoption of these polished Western musical forms served as conspicuous emblems of their collective ability to adapt themselves to the "higher" accomplishments of Western culture. Here lay the foundation of their future mastering of Europe's highest genres of art music. In virtually every more or less colonized region, from Japan, Korea, and China to Egypt, Lebanon, Madagascar, and sub-Saharan Africa, church choirs evolved into schools for choral singing and voice training, and military bands turned into instrumental academies. By the 1920s, many of these were consolidated into Western-style music conservatories, and an infrastructure for a burgeoning of Western concert music was in place.

But this whole development, as I have already suggested, is only part of a more intricate pattern of musical interchange between the Western and non-Western worlds that has unfolded in the present century. The slavish mimicry of an invading culture's forms, no matter how accomplished, is regarded by modern cultural anthropologists as a superficial facet of intercultural influence precisely because it is formally imposed. These scholars, whose field of research is itself a part of the intensive interchange of world cultures today, have come to recognize that, given sufficient contact between two cultures, a more informal and open interchange takes place. The host culture's response becomes more active; emulation leads to variation, adoption to adaption. Bruno Nettl was thinking primarily of this more fertile stage of musical response when he declared the "intensive imposition" of Western music abroad to be "the most significant phenomenon in the global history of music . . . of the last hundred years." "What is of concern to us here," he stated, "is the way in which the world's musical traditions have responded to the invasion . . . it is the variety of responses and of ways in which [they] have managed to maintain themselves in the face of the onslaught."[2]

Here, then, is a second view of musical globalization, a perhaps more advanced stage in that cultural reaction from beyond a strictly Eurocentric sphere of influence. If the acceleration of Western colonialism that began a century ago actively fostered the adoption of Western music, it also opened the door for the adaption of that music. Nettl stated it well: "As European and American nations began the business of colonizing more extensively even than before [the 1800s], Western technology clearly gained the upper hand, and there developed a musical system [the European] obviously symbolic of this superiority, but also adaptable to other musics."[3] This was a crucial moment in the evolution of world music. What had been an age-old process—the meeting and comingling of different musical cultures—that occurred infrequently and sporadically since it was dependent upon the migration of human groups was now, on the threshold of the twentieth century, poised to become a common event on a worldwide scale. And Nettl here identified the factor that, beyond all others, is fundamental to the globalization of music: technology.

To better understand the particulars of this adaptive "stage" of musical globalization and, indeed, to place the complex developments of twentieth-century world music in a comprehensible perspective, it would be well to examine the relationship between technology and music, particularly since the beginning of the industrial revolution. In the narrower sense, the technology of music refers to its handicrafts, chiefly the making of musical instruments but also the writing of musical scores. Both of these activities have become increasingly mechanized, beginning with mechanically printed musical scores in the sixteenth century and the factory production of instruments in the nineteenth century.

Since the industrial revolution and particularly in the past hundred years, technology has been increasingly linked to music as an ever more efficient means of dissemination. In all previous centuries, music circulated by means of travel—the transporting of instruments, of scores, or of the musicians themselves. Because travel before the nineteenth century was limited to "natural" methods of locomotion, such as horse-drawn vehicles and wind-driven vessels, it was an arduous and time-consuming endeavor. Distances between places were a major obstacles to communication and severely curtailed the spread of a given music from one region to another. In the Middle Ages, the compositions of even the greatest composers, each of which might exist in two or three manuscript copies, were known in only a few court circles, monasteries, and cathedral towns. As late as the eighteenth century, the works of Johann Sebastian Bach were virtually unknown outside Saxony, his immediate region of Germany. The nonliterate folk musics of the rural regions of Europe were utterly isolated from one another, as were the major music cultures in separate parts of the world. As I have shown, the meeting of such musics occurred through the uncommon and fitful processes of migration or exploration.

The achievements most central to nineteenth-century invention were those that significantly enhanced long-distance communication and, therefore, the dissemination of music. In the first half of the century—Carlyle's "mechanical age"—this took the form of two vital developments in rapid transportation, both made possible by James Watt's steam engine: steamships (in regular use from 1824) and railroads (in regular use from 1830). These twin land and sea media rapidly transformed the face of long-distance travel. By midcentury, a network of railroads interlocked Europe; by 1870, the Atlantic and Pacific coasts of the United States were linked by a transcontinental railroad line; and by 1891, the trans-Siberian railroad made it possible to travel by train through the entire Eurasian continent, from Lisbon to Vladivostok.

The steamship radically shortened transoceanic travel in these same years, beginning with the transatlantic crossing of the steam-powered American schooner *Savannah* in 1819. In 1838, Great Britain inaugurated regular steamship service across the Atlantic, and by the 1850s steam travel to Asia was offered by Great Britain, France, and the Netherlands. In 1869, the opening of the Suez Canal cut the length of Asian voyages virtually in half.

With the girding of the earth in rapid, mechanized transportation, distance ceased to be an insurmountable obstacle to communication; international exchange at every level became commonplace. The establishment of world's fairs and international time zones in the second half of the century symbolized this new global integration. Their effect on the dissemination of music can be exemplified by a single event in 1889.

In that year, the composer Claude Debussy attended the Grand World Exposition in Paris, where he first heard the exotic music of Southeast Asia. He was particularly struck by the shimmering sounds of the Javanese gamelan, an Indonesian orchestra composed of tuned metallic and wooden percussion instruments. The music was, in all respects, utterly different from any European music. Its complex interplay of bell-like timbres, pentatonic scales, and hypnotically repetitious rhythms were to affect Debussy's emerging compositional style more radically than the most progressive trends in European art music of the time. His mature style, a wholly original synthesis of European and Asian techniques, was to form one of the primary bridges to twentieth-century music.

The significant of this event, beyond the fact that it was the first direct encounter between a European composer and East Asian music, is that it could not have happened even a single generation earlier. The appearance of the Javanese musicians at the 1889 Paris exposition was only possible because a shortened steamship route to Asia, through the Suez Canal, had been completed just twenty years before. The era of international music tours had begun.

If the obstacle of distance was effectively reduced by advances in mechanized travel, it was virtually erased by the radically new technology of the second half of the century—telecommunications. Based upon the transmission and reception of electromagnetic waves between two remote parties, this was a true quantum leap in communications technology. It redefined the basis of technology itself, from the invention and building of mechanical apparatus to the discovery and control of electrical phenomena—a scientific process that runs from the development of telegraphy in the 1830s to the most sophisticated electronic automation today.

The first two telecommunications media, the telegraph and the telephone, firmly established the viability of electrical communication, but because they were vehicles of verbal information, they had no direct effect on the diffusion of music. The third medium, however, transformed it. This was the discovery and refinement of wireless communication at the end of the nineteenth century. The wireless transcended the unidirectional transmission of electrical signals through the closed medium of a cable or wire, by transmitting them omnidirectionally through the open medium of air. This rendered telecommunications universal by "broadcasting" signals to anyone with the proper receiving equipment. Wireless broadcasting was initially applied to the transmission of simple Morse code signals (called wireless telegraphy, refined in 1901). But its true potential was tapped when broadcasting was equipped with a newly developed vacuum tube capable of "modulating" the flexible sound patterns of speech (or music) onto the transmitted signal and amplifying them at the receiver end. This permitted the direct transmission of speech (or music) that came to be called "radio" broadcasting. Thus, to the universality of the medium (wireless telecommunication) was added the public utility of the message (information and entertainment), a combination that was to make radio one of the seminal mass communications media of the twentieth century. Statistics are eloquent: The first commercial radio station (KDKA in Pittsburgh) broadcast to 15,000 receivers in 1920; by 1927, there were 700 stations in the United States alone, broadcasting to nearly 8 million receivers.

As radio broadcasting began in earnest in the 1920s, it was powerfully reinforced by still another seminal nineteenth-century technology reaching commercial maturity at same time: the phonograph. This was the mechanism to artificially reproduce sound, discovered and invented by Thomas Edison in 1877. Though he conceived it as a means of recording telephone conversations and other human speech, its commercial potential quickly proved to lie in the reproduction of music. By 1900, a number of fledgling recording companies, such as Victor and Columbia, were competing with the Edison Talking Phonograph Company to produce recordings of famous performers, most of them classical artists such as the opera singer Enrico Caruso and the piano virtuoso Ignaz Paderewski. It was thought—naively—that this kind of music was the proper subject for recording because of its prestige and greater historical value. But this notion was forever erased by the spectacular sales of popular dance records, including the first jazz recordings in 1917. From 1920 until the present, popular records have been the profit-earning items that subsidize classical records.

It was at this juncture that the paths of radio and phonograph crossed. The year 1921 saw the release of inexpensive home models of both radios and phonographs. They quickly became fixtures in the American home and complemented each other nicely: Radio found in records a perfect medium for entertainment broadcasting, and listeners bought popular records heard on the radio. The two media came together in another important way, as well: In 1925, the electrical elements of the radio (vacuum tube amplification, microphone, electromagnetic speakers, and electrical power source) were applied to the phonograph and vastly improved its sound quality.

The phonograph record was a completely new element in musical life, eventually reaching and changing every aspect of it. Audiences, performers, music historians and critics, music educators, even composers—all were touched in some way by this invention. Sound recording, the first means of capturing a musical performance in a permanent and portable form, revolutionized the dissemination of music by sales of the records themselves and by the broadcasting of them over radio and television and on film sound tracks. As noted earlier, before this century, the exposure of all listeners and musicians to "live" music was sporadic and severely limited. If one lived in Vienna in Beethoven's day, one could hear his music only when a live performance took place, which was only moderately frequent. If one lived in Philadelphia at that time, opportunities to hear his music—and Philadelphia lacked a symphony orchestra in those days—were far less frequent, perhaps only an occasional evening of his chamber music. And if one lived in an American frontier town like Louisville, Kentucky, opportunities were virtually nonexistent—unless one had that rare commodity at this early date, a piano.

The comparison with the situation today is startling. In the twentieth century, we have an unprecedented awareness and knowledge of an incredible range of music, gained, in large part, by hearing this music on recordings. Just a century ago, orchestra conductors had to struggle from place to place to hear a performance of a Beethoven symphony—or to conduct a performance themselves. Today, anyone with a record player or tape recorder can listen to all nine symphonies in a single day. In a single afternoon, a listener can hear the music of Stephen Foster, J. S. Bach, Felix Mendelssohn, George Gershwin, the Rolling Stones, and Igor Stravinsky or a Javanese gamelan, a Navajo harvest dance, a Hindu raga, a Japanese koto ensemble, a mariachi band, and a Cajun band. In short, the sound recording has been a unique tool for exploring, with the greatest efficiency, both the history and geography of music.

To quite a remarkable degree, then, the developments in technology of the past century and a half have been central to the union of the world's musics that so distinguishes the present century. The forces that initiated the introduction of Western music into foreign cultures may have been military occupations and mission schools. But these have been supplanted and vastly superseded by the steadily progressive advancements in transportation and communication up to the present day.

To turn again to the question of adaptive responses to Western music, it must be said that, while this process has certainly been occurring, in different ways and at various speeds, since the early part of this century, the subject is by no means an already written history. This is true for several reasons. First, musical adaption is, by its very nature, an ongoing process, not a fixed musical product. It is a contemporary phenomenon that defies ready analysis in a historical context. Second, because it is a matter of subjective selection—each musician choosing those features of Western music most amenable to his or her own music—it does not lend itself to broad generalities or conclusions. The kind and degree of musical blend differs greatly from culture to culture. Last and by no means least, the musical scholars addressing the subject of non-Western musics were slow to realize the existence and importance of adaptive change in those musics.

The implications of this last point are significant. During the late nineteenth and early twentieth centuries, as the West was presenting itself to other societies, the non-Western world was also gradually being introduced to the peoples of Europe and North America. As noted, one fruitful result of this interchange was the interest taken by Western composers in the musical sounds of the world; Debussy's confrontation with Javanese music was the first in a continuous series of such discoveries by twentieth-century composers. A second result was the emergence of a subfield of musicology dealing with the systematic study of non-Western music, known today as ethnomusicology.

Modern ethnomusicologists, who study a foreign music in the context of its own cultural traditions, are the musical analogues of cultural anthropologists or ethnologists. But the founders of the field, active between 1900 and 1950, were European historical musicologists steeped in the nineteenth-century Germanic tradition of cultural evolution and trained to study the evolution of European art music through a systematic examination of musical scores. Because their first contacts with non-Western music were through the superficial channels of missionary and colonization movements and because these foreign musics—lacking any music notation—had no observable history, these early ethnomusicologists made the inevitable (and convenient) judgment that all non-Western musics were fixed, stable entities. This was in striking contrast to the manifest mutability of Western art music, an aspect considered by European scholars as one of its most characteristic qualities. Accordingly, these early ethnomusicologists, who called themselves comparative musicologists, adopted a contrastive approach to non-Western musics, which were conceived as a group of musics from which Western art music stood out.

Their methodology consisted of devising a simple framework for comparison that emphasized the departures from Western music common to all non-Western music; these included the absence of music notation and the dependence upon oral transmission; the lack of a system of harmony; the presence of scale tones (such as microtones) incompatible with the Western, equally tempered scale; and the absence of a regular, metrical rhythm. To early ethnomusicologists, notation, equally tempered scales, harmony, and metrical rhythm were the most essential features of Western music, and the fact that none of these was present in non-Western musics seemed of the highest significance. Whatever variables that existed between one music and another or between one performance and another within a culture were considered accidental rather than essential factors.

To modern ethnomusicologists, those entering the field after about 1960, this early emphasis on non-Western musics as fixed systems rather than dynamic processes seems myopic: Perhaps it was the inevitable myopia of an incipient field of research with too few samples for analysis, but it was also the myopia of historically oriented Western scholars attempting to cope with modern, ephemeral musics. Whatever the causes, today's ethnomusicologists have the improved perspective of nearly a half century of dramatically accelerated interchange between the Western and non-Western worlds, beginning after World War II. They have had a broader experience of Western music, including jazz, folk music, and the various strands of popular music. They have also lived in an environment in which the sounds of non-Western music are readily available (through radio, recordings, and so forth) and no longer a shock. And many of them have experienced direct contact with non-Western peoples through military occupation in World War II, Korea, and Vietnam, through organizations such as the Peace Corps, and, as jet travel increased accessibility, as tourists. The striking feature of "exotic" peoples and their cultures is no longer their fixed isolation but the ways in which rapid change has taken place and the problems of coping with Western values and technology.

These younger ethnomusicologists were thus predisposed to observe the mutability of non-Western musics and to take an active interest in the effects of adaptive change on a given musical system. Toward this end, they developed or borrowed a number of flexible concepts to explain and describe kinds and degrees of change. Basic to all of these is the concept of centrality, the notion that in any musical idiom, certain features are more central than others and function as hallmarks. They can be recognized by their pervasiveness in a musical repertory and how they symbolize the style of that repertory, both to its own society and to outsiders. Separating central and noncentral features of a music is important to a study of adaption since the adapting musician, rather than adopting a new music outright, selects certain traits and not others; on the other hand, he or she may choose to preserve at all costs certain central traits of his or her own music in the process. The concept of centrality enables scholars to define Western music, despite its great variety, as a unitary concept. However different the styles of classical, "Broadway," folk, jazz, or rock, they all share certain central features, easily recognizable to musicians of other cultures. In addition to the obvious elements of Western music—harmony, even-tempered scales, metrical rhythm, notation—defined by their predecessors, modern ethnomusicologists extend the concept of centrality to aspects of musical process or behavior in Western music: the predilection for ensemble performance, especially large orchestras; the importance placed on planning, with the norm being the carefully composed piece, meticulously rehearsed; the idea of presenting music as an end in itself, at a public concert; and the emphasis on doing what is difficult and showing it off.

Basic, too, is the concept of acculturation, which refers to the process of adaption itself. It is defined, variously, as the modification of a primitive culture by contact with an advanced culture or the process of intercultural borrowing between diverse peoples resulting in new and blended patterns, dictionary descriptions that perhaps reflect the changing biases of scholars toward the concept of cultural change. Degrees of acculturation are loosely measured by the complementary concepts of Westernization and modernization. Westernization is the substitution of central features of Western music for their non-Western analogues, often with the sacrifice of essential facets of the adapting musical tradition. Modernization is less drastic: the incidental movement of a music system or its components in the direction of Western music without, however, requiring major changes in those aspects of the non-Western tradition that are central and essential. Bearing on the process of acculturation is the basic idea of syncretism, that is, the confluence of similar or compatible culture traits to create new, mixed forms. This concept requires the recognition that certain cultures or musical forms are compatible, perhaps by having similar centralities.

The classic application of this concept to music is in the confrontation of African and Western musics in the New World, as opposed to the confrontation of Amerindian and Western musics. It is accepted by ethnomusicologists that African and Western musics have such compatibility (a major-sounding scale, use of harmonized thirds, underlying steady beat, and so on), while Amerindian and Western musics strikingly lack any compatibility. Hence, there is a rich variety of Afro-European musical blends in Afro-American musical styles and a singular dearth of any such blendings in Amerindian musics, even today.

The number of case studies bearing directly on the adaptive interaction between non-Western and Western music, though still small, is beginning to grow rapidly, and the conceptual framework of ethnomusicology since about 1950 has been changing to accommodate the new directions suggested by these studies. To describe the process of adaption on an individual case basis would easily require an entire volume.[4] For the purposes of this chapter, a few generalizations by region regarding the degree of adaption found in each will suffice.

To start with a richly documented area, it can be said that significant acculturative musical blends are the norm in sub-Saharan Africa. As mentioned, there is a fairly strong degree of syncretism between the two base cultures, Europe and Africa. Reinforcing this is the fact that African music was brought to America in the centuries of slavery and had already blended with European styles. The modern examples of blended African music have cross-fertilized with the Afro-American music of the United States and the Caribbean, resulting in such popular musics as highlife, Congo jazz, and juju, all marked by simplified Western harmony, emphasis on brass instruments, Latin American-style drum rhythms, and the use of string bass and guitar. All these musics have audible style influences from reggae, Mexican tropical, rhythm and blues, and samba.

In the Middle East, it is quite different. Various degrees of Westernization and modernization have occurred but only with difficulty. As Bruno Nettl indicated, the source musics—European and Muslim—are so fundamentally different, not only in sound ideals but also in the whole conception of the use of music, that the host music seems to be attempting to resolve the basic conflict. There are cases of outright adoption of Western classical music (with many pianos and violins) and the formation of large ensembles of Muslim string instruments in the manner of the Western orchestra, and a fad has developed for playing local instruments in Western-style concerts, with a strong emphasis on Western-style virtuosity. But in general, the basic Muslim functions of musical performance, never done for the pure pleasure of listening, have remained strongly intact. In sum, throughout the Middle East, there is a fitful mixture of Westernized and modernized tendencies.

The subcontinent of India has shown a remarkable resistance to a radical absorption of Western music. Where in Iran, for example, there are traditions of European classical recitals and concerts (on violin, piano, or guitar) as well as various nightclubs where a generic Western dance music is played, in India, the powerful institution of the country's own "classical" raga performances, rooted in a quasi-religious format and function, is still the central music tradition. In fact, such Western instruments as the violin and the guitar have been totally absorbed into these performances; some younger Indian violinists and guitarists have even hotly contested the suggestion that their instruments are from Europe!

Regarding Southeast Asia, I will quote Nettl's succinct characterization: "Southeast Asia may be the one [culture area] coming closest to
practicing virtual rejection of the impinging music; and perhaps, along
with Java and Bali, it comes closest to having a full-blown musical system
in a modern urban context built almost entirely on a repertory of non-
Western sound." [5]

Finally, the situation in Northeast Asia is completely different. In Japan
and Korea, Western music of all sorts has had a strong impact. In urban
areas, Western classical music and all kinds of Western popular music
and jazz have been so extensively and effectively cloned that these cities
can almost be regarded as annexes of Western cities. Interestingly, the
various forms of traditional musics in both nations have been perfectly
preserved as "shrines" to their histories. Japan and Korea have been
almost totally Westernized.

Bruno Nettl, who has been a great synthesizer of the collective achievements of modern ethnomusicology, is, like most of his colleagues and
students, an active believer in maintaining cultural diversity. Reflecting
on the growing body of evidence amassed over thirty years of field
research, he is cautiously optimistic about the global impact of Western
music. Writing in 1984, he commented: "While the coming of Western
music is often seen as the death-knell of musical variety in the world,
examination of its many effects shows the world's musics in the twentieth
century, partly as a result of the pressure generated by Western musical
culture, in a state of unprecedented diversity." Then, in a not entirely
value-free tone, he added: "Even so, this admittedly optimistic view of
the musical scene certainly does not imply approval of the colonization,
conquest, and exploitation of third-world peoples by Europeans and
North Americans. . . . In retrospect, the musical diversity of the modern
world may be one of the more acceptable results of the introduction of
Western culture to the rest of the world." [6]

Perhaps it is too soon to say. The trend toward the "indigenization" of
Western music in all parts of the world is, for all the diversity of responses, a single complex event, as is, for that matter, the ongoing attention
given to it by Western scholars. As a genuine manifestation of globalization in music, it surely deserves further investigation and corrobora-
tion—and, perhaps, encouragement.

But the processes of Westernization and modernization reflected therein are presently being superseded by more powerful Westernizing tendencies in global music, namely, urbanization and its close corollary,
industrialization. These concepts and the processes they describe are
hardly new. Cities have existed in non-Western societies for centuries,
and urbanization is not, in itself, an effect of Western culture. But the kind
of rapid urbanization that has taken place in the latter half of the twen-

tieth century is associated with the development of Western technology, Western-style nation-states, and large-scale immigration. Industrialization, on the other hand, is a distinctly Western development, but it began as early as the late Renaissance and developed to an initial peak in the century of the industrial revolution.

What is new is the extraordinary escalation of urbanization and industrialization in the past few decades into worldwide cultural forces. Recent urban growth, especially in Third World countries, has been phenomenal—an estimated 70 percent of the world's people now live in cities. Many of these cities are newly established urban centers in underdeveloped nations; others are older cities that have expanded into large, multicultural units.

Industrialization, for its part, has been virtually redefined by Western space-age technology and has been the trigger and central shaping force of the rapid urbanization of the globe. Jet travel has bound these cities into an integral worldwide urban network, and the ever-expanding advancements in electronic communications (radio, television, videocassette, cinema, satellite, and computer) have imposed on them all a single, Western-based social structure and a common set of Westernized living patterns. What has developed and developed swiftly from this is a new form of society: an international urban culture that operates on its own scale and follows its own trends, beyond the boundaries of the nation-state. Its significance to the process of globalization is, surely, central, if not yet entirely foreseen. Its significance to the future of global music is, on the other hand, already clear, namely, a phenomenally rapid expansion—through the new transnational urban infrastructure—of Western popular music around the globe.

This was surely an inevitable, if abrupt, event, given the urban nature of popular music and its intimate ties to electronic technology. In its characteristic twentieth-century form, popular music first coalesced in America in the 1920s, in conjunction with the twin emergence of commercial radio and the phonograph. From the beginning and throughout its history, this music has been commercially directed toward the large urban and suburban audience. Toward this end, popular music has exploited electronics not only as a means of efficient dissemination but increasingly as a part of its sound production and, hence, its communicative impact. By the 1960s, with the coming of American rock music and its mass youth audience, popular music had become almost purely a technological entity, using electronics as a means of amplification, of sound manipulation and distortion, and of developing new instruments, such as the electric violin and trumpet, the electronic piano, and the computerized sound synthesizer. It was at this stage and in this form that popular music began its dramatic expansion around the world.

The internationalization of Western popular music is an event of far greater potential significance than the nearly simultaneous internationalization of Western classical music. Despite a continuing "official" resistance in many nations to the former phenomenon and a continuing "official" encouragement of the latter, it is popular music that has proven the more hardy survivor in foreign soil and begun to develop an international life of its own. With the possible exceptions of Korea and Japan, Western classical music has made no more impact on the larger populace than it has in Europe and America.

This is, of course, partly attributable to the simpler nature of popular music—shorter in duration, simpler melodies, fewer chords, and, always, a pronounced and constant beat. Beyond this, there is the commercial dimension of all popular music. Reflecting its origins in America, popular music was, from the start, bought, adapted, and marketed by business enterprises dedicated to detecting and serving the tastes of an independent consumer public. As such, it has been an open, democratic music that was, in the apt phrase of S. Frederick Starr, "truly popular and, equally important, in no way beholden to the state for its creation and maintenance."[7] It is this capacity to thrive and develop outside the control of "official" approval or disapproval that accounts, as much as any factor, for its spectacular ability to travel.

For whatever reasons, the rise of a worldwide popular music linked to the West and to the United States in particular is a phenomenon that bids fair to produce the first music of genuinely global range. But it has thus far attracted the attention of only a few musical scholars. A modest number of ethnomusicologists have monitored the growth of various local and regional "hybrid" forms of Western popular music (such as West African highlife, Nigerian juju, Indonesian kroncong, and Indian "film music"), with an eye to the survival of local musical effects in the blend. But a consideration of the phenomenon as a whole, concentrating not on the adaptive variety among the individual urban samples but on the integral components of the popular styles worldwide, has yet to be addressed. Historical musicologists of the traditional sort—that is, historians of European and American art music—have no vested interest in the subject itself, nor would they be prepared, as a group, to apply the conventional historical method to such a volatile contemporary event. Even musicologists who are specialists in popular music tend to focus on the American scene and on European popular music to the extent that it affects musical trends in America, as in the case of the Beatles or Andrew Lloyd Webber. The fate of the music abroad, particularly in Third World and Asian cities, is treated by these specialists in a peripheral way, if at all.

One important exception to this is the German musicologist Walter Wiora. That the past hundred years have seen a change of special magnitude in the history of Western music was suggested in his innovative study, *The Four Ages of Music* (1965).[8] One of the first serious attempts to transcend the pervasive Eurocentrism of conventional music historiography, the book embraced the entire course of human music, dividing it into four broad periods: (1) the music of the prehistoric and early periods, (2) music in the high civilizations of antiquity and the Orient, (3) the "special position" of Western music, and (4) the music of "global industrial culture."

Although these periods or ages are broadly sequential, there is chronological overlap between them. The first age, for example, includes the music of present-day "primitive" peoples and the "archaic folk music" of modern Western cultures. The second age extends to the "folk and traditional music" of the modern Orient. The second and third ages are themselves largely contemporaneous, and the fourth age embraces the continuing evolution of the music of the third age. Only in the first and fourth ages did Wiora see a unified musical world. In the first, he surmised, musical cultures, operating with the same primitive materials and technology, were everywhere basically the same. In the second and third ages, the cultures of the world diverged, each developing a music suitable to its values, social structure, aesthetic, and technology. But in the fourth age, that of the "global industrial culture" since the industrial revolution, the world's musics converged again, united by the powerful dissemination of elements of Western civilization, including its whole musical system: its sound materials, its institutions, and its technology.

One aim of Wiora's universal approach was to place our Western musical tradition into clearer perspective.[9] By seeing the thousand-year epoch of Western music (the third age) as but one stage of a comprehensive chronicle of world music, we can begin to understand its "special position" therein—special in its complex polyphonic structure; its elaborate system of harmony; its monumental musical forms (such as opera and symphony); its large-scale ensembles; and its unique codependent institutions, the composer and the musical score.

A larger aim of the study was to establish a context for the unprecedented developments of the fourth age (the present century): Only by observing the strikingly divergent paths of the musics of the second and third ages can we realize the significance of their convergences in the modern age.

A singular feature of Wiora's scheme, given his own training in central European historical musicology, was his recognition of a "brave new world" beyond the grand European tradition. His characterization of the present "global industrial" age is a resounding challenge to the historical myopia of his musical colleagues:

> It is not to be denied that music is in fact taking part in a revolutionary change [that] goes far too deep to be understood simply as a reaction against the nineteenth century. It is leading not merely to a further period within the West . . . but out over the frontiers of Europe to a new age. This epochal change, emerging as it did in the French Revolution and with the beginnings of machine techniques, and thrusting rapidly ahead with the two world wars, is a caesura of the first order in world history.[10]

This remarkable declaration, which clearly delineated the key factors of the new century—the thrust of major musical trends beyond the limits of Europe and the new role of industrial technology as a fundamental driving force—provided a clear framework for a global approach to music history.

But Wiora (writing in 1965) also recognized the present as the pivotal moment of change, with the period from the French Revolution to the end of the two world wars as a preparatory stage. Moreover, he was able to identify, nearly at the time of its inception, what I am here suggesting is the primary "actor" in the future globalization of music: the emergence of an international urban culture. Perhaps Wiora's definition of the term *global industrial civilization* is more apt: "The dynamic drive of Western culture and the global industrial civilization that has grown out of it are working simultaneously in other dimensions."[11]

Wiora heralded the ascendancy of America as the seminal culture of the international popular music:[12]

> The diffusion of jazz belongs among the main counter-movements to the expansion of purely European music. In it one sees the changed situation at the beginning of the fourth age. What Europe has produced so far in our century in social dances and dance music is much too weak to fill the vacuum into which dance music from across the Atlantic is streaming; European youth sings and dances whatever jazz, and the American popular-hit industry that exploits it, offers as a model.[13]

In concluding his essay on the rounding of the globe by an international popular music, Wiora observed that it has been customary to contrast Western music with non-Western music. Such a contrast is implicit in the first two forms of musical globalization proposed in this chapter—the "triumph" of Western classical music in the non-West and of individual non-Western musics in the face of the onslaught of Western music. "This division of the world," he asserted, "corresponds only in part to the new reality . . . a universal musical culture is spreading out which in many respects is no longer geographically limited. Hence, this contrast holds only for a period that is already passing. In the new Age it is being covered over by relationships that reach around the whole globe."[14]

As Wiora added, concerning the geographic dimensions of an international urban popular music culture, "Progress in international circulation is broadening the range of musicians, who now travel by land, by sea, and by air, making possible a rapid succession of world music festivals, world congresses, world youth festivals, with participants from all parts of the globe. Tokyo is today nearer to Cologne than Prague was to Vienna in Mozart's time. And the radio 'brings the world into your home.'"[15]

On the extra-geographic dimensions of a globally expanding society, he noted that "the world we know and in which we function is expanding not only in space, but also in social, temporal, and organizational directions."[16]

These twin observations point up another dimension of a world popular music culture that may prove to have the most far-reaching implications for the ultimate globalization of music. This is what might be called the "Woodstock effect." An underlying element of American popular culture today, symbolized most powerfully by its music, is its near total enfranchisement by the young. This generation gap developed in the 1950s, in connection with the rise of rock and roll. Profound changes had taken place within America during and just after World War II. Millions of people from rural areas, particularly the South, flocked to the cities in search of jobs and a better way of life. Many large cities suddenly had greatly increased populations of rural whites and southern blacks, who brought their own cultures, creating a large urban audience for country and black music. At first, there was little contact between these types of music and the popular music of white, urban Americans, which consisted of melodically and harmonically sophisticated songs from musical theater and movies, sung by singers like Bing Crosby, Judy Garland, and Frank Sinatra. Most city radio stations continued to play this "Tin Pan Alley" music, black musicians played in bars and dance halls where whites never went, poor whites from rural areas continued listening to the music they had always liked, and small record shops sold black and country records. In the closing years of the 1940s, young, middle-class whites gradually became more interested and excited about this "fringe" music that they were not supposed to enjoy. The taboo seed had been planted.

The first half of the 1950s were a crucial time. Between 1950 and 1954, the programming on radio disc jockey shows changed gradually from a lineup of tunes all in the Tin Pan Alley style (sung by such radio stars as Doris Day, Rosemary Clooney, Tony Bennett, and Frank Sinatra) to tunes in alternative styles, including country songs (by Leadbelly, Patti Page, and Hank Williams) and songs in a black style (sung by white "cover" artists—that is, where the artist offers his or her own version of someone else's song—like Frankie Laine, Johnny Ray, and Bill Haley). As the latter styles gained rapidly in popularity among mainstream young, white listeners, the sophisticated songs gradually waned. The way had been paved for a revolution.

This came in 1955, when young country singers like Bill Haley and Elvis Presley began to gain more attention for their "cover" records of black rhythm and blues than for their straight country records. Bill Haley's cover of "Shake, Rattle, and Roll" (the original was by Joe Turner) and Elvis Presley's cover of "You Ain't Nothin' But A Hound Dog" (original by Big Mama Thornton) in the year 1954 opened the floodgates. Rock and roll preempted every other song style, on or off the radio.

From the beginning, rock and roll was accepted by young people as "their" music. They had, in a sense, discovered it (in those black and country record stores, in Chicago, Cleveland, St. Louis, Detroit, and Philadelphia). The vehement opposition to this "crude" music by parents, educators, churchpeople, politicians, and other representatives of the older generation only further entrenched the enthusiasm of the youth of America for this music. From the beginning, rock music, in its many variants, carried an aura of rebellion, of rejection of the values and habits of white middle America.

With rock and roll, the music industry had finally recognized that the number of adolescents and college students was so great that music geared to their tastes could be financially profitable, even though their parents disliked and even feared it. The older generation found rock loud, harsh, unpleasant, and often unintelligible; its sexual innuendos were plain, and for most older people in America and Europe in the later 1950s and 1960s, sex was not a proper subject for music of such a blatant and coarse character. Further, rock clearly contributed to such feared trends as racial mixing and the growing antagonism of younger people toward their parents.

When rock spread like a grass fire across Europe in the 1960s, even to the Soviet Union, it carried all this social baggage with it. In fact, when many young non-English-speaking foreigners first witnessed rock and roll concerts (which included British rock groups), they were as powerfully impressed by the visual effect of the events as they were by the sound of the music. The immediate sensation was of being "among their own," their fellow youth. By the middle 1960s, rock had grown beyond a mere music to become a social movement. Musically, it was a conglomeration of styles unified by a common spirit, a common environment, and a common objective. No matter that there was no single musical style at huge international concerts that featured the Rolling Stones, Country Joe and the Fish, The Grateful Dead, Ike and Tina Turner, Joni Mitchell,

Jefferson Airplane, the Doors, Led Zeppelin, Donovan, the Who, Jimi Hendrix, Paul Simon, and Cream—this myriad variety of musics served a function: It galvanized a mass youth event.

Thus, as we approach the year 2000, we may already have entered a global society through the world of music. Certainly, it has become clear that, in a world of total mass communication, music, that most fluid of human languages, has assumed an entirely new significance. It has become a form of energy in its own right that is capable, whatever its style or verbal message, of unifying people, regardless of race, region, or language. Just how this new potential will be played out in the coming years only time will tell.

Notes

1. Bruno Nettl, *The Western Impact on World Music* (New York: Schirmer, 1985), p. 3.

2. Ibid., p. 4.

3. Ibid., p. 10.

4. Ibid. is an excellent short reference for this.

5. Ibid., p. 157.

6. Ibid., p. xiv.

7. Frederick Starr, *Red and Hot: The Fate of Jazz in the Soviet Union* (New York: Oxford, 1983), p. 8.

8. Walter Wiora, *The Four Ages of Music* (New York: W. W. Norton, 1965).

9. Wiora considers himself a universal music historian; certainly his approach is universal, though covering a greater range than that of the standard universal historian.

10. Wiora, *The Four Ages of Music*, p. 150.

11. Ibid., p. 152.

12. Wiora considered jazz as the focal point of American music abroad, which it was before the advent of rock. In terms of the common social function of jazz and rock, S. Frederick Starr observed: "The rock rebellion against jazz [in the USSR] replicated the upheaval caused by jazz itself a half-century earlier" (*Red and Hot*, p. 294).

13. Wiora, *The Four Ages of Music*, p. 159.

14. Ibid., p. 155.

15. Ibid., p. 160.

16. Ibid., p. 152.

PART THREE

An Overview

10

On the Prospect
of Global History

Raymond Grew

The rising interest in global history obviously reflects the experience of our era, and that fact justifies confidence that programs for global history will prove attractive. But it also supports caution about expectations for what they are likely to accomplish.[1] Historians have long recognized that the visions of the past reflect the preoccupations of the present.[2] Indeed, those new concerns imposed by experience may be a more reliable source of fresh questions than the inventiveness of individual scholars. Current preoccupations provide, in any case, an aura of relevance and a sense of urgency irresistible to historians who are sufficiently products of their age to dislike having their research treated as a kind of cultural luxury or personal indulgence. Given such temptations and the dangers they may contain, it seems wise to begin reflections on global history with some consideration of what makes global history attractive to historians at the end of the twentieth century. Obvious as the explanations may be, it is not so obvious what they imply for history as a discipline.

This admittedly academic approach may be dangerously constrictive and disconcertingly pedestrian for so grand a topic, but it identifies some difficult problems. Visionaries who have some inspired conception of how the world's history hangs together should write that history. Moralists seeking to improve the world should and will find in global history a way to comprehend the past as a call to action. They need not wait for answers to the duller question this chapter poses of whether and then how global history might become a self-sustaining field of inquiry. That is a goal worth considering, however, and one that requires some critical awareness of the intellectual currents that now make global history an appealing possibility.

Making Global History

Global Contact

Few statements provoke so little controversy as the claim that human beings today are more in touch with their fellow beings around the world than ever before in history. The list of examples—instant communication of information, a culture of universal styles and experiences, the worldwide reach of markets and trade, the products composed of parts from several continents—has become a litany, and reference to the global village is a cliché that conference-going professors can hardly afford to challenge: "Historians no longer have to invent the world in order to study world history."[3] Obviously, these changes and our awareness of them are of major importance, and there is every reason to believe that they should be both an object of historical study and a welcome influence on the way historical scholarship is conducted and conceived.

There are also some reasons, less obvious perhaps, for skepticism, and I want to give these a little more attention not merely for the pleasures of perversity but also because a program for global history would do well to have them in mind from the start. Whenever a statement evokes nearly universal assent, we can assume that it reveals as much about the assentors as about the thing described. So the assertion that ours is an age transformed by global contact must be among the first subjects studied by global historians. Historians know, of course, that somewhat similar assumptions have been made in the past. That does not mean that facsimile transmissions, tape recordings, jet airplanes, and satellite communications may not be accomplishing something that railroads, steamships, literacy, the telegraph, motion pictures, the telephone, the radio, and the television did not. Perhaps it merely points to a very long process of globalization—one that could be extended much farther into the past.

This does suggest, however, that historians will want to ask who shares in this sense of transformation and to investigate the varied ways in which it is experienced and interpreted. What do modern communications communicate when the transistor radio, for example, is not really the same instrument and is certainly not carrying the same message in Omaha, the Mahgreb, the Andes, and Sri Lanka. When audiences in Indonesia, Dallas, Florence, and Sofia watch the same American film or soap opera, what do they really share? What interests and illusions might make it tempting to treat instant communication and constant contact as uniform experiences in a single global village? Global historians will need tools, many of which apparently have not yet been invented, for analyzing popular culture and local cultural filters. Similarly, discussions of world trade employ models and a language that proclaim their own universality and contain assumptions that must be exposed. The sophisticated body of theory on which such discussions are typically grounded will need to be reviewed in light of the wide range of experiences that can be considered global. Economists and political scientists have trouble distinguishing the role of politics, interests, and ideology in the development of the economy of the European Community. Consequently, there is certainly reason to be wary of descriptions of world trade that begin with some uniform concept of internationalization, dependency, or markets and then extend it in time and, in essence, stretch it around the world. Global historians will need techniques for exposing the parochialism of common assumptions and for writing about common processes in ways that leave room for many different histories.

Modernization

The concept of modernization as a process of development applicable to the entire world is frequently referred to (a little exaggeratedly) as *modernization theory*, and for the past decade, the term is most often brought up only to be denounced. There is no need to review those criticisms here. In fact, it seems to me that there is still much of value in a good deal of the literature that has been stimulated by ideas of modernization, including the perception that modern development should be seen as a process involving simultaneous change in many different aspects of society. Despite all the attacks on it, the concept of modernization seems unavoidable and probably useful.[4]

The impetus for global history has much in common with that earlier enthusiasm for modernization, beginning with the sense that history must be understood in terms of a transformation recently become visible but destined to be universal, extending to an emphasis upon the spread from Europe and North America of technology, institutions (military, political, administrative) and values (education and literacy, democracy, consumerism). Like much of the work on modernization, many of the calls for global history aspire toward general theories that can predict the future as an extension of the past, as well as specific studies that can influence public policy to properly prepare for that future. Given these similarities, global historians especially need to consider how they will avoid parochialism, linearity, and the other weaknesses and excesses that mar the literature on modernization.

That will not be easy. Perhaps the dangers of a mechanical functionalism or a preference for system maintenance—charges often leveled against theories of modernization—can be readily avoided. Maybe the fading of the Cold War will lighten the ideological baggage that ideas of modernization have been accused of carrying (although anti-Marxism is hardly weaker in the 1990s than it was in the 1950s). But how will this conception of historical change, which looks back from a future it prophesies, avoid the stranglehold of teleology any better than modernization did? If the process of globalization is considered to be universal, is there a method that will remind global historians (as modernizers so often forgot) that they should not assume that the West is the model all the world must follow? An emphasis upon modernity, as a particular state of being rather than as a process, is certainly a help;[5] it is not enough, however, simply to assert the possibility of continued diversity, of multidirectional development, and many models. Nor do good intentions offer much protection. Convergence theory, after all, was a special form of modernization theory that sought to escape Cold War rhetoric and more generously permit alternative paths to a common destiny. Yet the idea that the Soviet and capitalist systems would advance, each in its own way, until the two became increasingly similar, which was tellingly criticized even when new, seems ludicrous now.[6]

Global histories could easily run the risk of recapitulating all the errors of modernization theories. Assumptions of universalism are too close for comfort to ideas enwrapped in Eurocentrism from the Enlightenment to the present. Even the ethical and scientific claims that give the case for global awareness such power often sound disquietingly like the language of rationalist believers in progress who, over the last several centuries, have, alas, so often been proved wrong in their optimistic assurance that moral good can be identified through applied reason and realized through history. In addition, recent events—the new regimes of Eastern Europe, the development of the European Community, and the growing wealth of the Pacific rim—could revive the temptation to cultural narrowness so objectionable in some older visions of modernization and convergence.[7] Global history, in short, needs some methodological protection against flaws that have undermined its predecessors in order to be convincingly established as a field of scholarship. And to be a truly lively one, it must be open to the findings, techniques, and theoretical frameworks of the most exciting contemporary scholarship (including that which rejects all metahistorical narrative).

Global Ecology

That we live in a single, global ecology in which all of the parts are interdependent is now almost universally accepted, and this perception can be expected to affect our view of history as much as ideas of geology and evolution affected historical practice in the nineteenth century. The parallels are striking. Ecological awareness, like theories of evolution, benefits from the prestige of natural science and the excitement of inter-disciplinary research. Both produce evidence a broad public can appreciate, although satellite photography is even more compelling than old bones. Both suggest that human beings are part of a biological chain, that the laws their science has discovered apply to human beings, and that this is true not just in the physical realm but in the social and moral spheres as well, where failure to learn the lessons of these sciences could be fatal. And just as evolutionism quickly became tied to anticlericalism and pro-gressive politics, so environmentalism has special attractions for ideol-ogies critical of capitalism and distrustful of technology.

Awareness of our global ecology is a stimulus to global history as legitimate as it is inevitable.[8] If it can help the historical discipline to break the stranglehold of the national state as the preferred unit of analysis, that alone would be a major contribution. There are also dangers against which a serious plan for global history should try to protect itself. The ecological vocabulary offers a basket of metaphors—about nature, renew-able resources, equilibrium, global system, and so on—so easily misap-plied to history as to be frightening. The issue is not how much civilization is like a forest or society is like an anthill but rather that a polyvalent, scientifically certified, and morally attractive terminology can easily invite loose analogies and mechanical applications that will make for poor historical thinking. A call for global history needs, therefore, to include some fairly practical suggestions about the problematics of global history, indicating the kinds of questions that can be addressed and how a historical context can be recognized and taken into account.

A Common Destiny

The discussion thus far has treated the idea of global history in a highly intellectualized way, as the product of certain lines of thought already well established in the natural and social sciences or as a response to contemporary experience so intellectual (and academic) that it creates an agenda for new research.[9] We need not assume, however, that academic disciplines are or should be semi-isolated, semi-autonomous, institution-alized forms of inquiry. There have always been those, including profes-sors of history, less concerned with history as a branch of science than as a form of action, and this is somewhat true in regard to the interest in global history, which is often luminous with moral awareness.

The desire to conceive history differently is, in short, part of a larger movement, and there are a number of things to say about that, beginning with the fact that it is not at all new.[10] Because some believe that historians should write without a political purpose—or at least that historians should try to write without a conscious political purpose—those who embrace the idea of global history must concede from the first that their history is redolent of politics, that it cares about policy, and that it hopes to have some influence on both. There are, after all, plenty of precedents for such engagement even among the most professional of historians. The development of history as a discipline owes a great deal to the belief that history is relevant to the present and the future—that history can help make nations, contribute to democracy, nudge progress along, increase the chances for social justice, or just give the oppressed a voice. If the history stimulated by such visions was often better and more lasting than the policies that resulted, academics can find comfort in that. We need not blush, therefore, to argue that the awareness that created movements to address the dangers of nuclear war, ecological disasters, or starvation and disease should affect the way we look at and use history.

But at the same time, we must acknowledge some very real dangers. There are plenty of examples all around us of historical work that is not very good, work in which shoddy research, lack of imagination, and limited analysis were acceptable simply due to the cause supposedly served or the fashionable vocabulary employed. The community of believers tends to have different standards for membership than the community of scholars.

Global history will be vulnerable to all of that. And it will, in addition, be subject to special pressures to compensate for past wrongs (increasing the need to distinguish our era from all previous ones); to privilege any evidence of interconnectedness, no matter how bland, over distinctiveness, no matter how creative; to treat all conflicts of values and interests as mistaken and always subject to resolution; and to welcome narratives of accommodation and pacification. The greening of history and history as a salute to global diversity are certainly likely to win applause, and we should fear the temptations in that. Following fashion, however grandiloquently framed, invites loose thinking. Notoriously ahistorical, the questions that most immediately arise from current preoccupations may not only lack historical perspective but also may tend to exclude it in ways easily overlooked. Political engagement need not conflict with some sense of historical understanding as a cumulative process, but merely rewriting the past to fit (an ephemeral and probably mistaken) view of the present adds little to policy or history. Plans to establish global history as a field of inquiry should include some protection against such obvious dangers.

The Lessons of History

To avoid these dangers to the autonomy and intellectual vitality of global history, we might do well to consider the recent history of the historical discipline itself, which has both embraced and suffered from similar threats before. Awkwardly hortatory, the list that follows is skewed to emphasize temptations that global historians might find attractive.

1. *Avoid technological determinism.* Affix the adjective global to any topic and the discussion is likely to turn to technology. In our era, historical change is associated with technology, and people who have never read a major philosopher or a single important work of history are prepared to discuss at some length the computer revolution or the television revolution. When explaining why ours is a global age, the increased communication made possible by technology is the first point that comes to mind. But it is useful to remember that emphasis upon the steam engine and spinning jenny has not provided the most fruitful path to analysis of the industrial revolution. Similarly, even if the evidence for its impact were better, lead poisoning cannot explain what really interests us in the fall of Rome. The sextant cannot tell us what we want to know about the age of discovery, nor can the need for coaling stations explain the thrust of imperialism. Technology is obviously very important, but it can address only indirectly the questions about human behaviors that global history will seek to explore. Rather, it is the complicated scholarly effort to understand technology in terms of its social and intellectual context that can contribute subtlety and sophistication to global history.

2. *Reject the dichotomy of traditional and modern.* There is often an embarrassing circularity in naming some practices as modern (and therefore destined to spread) and labeling some other values or practices as traditional (and thus unchanging and therefore doomed). Again and again, these implied predictions have also turned out to be wrong. But the truly harmful myth lies in the distinction between traditional and modern. Much that is thought to be traditional has proved to be as flexible, easily reinvented, and intangible as any definition of progress. The modern in any society, however we identify it, incorporates and assimilates much that was there before, and there is no way to determine what proportion of parliaments, double-entry bookkeeping, or religion is traditional or modern. Paradoxically, the tendency to reify the traditional as indigenous, atavistic, or primordial is ideological rather than analytic, allowing reactionaries and radicals alike to identify concepts like social identity or love of family as antedating (and maybe antithetical to) the modern world. Traditional and modern, in short, cannot be separated, and efforts to do so are both ahistorical because they deny context and falsely historical because they tend to label the borrowed as forever foreign and the indigenous as traditional. Not surprisingly, the concepts such terms refer to have come to be radically reconsidered, and the habit of falling back on them is especially misleading for global history.

3. *Genealogy does not determine identity.* The transistor in Japan is no

more American than paper in Europe is Chinese. Like rubber, maize, or the potato, elections or political parties or corporate hierarchies may carry names that reflect a foreign origin, but they have been woven into diverse societies. Sometimes altered in the process, ideas and technologies have generally found their place in receiving societies more easily than human immigrants. That is important for the global historian because it means that there is no way to know in advance, automatically or by definition, what is universal among societies. Institutions, concepts, or devices that appear to be essentially identical across different societies may actually have been domesticated differently and may turn out to play quite different roles despite the similarity of their origins or names.

4. *Globalization need not mean homogeneity.* Enthusiasts of globalization tend to conceive it as an irresistible process and to describe it as a sequence of waves washing over the world. Such rhetoric easily implies that homogeneity is inevitable, and some people already lament the concomitant loss of colorful diversity. There may be reason for such fears (or hopes), but the point is that the history of history should warn us to be cautious with such assumptions about how the process works. Neither Christianity nor a Latin-speaking church eliminated the diverse tongues of Europe, yet nation-builders in the nineteenth century were sure that literacy and railroads would destroy dialects, local costumes, and regional loyalty. Some of that happened but not enough to prevent a similar prediction a generation or two later, expected this time to result from the effects of popular journalism and the cinema; these expectations were renewed a generation after that as inevitable effects first of radio and then of television. Yet regionalism has been as strong a political (and maybe social) force in Europe during the second half of the twentieth century as at any time since the invention of the national state. Global history should at least avoid the demonstrable errors of Western history.

5. *Global history should not be limited to recent history.* We are discussing global history now because we think the world has changed in modern times and provided us with a new outlook. Even so, global history should not be limited to the recent past, the period since World War II or this century. The historical discipline, after all, has flourished by applying to the past new questions that arise from present concerns. For the historian advocating global history, one measure of its value will be whether this new perspective (reflecting the experience of the twentieth century and an anticipation of the twenty-first) illuminates connections so fundamental and universal that their study can prove revealing about other societies and eras.[11] Both a limited belief in the capacity of historical analysis to bridge the gulf of time and the moral conviction that there is significant universality in human experience argue against designing global history as a modern subject.

Chronological constriction is a price historians should not pay for expanding their geographical horizons. In any case, the strongest argument for limiting global history to the recent past is that the global consciousness now developing demarcates a new era, significantly different from all previous history. That important perception may be profound, and the emphasis on mentalities and the questions about modern life that follow can open valuable lines of research. But a field of study should not be designed to determine the questions that can be asked for it is methodologically dangerous to quarantine one's assumptions. Periodization, in particular, is so fundamental to the conception and identification of historical problems that it must always be subject to challenge, which means that the impression of change in the world and of our views of it must be tested by studying other periods. It may be that there have been other global consciousnesses—for example, the belief that people are naturally organized by nationality, that technology is the source of power, that class conflict is the mechanism of change, that the laws of markets are universal, that states are a necessary form of social organization, or that God has a destiny and purpose for His people. And it may be that what marks our new era is not the fact of global consciousness but a particular set of beliefs about it (including the view that this era is unique). All that needs to be considered in the light of—and, in turn, to cast light upon—the past.

6. *A field of history must generate research.* Despite its immensity, the field of global history must lead to more than reflective essays, however impassioned, or wide-ranging descriptions based on secondary works, however stimulating. To thrive, it must, like any other field of historical inquiry, be the locus of research. The global historian obviously can never know enough, but historians who work on a much smaller scale have always faced that problem, too, and in principle, at least, it is hardly a new dilemma. Familiar devices for combining original research with the work of others can certainly be used, and imaginative new approaches to team research offer promising possibilities. The question of what to investigate is more difficult, although many of the issues in the established fields of history can also be approached globally. But how global must global history be? And is it possible to achieve the kind of focus that marks most research on the history of a single country or period? The issue is important for it raises the question of how global history can, in the current jargon, be problematized and made the locus of fresh and important questions specific to global history but possibly valid for other kinds of history, too.

Global historians might, for example, begin in the present by identifying some of the characteristics of today's global society, such as universal material conditions (climate or disease, for example); universal needs (like food, shelter, and protection); universal institutions (government, administrators, religions, or police); even universal values (love, strength, family, or life) or universal social practices (recreation, roles assigned by gender, childhood as a distinctive period of life). For any category of this sort, it would then be possible to ask whether certain patterns of behavior fall into geographical zones, that is, whether there are regional groupings within which specific behaviors are more similar than those between the zone and the rest of the world. Some such empirical approach, beginning with the present and avoiding such traditional categories as nations or civilizations, would have the merit of admitting the possibility that a global perspective could challenge perceptions of how the world is organized and allow the discovery of diverse patterns among different variables. Then the global historian might inquire about the chronology of these zones, establishing a periodization on the basis of when there was greater similarity or difference and less or more interaction among these zones.

Anthropologists have largely abandoned the effort to establish universal taxonomies, and global history should not repeat those efforts. It is not enough to avoid the assumption that global history marches in a single direction. One purpose in identifying these various zones of similarity and contact should be to recognize the great range in patterns of change and the differing rhythms within and between them. Even time itself—its different pace and significance—might be studied in this way.[12] Posed globally, historical questions can also establish the need to investigate more imaginatively and closely the diversity in cultural practices— why, for example, television is more universal than painting or cuisine more distinctive than coinage.[13] Thus, global historical research could lead to some radical reassessment of common assumptions about how such universals as science, language, or religion integrate and divide single societies and the world as a whole, and it can lead to fresh and specific historical questions that might, in turn, stimulate new, quite comfortably local research.

7. *Global history should be open to the new currents in other historical fields.* If new research is to be one of the products of global history, the field should not be deprived of those questions, paradigms, methods, and theories currently most stimulating in ordinary historical study. A field, that is, should not be limited to the methods or paradigms from which and in terms of which it developed. Fifty years ago, diplomatic history set the standard for methodological rigor in history, an achievement that tended to tie research to an established set of questions and approaches. Subsequently, diplomatic history has come to be overlooked to a considerable degree, in part because it did not participate in the methodological shifts in the historical discipline as a whole. That left the impression that

the most interesting questions and the most penetrating methods not only lie elsewhere but are also alien to issues of international relations. The prospects for global history as a vigorous field would obviously be dimmed if its special demands and preoccupations should, in practice, largely exclude the kinds of history—the history of gender or the social, cultural, interdisciplinary, anthropological, sociological, or comparative history—that underlie much of today's most exciting historical work.

As scholars break global history down into a series of problems, there should be plenty of room for the imaginative, heavily contextualized reconstruction characteristic of some of the best historical research, as well as for creative borrowing from other histories.[14] Then global history can, in turn, make its own contribution to historical research within traditional fields, helping specialists to reconceive some of the classic problems of their subdisciplines. There is, after all, an embarrassingly long list of topics on which social scientists in general have not done awfully well. Contemporary issues like the persistence of nationalism or the continued importance of religion, hard to explain in terms of theories that predict their imminent disappearance (theories rooted, of course, in the intellectual history of nineteenth-century Europe) may be understood quite differently when investigated in terms of the world's multiple communities.[15]

8. *The challenge of global history is to construct global perspectives.* This, I think, is where global history differs somewhat from the great tradition of world history. There, it is the narrative itself that connects the human species from its common roots in the cradle of civilization through its organic growth in patterned developments that spread through time and space. Writing from a celestial perspective, the author discerns relationships and draws lessons invisible to human beings who can rarely see beyond their own horizons. With civilizations or ecumenes as the unit of analysis, the tale told with biblical power provides momentum and meaning. There are, in short, special strengths to this approach, and narrative may, indeed, be more translatable than analytic frameworks, which are more fundamentally culture bound even when designed to be less so.[16] Thus, the famous works of narrative world history, notably those by McNeill, Toynbee, and Spengler, may well deserve to be read much more and much more closely than they usually are.[17] In addition, all sorts of promising new ventures in the genre are under way, stimulated by public interest, the demand for new undergraduate courses, and new scholarly work.[18]

Nevertheless, if it is true that global history represents a different approach, then the opportunities afforded by that difference, as well as the limitations inherent in it, need to be recognized. Global history may, in fact, be easier than world history in the double sense that reliance upon narrative and a single comprehensive vision is not only more than most academics can tackle but is also bound to leave unsatisfied some of the fundamental demands of modern scholarship. Global history that breaks the field into problems, generates new research, and uses the most fashionable approaches may be able to borrow more readily from the other social sciences and, while acknowledging how much is relative, to appropriate both the reflexivity and the methods of the humanities. There is, in short, some solace for the global historian in the difficulties modern scholarship of all sorts have encountered and widely advertised in trying to study culture across cultures.[19] But that will require global historians to join in creating new theoretical frameworks and avoid the temptation to draw straight lines from one time and place to another.

The Practice of Global History

To reject tendencies dangerous to fresh scholarship that are part of global history's appeal and to eschew historical shortcuts that have proved dead ends is to increasingly expose the question of what global history should be, of where the global connections lie that could constitute a field of study. If there were a hundred thousand historians around the world who considered themselves to be global historians, they would form thousands of subgroups. Some of these subgroups would be organized around particular sets of universal experiences (e.g., disease, family life, markets); some would be based on the use of particular methods or theories and coordination with other disciplines; some would group those who specialize in the same region or era. As they were institutionalized (and they soon would be), these foci—topical, methodological, and contextual—would segregate research in familiar ways. Some global historians would study the family, some would emphasize quantitative methods, and some would concentrate on a particular region. Current historical conventions do have a rationale, and global history should not require their elimination.

Because the mills of scholarship will tend to grind the seeds of global history into more easily managed mixtures, it may be useful to think of alternative ways of grouping approaches to global history that will permit the specialization research demands while preserving a global vision. Such groupings should fit with the way historians actually work; help identify historical problems that can be conceived globally and investigated within much narrower frameworks; and acknowledge the historian's preoccupation with time, respect for geography, and devotion to cultural context. The following categories are intended to meet these criteria, with the credibility that comes from not being very surprising. For those who would establish global history as a new field, they provide encouraging evidence that a lot of excellent global history has already been written.[20]

Global Diffusion

One way to think of global history is to treat it as the world history of diffusion, example by example. That initiates that process of paring down the subject that the historian's comfort requires, and in a reassuring way, it emphasizes time as sequence. Indeed, the study of diffusion tends to work best when taken one item at a time—a single invention, design, or disease[21]—but in capable hands, it can provide a stunning perspective on a broad scale.[22] As these examples suggest, there is a tendency for studies of diffusion to emphasize material conditions, but anthropologists and archaeologists have a long interest in cultural diffusion. So do historians of ideas, and we have brilliant examples on topics as diverse as nationalism or the diffusion of manners.[23]

For the global historian, there are some troubling tendencies in diffusionist studies, including possibilities that the approach itself has an inherently materialist bias, easily incorporates teleology when pursued one innovation at a time, encourages any penchant for presenting mere chronological sequence as progressive stages,[24] and often uses a vocabulary that permits diffusion to substitute for causation as if ideas (or techniques) were like germs. Diffusion will nevertheless remain a valuable way to construct global history, and shifting the focus to the *process* of diffusion will allow research on diffusion to address many of the historical problems important in global history. (Significantly enough, this is readily done in studies of migration, the diffusion of people.) Then the object of study becomes the process of adoption, resistance, assimilation, adaptation, and transformation, and the analysis uses comparison more than sequence.

The Web of Connection

In another approach to global history, time is, at least conceptually, forever experienced simultaneously, and the interactions among societies become the subject of global history. Here, too, much impressive work has already been done, especially on markets and trade.[25] In principle, of course, modern communication or science could be analyzed in similar terms, although the multiplicity of such exchanges today (but not their speed) creates enormous practical difficulties. Rather, the web of connections has proved an especially fruitful subject of study for the sixteenth, seventeenth, and eighteenth centuries. This research has revealed connections often overlooked, emphasized asymmetrical power relations, and, especially in Wallerstein's influential work, expanded into a history of the development of capitalism as a world system that also becomes a paradigm of how capitalism has operated ever since.[26] Dependency theories have worked in a similar vein to expose the techniques of domination within international economic relations during the last century, especially in Latin America; and Eric Wolf wrote truly global history in his powerful assessment of the world's encounter with Europe's expansive capitalist culture.[27]

Evidence of global history's potential, this literature provides a foundation upon which the field can build. In doing so, it need not be constrained by the perspective that has commonly accompanied this approach. The emphasis upon capitalism has tended to mean putting Europe at the center of the world and tracking the spread of European dominance. The emphasis upon power has led to conceptions of center and periphery that can inadvertently close off fertile lines of inquiry.

New research will need to be more attentive to the remarkable durability, inventiveness, creativity, and simple intransigence of cultures too readily cataloged as peripheral, subordinate, or dominated. Ecological models (and maybe genetic and evolutionary ones, as well) may offer some alternatives to the rigidity of fixed systems and to this preoccupation with power. All this, then, should result in a subtler, more complex analysis of the process of change within any one society, reducing the tendency to associate cause with an impinging other and effect with the indigenous internal. Increased allowance for cultural creativity will also make it easier to explore the global web of connections outside the cash nexus. Markets are nodes of cultural as well as financial exchange,[28] and all sorts of techniques, institutions, and ideas also constitute the stuff from which such webs are woven. This sort of global history can be especially useful in overcoming the artificial boundaries created by our own categories, reminding us that the economy of one society may intersect the military of another, the religion of a third, and so forth. That is an especially valuable corrective for global historians investigating particular kinds of experience on the grounds that they are universal.

Global Experiences

Research on global history can also begin from almost any general theory of society for such theories assume that societies have significant qualities in common. Global history then becomes a means of investigating those commonalities through historical comparisons, and history itself, for all its glorious particularity, can partake of the universal as well. The critical element in this approach is the analytic categories used, which can be as fundamental as kinship, division of labor, or property (the kind of issues that are the foundation of anthropology). Or the categories can be based on such complex but nevertheless apparently universal matters as religion or statemaking or social control (the kinds of topics that lie at the heart of historical sociology). Or they may simply define certain interesting kinds of behavior or be the invention of a scholar.[29] Familiar categories are more easily connected to the established literature, theoretical and empirical, but their application to specific historical examples and their value in analytic comparison is likely to be contested. Newly invented categories may fit specific cases very nicely but tend to be more loosely tied to broader examples and theories.

The vast literature relevant to global history produced in anthropology and sociology, in particular, offers inspiration and models, caution and alarms for historians. In the 1950s and 1960s, Weberian ideal types and Parsonian functionalism stimulated an extraordinary outpouring of major works,[30] including an enormous literature on political development.[31] As mentioned earlier, much of that has subsequently come under severe attack, but the global historian would be foolish not to make extensive use of this rich literature, both for its often striking findings and for the many questions it opened up that remain inadequately explored.

There is also reason for disquiet. The typologies on which this work rests are almost totally Western in terms of the examples from which they are derived and the conceptions on which they rest,[32] even when treating such seemingly universal categories as class, family, the idea of the state, or the role of religion. In addition, historians are likely to worry that the analysis is insufficiently contextual, retreating too rapidly to abstract and essentially nineteenth-century models with their overwhelming implication that the ultimate purpose is the discovery of universal laws. Even the comparisons in this literature, which reach so promisingly toward a worldwide range, often rest on dangerous puns, in which terms make comparable what culture and society may have constructed very differently.[33] Yet if the categories in question are really not meant to apply everywhere, then the comparisons lack either the universality or the interconnectedness that would lead to global history.

Current trends, however, can be helpful here. Literary theories, Foucauldian concepts of discourse, Edward Said's animadversions on Orientalism, and Pierre Bourdieu's ideas of habitus provide a popular kind of toolkit with which to deconstruct these sorts of categories and typologies.[34] They suggest a way of replacing a Eurocentric and progressivist vision with multiple perspectives from different (and changing) cultural and social positions. When they stimulate real rethinking and not just writing in a new vocabulary (discourse and gaze can express old-fashioned and provincial ideas), such concepts can lead to a different kind of global history—multicentered, reflexive, ambivalent, and open-ended. This kind of a history is also comparative, but it compares not fixed functions or defined categories but rather the fluid processes and rituals that create and mark social boundaries, define and punish criminals, segregate by age and gender, rear children, and reproduce culture. Global history will require a cautious, fluid, self-conscious, but courageous re-creation of multivalent categories in addition to the courage of a common analytic vocabulary. The recognition of different histories can also contribute to theory while provoking new questions that invite a global perspective.

Cultural Encounters

Research on global history can also proceed as the study of cultural encounters, by which I mean not just a topic but rather an approach that shares certain qualities with each of the three already described, even though it need not trace influences spreading through time, explore connections working simultaneously, nor define categories of comparison. Rather, the interrelation of local and global cultures can, in itself, be the subject of research. That research is now more promising than ever and for several reasons. We are obviously more aware than ever before of the multiplicity and subtlety of global relationships. More important, concepts of culture (and therefore of encounters across cultures) have changed with the recognition that all cultures are always in flux and need not be coherent. Most basic of all is the understanding that self and other are shifting constructions, so that "the West" itself can be seen as an invention (and essentially an imperial one) responding to global experience.[35] (This does not assume that culture is something fixed or even coherent, that interactions across the globe are necessarily different in impact from those with neighbors, or that encounters must have a single vector.) All societies define themselves in terms of an Other, and encounters with other cultures provide the basis on which each, at various times, tends to label certain of its attributes as fundamental and enduring and considers others to be more incidental or ephemeral. Through this process, some qualities (or aspects of cultures) come to be perceived as general, universal, or global, and some come to be perceived as local. Both the local and the global are thus continually reshaped. African art, for example, developed as part of various groups' identities, distinguishing them from their neighbors even while they borrowed from each other. Europeans, in turn, perceived African artifacts as art in European terms, creating interests, aesthetic and economic, that changed the art of Europe and Africa, redefining what was global and what was local. One kind of global history could thus be built upon the study of this sort of symbiosis.

Aspiring neither to the discovery of universal laws nor to the creation of a dominant formal model, students of cultural encounter would look at the process of intersecting cultures without assuming that cultures have sharp boundaries or fixed identities—an approach that can incorporate much of the powerful postmodern rejection of claims to objectivity. The historian's predilection for the ironic voice need not stop with an author's knowing wink;[36] it can also lead to the recognition of multiple meanings and outcomes, giving researchers their best chance to recognize recurring patterns without becoming the minstrels of power. Nor need their efforts end in pallid relativism.

What from one perspective (often revealingly labeled the "center") looks like the spread of a universal requirement and from another perspective is seen as a new challenge to an established culture (often, though improbably, described as traditional and autonomous) becomes a quite different phenomenon when those—and other—perspectives are combined, taking the encounter itself as the universal, cultural phenomenon and the object of study. Understood as a continuing process of creativity, cultural encounters between global and local cultures, re-creating both, need not be framed in terms of winners and losers, imperial hegemony and subaltern alternatives, aggression and resistance.[37] Rather, they are particularly visible instances of continuing processes of assimilation, transformation, reassertion, and re-creation—processes as essential to culture as cell division is to life.

The encounters of global and local cultures, then, are not just conflicts, but they include real and multiple conflicts that can be part of the creative process. Machiavelli noted that opponents tend to become more alike—affected, we would say, by the common discourse through which their conflict is focused. Thus, certain concerns, customs, practices, and values come to be excluded, included, or privileged as the discourse of rituals and exchanges serve to maintain, create, or shift cultural boundaries. Global culture is distilled in this process of encountering local cultures, while local culture is constantly re-created in an unending process that reveals new possibilities and challenges, redefines tradition, and alters the markers of the alien. Global history forms the ecological niches in which various cultures prosper.

Anthropologists have led in the exploration of these issues (and have increasingly come to work along the lines suggested here),[38] but scholars in all the social sciences and humanities have much to say about them. Among the most exciting possibilities are analyses in terms of gender and applications of feminist theory to the study of global and local cultural encounters.[39] But the possibilities extend beyond strictly cultural issues to the international division of labor under capitalism or international relations.[40] Furthermore, the problems and evidence encompassed in a global history studying the intersections of global and local cultures should provide protection from the risks listed earlier of teleology, materialism, determinism, contemporaneity, and so forth. Cultural encounters create altered forms and new mixtures, the equivalent of biological sports, and not just hegemony or homogeneity. Tape recorders, like literacy and printing, can simultaneously increase access to global culture; redefine, codify, and elevate the local; and conflate the two in endlessly unpredictable ways.[41] The locally established cultural hierarchies of high and popular, secular and religious may be undone or actually reversed by global encounters for there are cultural creations—like American movies, some folk music, or certain foods—that appear to gain in translation, their roots in local soil transformed as they come to be seen as universal. The study of cultural encounters may even enable us to escape the shadow of imperialism sufficiently to address forbidden questions about whether, globally, some ideas are more communicable, and some cultures more appealing. We can also explore whether some values are more adoptable, some practices more acceptable, some institutions more imitable, some technology more importable, and some knowledge more credible than others. Answers to these questions could help define the shape of the future.

Conclusion

The urge to see the world as one, expressed in the ecological movement's conviction of our common destiny, has long been part of the interest in history and central to the belief that it could be written. Historians have written the global history of God's plan, the global history of evolutionary progress, and the global history of spreading (and declining) power. Although the confidence that informed those visions is available to few scholars today, a paler but enduring curiosity remains to express in sometimes tedious research the belief that all human societies have something of value to say to all others and that they say it across time and continents.

The conclusion is modest. The best chance for global history lies in its becoming just another among the many fields of history. There should be room within it for all the various methods that historians use elsewhere, and it should be open to more than one ideology. As another way of regrouping interdisciplinary and cross-cultural research—a continuing project and not the expression of a single theory—global history would not necessarily replace nor even challenge historical specialization.[42] Such limited goals should help global historians avoid some of the obvious pitfalls, and this more modest and less imperious global history can prove useful to all the other fields of history. They would reunite questions of structure and culture too often separated, bring together points of view often assumed to be opposed, and make comparison a commonplace tool.

A product of our times, it will offer some historical insight into contemporary concerns and therefore into the past as well. And it will do so while substituting multicultural, global analysis for the heroic, national narratives on which our discipline was founded.

Notes

1. I am grateful to the participants at the Bellagio conference for their stimulating and helpful comments and to many friends, especially Marvin Becker, Charles Bright, Fernando Coronil, and Albert Feuerwerker, whose criticisms and suggestions were invaluable even when they called for a higher standard than I could meet.

2. In fact, current writing on historical method may even exaggerate this effect. Historicism always made much of it but left room for history to be considered as a cumulative science nevertheless because, as R. G. Collingwood argued, new answers and new questions are necessarily evaluated in the light of previous findings. More recent criticisms have undermined this position by suggesting that the historiographical literature is not the record of multiple investigations brought to bear on historical problems that have an independent existence. Rather, they suggest that the whole disciplinary discourse can—and indeed must—be rethought. This view, which hardly argues for the possibility of an objective history, may tend to exaggerate the role of the present concerns in shaping historical research by treating that research (even over a century or more) as fairly uniform in purpose despite different methods, ideologies, and purposes and also by underestimating the independent challenge that inconvenient evidence can create.

3. Michael Geyer and Charles Bright, "For a Unified History of the World in the Twentieth Century," *Radical History Review* 39 (September 1987): 69-91. Significantly, the whole issue is devoted to world history. The twenty-volume "One World Archaeology" series provides a fascinating example of the impact of global consciousness on current scholarship.

4. The literature on modernization is vast. In reviewing some recent contributions, Ian Roxborough commented that "a few years ago, the demise of modernization theory was widely celebrated. Under a sustained barrage of criticism from dependency and neo-Marxist theories, it was in poor health and funeral orations were pronounced. Now, however, modernization theory appears alive and well, while the practitioners of dependency and neo-Marxist theories are bemoaning an apparent stagnation in theoretical work, "Modernization Theory Revisited," *Comparative Studies in Society and History* 30:4 (October 1988): 753. My own comments were made in "Modernization and Its Discontents," *American Behavioral Scientist* 21:2 (November/December 1977): 289-312, and "More on Modernization," *Journal of Social History* 14:2 (October 1980): 763-778.

5. S. N. Eisenstadt, ed., *Patterns of Modernity*, 2 vols. (London, 1987); Alex Inkeles, *Exploring Individual Modernity* (New York, 1983); Anthony Giddens, *The Consequences of Modernity* (London, 1990).

6. Ian Weinberg, "The Problem of the Convergence of Industrial Societies: A

Critical Look at the State of a Theory," *Comparative Studies in Society and History* 11:1 (January 1969): 1-15; two anonymous Eastern Europeans, "The Two Systems in Action," *Comparative Studies in Society and History* 20:2 (April 1978): 236-258.

7. John McCormick, *Redeeming Paradise: The Global Environmental Movement* (Bloomington, Ind., 1989); for a different example, see Francis Fukuyama, "The End of History?" *The National Interest*, no. 16 (Summer 1989): 3-18; and comments, *The National Interest*, no. 16 (Summer 1989): 19-35; no. 17 (Fall 1989): 1-16; no. 17 (Winter 1990): 21-28.

8. Philip D. Curtin, "The Environment Beyond Europe and the European Theory of Empire," *Journal of World History* 1:2 (Fall 1990): 131-150; William H. McNeill, *The Human Condition* (Princeton, N.J., 1980); Alfred W. Crosby, *Ecological Imperialism: The Biological Expansion of Europe, 900-1900* (Cambridge, England, 1986); Donald Worster, ed., *The Ends of the Earth: Perspectives on Modern Environmental History* (Cambridge, Mass., 1988); and P. Burnham and R. F. Ellen, eds., *Social and Ecological Systems* (New York, 1979). See also the special issue of *World Development* 19:1 (January 1991), edited by N. R. Goodwin, in which the historical and contemporary fruitfully intermesh.

9. Good examples are Neil J. Smelser, "The Social Sciences in a Changing World Society," and William Foote Whyte, "Social Sciences in the University," in *American Behavioral Scientist* 34:5 (May/June 1991): 518-529, 618-633.

10. Henri Berr's journal, *Revue de synthèse*, still has lessons to teach, and note the optimist in his *La synthèse en histoire* (Paris, 1911); Georges Bataille could combine his earlier ideas on culture and philosophy and economics with reflections on the Marshall Plan to produce an essay that can be taken as a schema for global history, *La Part Maudite* (Paris, 1967).

11. For a striking example of the possibilities, see Janet L. Abu-Lughod, *Before European Hegemony: The World System A.D. 1250-1350* (Oxford, 1989). Without a strong theoretical framework, Guy Martinière and Consuelo Varela, eds., *L'état du monde en 1492* (Paris, 1992), remains a topical collection of essays rather than a global history.

12. Consider the possibilities raised by relating studies like those of Samuel G. Brandon, *History, Time, and Diety* (Manchester, 1965); Nancy M. Farriss, "Remembering the Future, Anticipating the Past: History, Time, and Cosmology Among the Maya of Yucatan," *Comparative Studies in Society and History* 29:3 (July 1987): 566-593; George Kubler, *The Shape of Time: Remarks on the History of Things* (New Haven, Conn., 1962); Walter Ong, *Orality and Literacy: The Technologizing of the Word* (London, 1982); Marshall Sahlins, *Historical Metaphors and Mythical Realities: Structure in the Early History of the Sandwich Islands Kingdom* (Ann Arbor, Mich., 1981); Sahlins, *Islands of History* (Chicago, 1985); and G. J. Whitrow, *Time in History* (Oxford,, 1988).

13. Although anthropologists have long dealt with such questions (for example, A.L. Kroeber), they have been the object of relatively little historical research in terms so specific that the larger issue often disappears.

14. Can a historian thinking globally but working locally employ the kind of intensely local and personal techniques advocated by the British historian, R. G. Collingwood?

15. I have commented on these issues in "Rethinking the Assumptions and Purposes of Nineteenth-Century Social Science," in Francisco O. Ramirez, ed., *Rethinking the Nineteenth Century: Contradictions and Movements* (New York, 1988), 203-209; and "The Construction of National Identity," in Peter Boerner, ed., *Concepts of National Identity: An Interdisciplinary Dialogue* (Baden-Baden, 1986), 31-43.

16. See John Terrell, "Storytelling and Prehistory," *Archaeological Method and Theory* 2 (1990), 1-29, and especially Hayden White, *The Content of the Form: Narrative Discourse and Historical Representation* (Baltimore, Md., 1987).

17. And there are many other interesting efforts. Alexander Rüstow, *Freedom and Domination: A Historical Critique of Civilization* (Princeton, N.J., 1980) sought to avoid the limits of a narrative framework; Oroon Kumar Ghosh, *Convergence of Civilizations: Beyond Marxism, Liberalism and Ultra-Nationalism* (Calcutta, 1988) meant to overcome Eurocentrism. Significantly, neither was entirely successful. Discussions of religion and values also continue to be put in global frameworks, for example, in Géryke Young, *Cross-Purposes East and West* (London, 1991).

18. See *Journal of World History*, Official Journal of the World History Association, 1:1 (Spring 1990).

19. James Clifford, *The Predicament of Culture: Twentieth-Century Ethnography, Literature, and Art* ((Cambridge, Mass., 1988); Edward Said, *Orientalism* (New York, 1979); Gyan Prakash, "Writing Post-Orientalist Histories of the Third World: Perspective from Indian Historiography," *Comparative Studies in Society and History* 32:2 (April 1990): 383-408; Michel de Certeau, *The Writing of History* (New York, 1988); and the issue of *Representations* no. 33 (Winter 1991), devoted to Certeau.

20. The topic, it should be added, does not determine which of the following approaches is dominant in a given study. Compare William H. McNeill, *The Pursuit of Power: Technology, Armed Force, and Society Since A.D. 1000* (Oxford, 1983), and Michael Mann, *The Sources of Social Power: A History of Power from the Beginning to A.D. 1760* (Cambridge, England, 1986).

21. Even a vegetable can be treated in this manner! See Redcliffe N. Salaman, *The History and Social Influence of the Potato* (Cambridge, England, 1949), an early but prototypical example.

22. William H. McNeill, *Plagues and Peoples* (Garden City, N.J., 1977); Fernand Braudel, *Capitalism and Material Life, 1400-1800* (New York, 1973).

23. The history of science, which is most often written in a diffusionist mode, seems to offer little resistance to global extension. Diffusionist accounts of the history of ideas raise more problems. The standard approach to the history of political theory is certainly diffusionist but also heavily Eurocentric. Norbert Elias, *The Civilizing Process: The History of Manners* (New York, 1978) offered a challenging model that begged to be extended on a global scale, and Benedict Anderson, *Imagined Communities: Reflections on the Origin and Spread of Nationalism* (London, 1983) showed what can be accomplished when cultural and structural approaches to diffusion are combined.

24. Recapitulating nineteenth-century errors, J. W. Burrow authored *Evolution and Society: A Study in Victorian Social Theory* (Cambridge, England, 1966).

25. Sidney W. Mintz, *Sweetness and Power: The Place of Sugar in Modern History* (New York, 1985); Philip D. Curtin, *Cross-Cultural Trade in World History* (Cambridge, 1984). Illicit trade (in opium, for example) can be treated similarly. Marxist theories have not only led to some of the most valuable research but also have an explanation for the topic itself: "Global history comes with the expansion of the world market, which 'produced world history for the first time,'" as William Roseberry noted, citing Marx, in "Marxism and Culture," in Brett Williams, ed., *The Politics of Culture* (Washington, D.C., 1991), 39. He added that it therefore came to Latin America sooner than China, while acknowledging Sherry Ortner's warning that a capitalist-centered worldview leads to histories not of other societies but of the impact of our society on those others (p. 43). Compare *Radical History Review*, no. 39 (1987), devoted to "Structures and Consciousness in World History."

26. Christopher Chase-Dunn, *Global Formation: Structures of the World-Economy* (Oxford, 1989), provided a firmly Marxist exposition strongly directed toward the contemporary period but still much influenced by Immanuel Wallerstein, *The Modern World System*, vol. 1, *Capitalist Agriculture and the Origins of the European World Economy in the Sixteenth Century* (New York, 1974) and *The Modern World System*, vol. 2, *Mercantilism and the Consolidation of the European World Economy, 1600-1750* (New York, 1980). Jack A. Goldstone, on the other hand, used formal comparison to emphasize the importance of population growth, in "East and West in the Seventeenth Century: Political Crises in Stuart England, Ottoman Turkey, and Ming China," *Comparative Studies in Society and History* 30:1 (January 1988): 103-142. See also Jean Baechler, John A. Hall, and Michael Mann, eds., *Europe and the Rise of Capitalism* (Oxford, 1988), in which more of a non-European perspective is featured.

27. Eric A. Wolf, *Europe and the People Without History* (Berkeley, Calif., 1982); John A. Hall, *Powers and Liberties: The Causes and Consequences of the Rise of the West* (Oxford, 1985), employed related concerns but wrote from a more specifically European perspective.

28. G. William Skinner, ed., *The City in Late Imperial China* (Stanford, Calif., 1977). Even an analysis that begins as economic can rapidly spread beyond; see William M. Reddy, *The Rise of Market Culture: The Textile Trade and French Society, 1750-1900* (Cambridge, England, 1984).

29. Graduate students in a course I recently taught wrote essays on the world history of banditry, religious conversion, and ethnic enclaves.

30. S. N. Eisenstadt, *The Political Systems of Empires* (Glencoe, Il., 1963).

31. This is exemplified by the "Studies in Political Development" series sponsored by the Committee on Comparative Politics of the Social Science Research Council; the last three volumes in that series attempted to establish a general pattern; see Leonard Binder et al., *Crises and Sequences in Political Development* (Princeton, N.J., 1971), and to test it historically but not to apply it globally, see Charles Tilly, ed., *The Formation of National States in Western Europe* (Princeton, N.J., 1975) and Raymond Grew, ed., *Crises of Political Development in Europe and the United States* (Princeton, N.J., 1978). Earlier volumes in this series, like most of this literature, had looked primarily outside Europe and North America, however

much they applied models rooted in European experience. See as a good example David E. Apter, *The Politics of Modernization* (Chicago, 1965).

32. Note the comment of David L. Sills and Robert K. Merton on their volume *International Encyclopedia of the Social Sciences—Social Science Quotations*, regretting that their citations were almost exclusively Western, in "Social Science Quotations: Who Said What, When, and Where," *Items* 45:1 (March 1991): 3.

33. Sociologists have become very conscious of these problems; Else Oyen, *Comparative Methodology: Theory and Practice in International Social Research* (London, 1990). Nevertheless, extraordinarily venturesome historical comparison remains possible; John Gledhill, Barbara Bender, and Mogens Trolle Larsen, eds., *State and Society: The Emergence and Development of Social Hierarchy and Political Centralization* (London, 1988).

34. See Michel de Certeau, *The Practice of Everyday Life* (Berkeley, Calif., 1984).

35. The point has been influenced by Fernando Coronil, "Beyond Occidentalism: Towards *Post*-Imperial Geohistorical Categories," an unpublished paper.

36. Hayden Whyte, *Metahistory: The Historical Imagination in Nineteenth-Century Europe* (Baltimore, Md., 1973).

37. Vittorio Lanternari, *The Religions of the Oppressed: A Study of Modern Messianic Cults* ((New York, 1963) is a classic that surprisingly has stimulated less subsequent work than might have been expected. There is much interest, on the other hand, in popular culture, with a good deal of new work influenced by Dick Hebidige, *Subculture: The Meaning of Style* (London, 1979).

38. Marshall Sahlins, *Islands of History* (Chicago, 1985) is an especially well-known example, but see also the provocative warnings of Lawrence Rosen, "The Integrity of Cultures," *American Behavioral Scientist* 34:5 (May/June 1991): 594-617.

39. Jessie Barnard, *The Female World from a Global Perspective* (Bloomington, Ind., 1987).

40. See Claude Meillassoux, *Maidens, Meal and Money: Capitalism and the Domestic Community* (Cambridge, England, 1975), and Hidemi Suganami, *The Domestic Analogy and World Order Proposals* (Cambridge, England, 1989).

41. René T.A. Lysloff, "Shrikandhi Dances Lengger: A Performance of Music and Shadow Theater in Banyumas," Ph.D. diss. University of Michigan, 1990.

42. All this does suggest one form of institutionalization: a serial publication containing studies conceived in a global perspective by historians who were nevertheless working within the more feasible and familiar frameworks delimited by place and time. Each article would be accompanied, however, by essays written by other historians specializing in other cultures and eras. Using the historical evidence they knew best, they would sketch out how the topic would look if seen as an instance of global diffusion, as part of a web of connection, as a type of experience to be discussed comparatively, and as a kind of encounter between global and local cultures. One piece of research would thus become the basis for several research agendas in global history. Global history should have no difficulty generating new projects.

About the Book

As we enter a truly global epoch we need a historical awareness to match the times. This book offers a new scholarly perspective, a new historical consciousness, and a new subfield of history—global history—that will have a major impact on the way we write history and make policy in the future. The need for a new approach can be seen everywhere: in environmental problems that ignore national boundaries; in nuclear threats that have no territorial limitations; in the rapid increase in multinational economic activity; and in advances in space exploration and communication satellites that link peoples to a degree hitherto unimagined. The contributors to this book offer both a theoretical treatment and a number of examples of what global history is and how it might be written.

Bruce Mazlish is professor of history at the Massachusetts Institute of Technology. **Ralph Buultjens** teaches international affairs and Asian religions at the New School for Social Research in New York and at New York University.

About the Editors
and Contributors

Richard J. Barnet is a fellow at the Institute for Policy Studies in Washington, D.C.

Ralph Buultjens teaches at the New School for Social Research and at New York University. He is the Nehru Professor at the University of Cambridge, England, 1992-1993.

John Cavanagh is a fellow at the Institute for Policy Studies in Washington, D.C.

Neva R. Goodwin is director of the Program for the Study of Sustainable Change and Development, Tufts University.

Raymond Grew is professor of history, University of Michigan, and editor of *Comparative Studies in Society and History*.

John Joyce is professor of music, Tulane University.

Manfred Kossok was professor of history, Karl Marx University in Leipzig. He died on February 27, 1993.

Bruce Mazlish is professor of history, Massachusetts Institute of Technology.

Louis Menand III is emeritus senior lecturer in political science, Massachusetts Institute of Technology.

Wolf Schäfer is professor of history, State University of New York, Stony Brook.

Wang Gungwu is vice-chancellor, University of Hong Kong.

Printed in the United States
1694

9 780813 316840